THE LIBRARY
OF ALEXANDRIA

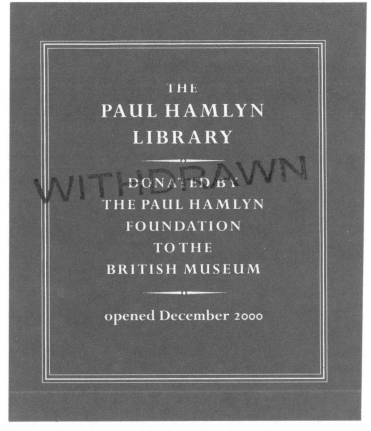

THE LIBRARY
OF ALEXANDRIA

CENTRE OF LEARNING IN
THE ANCIENT WORLD

Edited by

ROY MACLEOD

I.B. Tauris *Publishers*
LONDON • NEW YORK

Paperback edition published in 2002 by I.B.Tauris & Co Ltd
6 Salem Road, London W2 4BU
175 Fifth Avenue, New York NY 10010
www.ibtauris.com

In the United States of America and in Canada distributed by
St Martins Press, 175 Fifth Avenue, New York NY 10010

First published in 2000 by I.B.Tauris & Co Ltd

ISBN 1 86064 821 5

A full CIP record for this book is available from the British Library
A full CIP record for this book is available from the Library of Congress

Library of Congress catalog card: available

Printed in Egypt

Contents

Notes on Contributors

Robert Barnes is a Senior Lecturer in Classics at the Australian National University, with interests in ancient philosophy and religion, and in bibliography and the history of libraries. He has been much concerned to arouse public discussion of the recent narrowing of its collecting policy by the National Library of Australia.

Wendy Brazil took her BA at the University of Sydney, MA degrees in Classics and Linguistics at the Australian National University, and a MEd degree at the University of Canberra. She has been a research officer in Parliament House, a librarian at the National Library of Australia, a tutor in education at the University of Canberra, a theatre reviewer, and is currently a Fellow of University House at the ANU. She also is a teacher of Latin and Greek in secondary schools and at the Centre for Continuing Education (ANU). She is the author of articles in the *IPA Review and Education Monitor*, and has written a new curriculum for Latin, entitled *Fabulous Latin*. She is also the convenor of the Latin Reading Symposium at University House 'in uino latinitas', and 'Latin with Lunch' at the University of Canberra.

J.R. Green is Professor of Classical Archaeology at the University of Sydney and is the author of numerous books and articles on ancient theatre, including *Images of the Greek Theatre* (British Museum Press 1995; Greek translation, Crete University Press 1996) and *Theatre in Ancient Greek Society* (Routledge 1994, paperback 1996). He is Director of the University's excavations in Paphos, Cyprus, and a Senior Research Fellow of the Institute of Classical Studies, London.

Patricia Cannon Johnson was born in England, and studied conservation of antiquities at the University of London Institute of Archaeology. She then worked for thirteen years in the Egyptian and Greek and Roman departments of the British Museum. In 1980, after a period as a freelance, she became Conservator at the Nicholson Museum of the University of Sydney, from which she retired in 1997. She now works as a writer, restorer, and teacher of Mystery studies.

Samuel N.C. Lieu is the Professor of Ancient History at Macquarie University, and co-Director of its Ancient History Documentary Research Centre. He was previously Professor of Classics and Ancient History at Warwick University, and Director of its Centre for Research in East Roman Studies. He read Ancient History at Cambridge and took his doctorate at Oxford with a thesis on the comparative study of Manichaeism in Rome and China. Since 1990, he has been co-ordinator of the Corpus Fontium Manichaeorum Project – a UNESCO sponsored project which aims to publish 60+ volumes Manichaean texts discovered by archaeologists from sites along the Silk Road in Central Asia and from sites in Egypt. In 1996 he was awarded a grant by the Australian Research Council for a project on Manichaean texts. His research interests include the comparative study of historiography in Rome and Chain, the military history of Rome's eastern frontier, the conflict of paganism and Christianity in Late Antiquity, and the use of computers for research and teaching in ancient history. He is a Fellow of the Society of Antiquaries (London) and the Australian Academy of the Humanities.

Roy MacLeod is the Professor of History at the University of Sydney. Educated at Harvard, the London School of Economics, and Cambridge, he has written extensively on the history of European science, technology and medicine, and on the history of European expansion overseas. He has taught in England, France, the Netherlands and the United States, and has held senior appointments at several universities. He is a Fellow of the Society of Antiquaries of London, and of the Academy for the Social Sciences in Australia. He is currently writing on the transmission of ideas from Europe to the 'periphery', as seen through the idea, ideology and architecture of the modern museum.

D.T. Potts is Edwin Cuthbert Hall Professor of Middle Eastern Archaeology at the University of Sydney. He has excavated extensively in the United Arab Emirates in recent years and has written extensively on a wide range of topics in the archaeology and early history of Iran, Mesopotamia and Arabia. He is best known for his two volume work, *The Arabian Gulf in Antiquity*, published by Oxford University Press in 1990; for his two volumes on the *Pre-Islamic Coinage of Eastern Arabia*, published in Copenhagen in 1991 and 1994; for his recent *Mesopotamian Civilization: The Material Foundations*, co-published by Athlone (London) and Cornell University Press in 1997; and for *The Archaeology of Elam* published by Cambridge University Press in 1999. He is the founder and editor of the international journal *Arabian Archaeology & Epigraphy* published by Munksgaard in Denmark, as well as the founder and co-editor of ABIEL, a monograph series focusing on Arabian archaeology and epigraphy, published by Brepols in Belgium. He is Fellow of the Society of Antiquaries (London) and the Australian Academy of the Humanities.

R.G. Tanner is Professor Emeritus of Classics and Lecturer in Sanskrit at the University of Newcastle, New South Wales. He graduated from Cambridge in 1952, and subsequently taught at Melbourne University, 1953–5, and at The King's School Parramatta, 1957–1959, before moving to Newcastle as a Senior Lecturer in 1960. He was Foundation Professor of Classics at Newcastle from 1964 to 1993. He was Commonwealth Fellow at St. John's, Cambridge, 1967–68, and President of ASCS, 1992–95. He has published widely in ancient drama, Latin literature, Greek philosophy, patristic studies and Sanskrit. His publications on Artistotle include 'Aristotle as a Structural Linguist' *TPS* (London, 1969), 94–164, and 'Form and Substance in Aristotle', *Prudentia*, XV, 2, (1983), 87–108.

John Vallance is Head master of Sydney Grammar School. He read Classics at the University of Sydney, and St. John's College Cambridge. Between 1986 and 1993, he was a Fellow and Tutor of Gonville and Caius College, Cambridge, lecturing in Classics and the History of Science. He is the author of articles on ancient philosophy, science and medicine, including many in the third edition of the *Oxford Classical Dictionary* (1996), and is an editorial adviser and contributor to the *Enciclopedia Italiana*. His publications include *The Lost Theory of Asclepiades of Bithynia* (Oxford, 1990). He is completing a *Source Book in Greek Science* for Cambridge University Press.

J.O. Ward is a Senior Lecturer in the Department of History at the University of Sydney. He has written a number of books and articles on medieval intellectual life, general medieval history, monastic history, witchcraft, the crusades and the Templars. He has an international reputation for his work on Ciceronian rhetoric in the Middle Ages. He has recently published *Ciceronian Rhetoric in Treatise, Scholion, and Commentary* (Brepols, 1995)

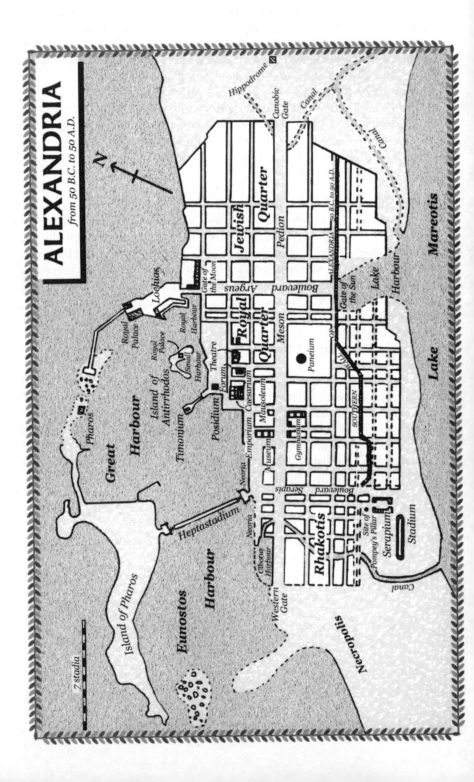

PREFACE

When Julius Caesar captured Alexandria in 47 BC, the ancient library that bore the Macedonian's name was in ruins. In the fires that raged along the harbourside, and ravaged Ptolemy's fleet, thousands of scrolls collected and composed by nine generations of resident scholars and philosophers were consumed. More destruction in AD 450 removed from scholarship a priceless inheritance of Greek, Hebrew, and probably Mesopotamian literature, and much of what was then known of ancient Egypt. What had been not the only, but perhaps the most famous library, museum and even garden of the Hellenistic period, was banished to the attics of legend and myth.

Despite this loss, or rather because of it, the ancient Library has never lost its hold on the European imagination, and in recent years, has begun to win increasing attention from historians and students of literature and science. Scholars, who for years have taken its legacy for granted, are now re-examining its history for what it can tell us about classical methods of studying literature and science, and about the transmission of ideas across cultural frontiers. Today, this interest in the past is being encouraged by a vision of the future – the Bibliotheca Alexandrina, an ultra-modern library and conference center, developed under the auspices of UNESCO and the Egyptian government, and rising on the shoreline of Alexandria, near the place where the ancient buildings are thought to have been. This international enterprise is dedicated to the advancement of knowledge, and will attract scholars from many countries. It will celebrate the cosmopolitanism that is the city and culture of Alexandria, and the traditions of internationalism, critical questioning, and freedom of enquiry that were at varying times the hallmarks of the ancient Library.

To assist the new project, and to broaden its range of acquisitions, organisations of Friends of the Alexandria Library have been established throughout the world. In Sydney, the Australian Friends have undertaken a range of programs and activities in music, art and literature. As a contribution to this activity, and in homage to the Library's legacy, a group of Australian historians, archaeologists, classicists and medievalists embraced an opportunity to share recent work on the Library's significance. This volume is the result.

It seems particularly fitting that scholars from one of the younger nations in the academic world can in this way participate in the renewal of this renowned center of ancient learning. In so doing, we celebrate Alexandria's contribution to the common culture of European nations, and to the international exchange of ideas about the natural world.

I should like to express thanks to Ms Jill Barnes for her excellent assistance in bringing this book to completion and to my authors, who made it such a fascinating adventure. Finally, it is a special pleasure to pay tribute to the work of Lorenzo Montesini, and to the Australian Friends of the Alexandria Library, to whose efforts and enterprise this book is dedicated.

Roy MacLeod
University of Sydney

Introduction: Alexandria in History and Myth

Roy MacLeod [*]

In his encyclopedic work on etymologies, the 6th century Spanish prelate and scholar, Isidore of Seville, devoted a chapter to *De Bibliothecis* – defining a *biblion*, (scroll) and *theke*, (depository) – both as places, but also as symbols of Western culture. In narratives that preceded him by seven centuries, and that outlived him by many more, there grew a tradition of scholarship that centred upon the history, legend, and influence of what some have called the 'vanished library' of Alexandria. The famous Library's origins lie among the more distant echoes of European memory, and await our rediscovery.

The story begins before Alexandria itself. Among the Greeks, it is said, Peisistratus, tyrant of Athens, was the first to found a library – subsequently taken by Xerxes to Persia, an act which set a fashion for sovereigns and sovereign cities, to seek out the books of all peoples, especially those of alien and conquered lands; and by the act of translating, render them, their languages, and their peoples members of the dominant culture.[1] According to Arrian, when Alexander the Great, Aristotle's most famous pupil, halted during one of his journeys at the western end of the Nile Delta between Lake Mareotis and the sea, he noted that 'the site was the very best in which to found a city, and that the city would prosper'. Looking to a place remote from the shrines of Olympus, he commanded that there should be dedicated to the Muses a 'library' in the new city, the most important to bear his name.[2] Flushed with imperial ambition, Alexander's successors in Egypt, the first three Macedonian kings, obeyed his instructions, and created an institution whose history and influence would reach outward in space and endure in time, bequeathing a vast legacy to the European intellectual tradition.[3] This legacy survives in the restoration of the Bibliotheca Alexandrina at the close of the present century.[4]

The story of the Great Library at Alexandria is part history, part myth. Ten years ago, Luciano Canfora published a literary account – perhaps

1

'non-fiction novel' is a better description – that scanned the cultural milieu of Hellenic Egypt at a time when the Alexandrian rulers chose to project power and influence through the encouragement and control of scholarly research.[5] That project focused upon a community of people, objects and texts within the palace at the Brucheion, the Greek section of the city.[6] For the next two thousand years – for linguists, archaeologists, historians, and scholars of religion, culture, and the book – that community became a place within a place, a constellation of identities, a heterotopia, in the language of Foucault, where text elides into subtext, and myth endures long after masonry disappears.[7]

The first extended discussion of the Library that survives is the *Letter of Aristeas* (c180–145 BC), by legend written by a Jewish scholar employed at the Library, which chronicles the history of a project to translate the Hebrew scriptures known as the Septuagint into Greek. The name survives from the belief that seventy Jewish scholars were assembled and secluded by the king until the translation was complete. Whilst the story is now not widely believed, this letter and other fragments lend support to the theory that the Library was commissioned by Ptolemy I (Soter), one of Alexander's successful generals, who after Alexander's death secured the kingship of conquered Egypt. Following Alexander's wishes, Soter (whose dynastic name continued until the XVth of the same), sought out Demetrius of Phaleron – a former tyrant of Athens, a man of affairs, and a student of Aristotle – to establish a library. (As the story goes, Ptolemy invited Theophrastus to tutor Ptolemy's heir, but the Athenian declined the position and recommended Demetrius in his place.) Demetrius, who had helped Theophrastus found a school modelled on Aristotle's Lyceum and the Academy of Plato, agreed. Seeking sanctuary from the political turbulence of the metropolis, Demetrius saw the possibilities of a well-patronised position at the periphery, and seized the opportunity.

The originality, as well as the origin, of the Alexandrian enterprise has been endlessly debated. It is clear that these Hellenes of the 3rd century were neither alone nor the first to grasp the importance of collecting and translating books in many languages as tools of commercial and political intelligence and cultural information. The ancient kingdoms of the Hittites and the Assyrians had impressive archives, reportedly in many languages, and a great library can be dated to Babylonia in the time of Nebuchadnezzar (605–562 BC).[8] Alexandria, however, promised something different. Moreover, it drew upon an appreciation of both Hellenic and Mesopotamian traditions. Fortunately, rival 'Greek' and 'orientalist' theories of genesis have been by and large resolved in favour of a view that sees Alexandria as the beneficiary of a mixed inheritance. Conceived after the manner of the Peripatetics, the special character of the Library was informed by

Macedonian rulers who had a vested interest in accumulating oriental knowledge, with the intention of installing a syncretistic Hellenism throughout the imperial world.[9]

As it unfolded, this special Alexandrian project was to become, if not unprecedented in kingly purpose, certainly unique in scope and scale. The Library was destined to be a far more ambitious undertaking than a mere repository of scrolls. It was the first to underwrite a programme of cultural imperialism, to become a 'centre of calculation', in Bruno Latour's phrase.[10] For similar reasons, royal libraries were later established in all the Hellenistic centres – for prestige, for cultural intelligence, and for the practical purposes of administration and rule.[11] Moreover, unlike its rivals at Pergamun or Ephesus, Alexandria would welcome learned Greeks to come and work together, to pursue mathematics and medicine, literature and poetry, physics and philosophy. Such would be works in whose reflected glory the Ptolemies would shine. Finally, unlike its rivals, the new Library was to be universal. It would aim for complete coverage of everything ever written. In the half century after the Stoa of Zeno and the school of Epicurus, this was to happen in one place, at which all the written works of the world would be assembled.

Thus, in this paradigmatic place, at the confluence of Mediterranean trade, was launched an industry of learning. As the king's consultant, Demetrius began its collections in the manner of Plato, with works of statecraft, on kingship and ruling – for the advancement of government and culture were the twin objectives of a wise ruler. It was an axiom of Alexander that in order to govern, conquerors must first know whom they govern. By extension, this required the collection and translation of local literatures into Greek. But the Ptolemies found it equally prestigious to collect and conserve the Hellenistic legacy itself. As Alexandria grew and prospered, so the Library would prosper, becoming an epicentre of Hellenism more Hellenic than Greece – where the Peripatetic model would flourish beyond Aristotle's dreams.

In the precinct of the Library were two institutions, the Museum and the Library itself, with overlapping purposes but separate jurisdiction – a *biblion* (or place of books) for scholars and a *museion* dedicated to the Muses. The precise location remains uncertain, but circumstantial evidence places it central to the city and its port. Its architectural style is not known, but we have clues suggesting it was built upon the plan of a *rameseseum* – as such, a combination of palace, museum, and shrine. As a shrine dedicated to the Muses, the Museum had the same legal form as Plato's school in Athens, where a school required religious status to gain the protection of Athenian law. It was presided over by a priest of the Muses, called an *epistates*, or director, appointed by analogy with the priests who managed the temples of Egypt.[12] Under his gaze, and encouraged by Ptolemy II (Philadelphus), as early as 283 BC there came together what Strabo later called a *synodos* (community) of perhaps 30–50 learned men (there were no women), salaried members of a 'civil list' for their services as tutors, granted exemption from taxes, and given free board and lodging in the royal quarter of the city, where in a circular-domed dining hall, they communally dined.[13] Outside, there were classrooms, for the residents were from time to time called upon to teach.

Perhaps not all the learned scholars were popular with the local people, as tax-exempt foreigners rarely are, particularly if, as we learn from a Roman papyrus, they are paid from public funds. But the gilded residents of the Museum often made news. Among the earliest invited by Demetrius was Euclid, the mathematician, who is supposed to have told Ptolemy I (Soter), in response to a request for coaching, that 'there is no Royal Road to Geometry'. Euclid may have compiled his *Elements* during the reign of Philadelphus; he also taught Apollonius of Perga (fl.250–220 BC), the 'great geometer', who wrote eight books on conic sections, seven of which survive – four in Greek and three in Arabic.[14] Mathematics and metaphysics seem to have lived in harmony together, alongside natural history and astronomy. Ptolemy Philadelphus, it is said, was interested in zoology; and so the Museum may also have contained a garden, a zoo, and an observatory. From the time of Ptolemy V (205–180 BC), its scholars organised games, festivals and literary competitions. It remained a cult centre, directed by a priest. If the principal shrine of Apollo was Delphi, and that of Zeus, Olympus, then surely the shrine of the Muses would be Alexandria.[15]

Near the Museum was the Library itself, directed by a scholar-librarian, appointed by the king, who also held the post of royal tutor.[16] The Library comprised several wings and porticos, with lines of shelves, or *theke*, arranged along covered walkways (which one can perhaps too easily reconstruct in the mind as cloisters). We are told that separate niches were devoted to different classes of authors, and to different categories of learning. With an enthusiasm reminiscent of latter-day saints bringing Bibles to Babylon, the agents of Ptolemy III scoured the Mediterranean for books, which swelled the growing collection.

That books are a passion, and collecting them, a pathology, should be an Alexandrian saying. The Library had little regard for intellectual property – or even for property rights *per se*. It is said that Ptolemy III (246–221 BC) wrote to all the world's sovereigns, asking to borrow their books for copying. When Athens lent him texts of Euripides, Aeschylus and Sophocles, he had them copied, but kept the originals, cheerfully forfeiting the fortune of fifteen talents he had deposited as bond. Recalling similar treatment accorded medical texts, Galen recounts that customs officials had orders to confiscate from passing ships all books they had, which were then copied.[17] The originals were deposited in the Library, and marked in the catalogue "from the ships" – thus the expression, 'ship libraries' for the larger collection. If they were lucky, owners received copies, but one suspects many travellers sailed from Alexandria minus their first editions.

The Library and Museion were not linked to any particular philosophical school or doctrine.[18] We are told that resident scholars had a degree of academic freedom, perhaps even tenure. But there were ways to cancel contracts. The rare birds who scribbled in the muses' cage, whether philosophers or systematisers, were in the service of the king, and it was wise not to invoke their wrath. A tale is told of Sotades of Maronea who, with possibly more wit than tact, wrote a ribald verse about the marriage of Ptolemy II (Philadelphus) to his sister. When identified, the unhappy poet was jailed; when he escaped, he was recaptured, put in a leaden jar, and dropped into the sea. His experience was recounted widely – perhaps invented – to caution the unruly. Knowledge and control were epigraphic in the Library's origins, and in its methods.

By the time of Callimachus, the Library possessed over 400,000 mixed scrolls with multiple works, plus another 90,000 single scrolls. As the collection grew, so at least one satellite – daughter (some say, branch) library – emerged, the Serapeion, housed in the temple of Serapis, home to a new Greco-Egyptian cult established by Ptolemy III in the southwest of the city, at some distance from the royal quarters.[19] Demetrius was himself a convert of Serapis, and the new library soon held over 40,000 books. Eventually, many other smaller libraries sprang up throughout in the city – foreshadowing the proliferation of bibliothèques and parcheminères in the Latin Quarter of medieval Paris, and the university towns of Bologna and Oxford.

Following Demetrius, the first Librarian, in what remains a problematic and incomplete list, was Zenodotus of Ephesus (283–245 BCE). Among his most famous assistants was Callimachus of Cyrene, who may never formally have held the position of Librarian,[20] but who began for the Library the first subject catalogue in the world – the *Pinakes* (tablets). This was composed of six sections, and listed some 120,000 scrolls of classical poetry and prose.[21] For the seven hundred years, until the 4th century AD, as many as a hundred scholars at a time came to the Library to consult this collection, to read, talk, and write. They wrote first on papyrus, of which Alexandria had a monopoly; and then on parchment, when the Ptolemies stopped exporting papyrus in an attempt to strangle the young library set up by the Selucids in Pergamon. At first they wrote on scrolls, which were stored in linen or leather jackets, and kept in racks in the hall, or in the cloisters. Later, in Roman times, they wrote manuscripts, in codex form, which were stored in wooden chests (*armaria*).[22]

Among the Library's staff, translators were the most numerous, called scribblers (*charakitai*) and – because they wrote on papyrus – *charta*. Their time was spent 'pecking away', as Timon of Athens put it, in the cage of the Muses. But the Library's work was not limited to the classics. About 270 BC, the Librarian's torch passed to Apollonius of Rhodes, author of the scholarly epic *Argonautica*, who reputedly made welcome the young Archimedes of Syracuse (287–212 BC). Archimedes, the genius of 'Eureka', spent some time at the Museum, observing the rise and fall of the Nile and inventing the famous 'screw' that bears his name. There he also began the science of hydrostatics, and outlined methods for calculating areas and volumes that 1800 years later formed the basis of calculus. Perhaps impelled by necessity, Archimedes turned his hand to warfare – designing siege engines for the defence of his native city against the Romans, in a contest that was to cost him his life.[23]

At the Museum and the Library, Archimedes was not alone in cultivating the practical arts. After all, the city was renowned for its Pharos, towering over 100 metres high over Alexandria's harbour – commissioned by Ptolemy II, designed by the Greek architect Sostratus of Knidos, and considered one of the seven wonders of the world. Fires lit at its top, and focussed by a plane mirror, were visible thirty miles out to sea. Within the Museum, the special demands of a culture based on agriculture and seafaring were abundantly clear. Annual inundations of the Nile altered physical landmarks, and celestial observations could help determine terrestrial property boundaries. Merchants sending ships from port, Alexandria's essential business, depended upon celestial navigation to navigate once out of sight of land. It was not accidental that men at the Museum turned their minds to the applications of mathematics and geography.

Apollonius was succeeded in 235 BC by Eratosthenes of Cyrene (c276–194 BC), the Stoic geographer and mathematician, who delighted in geometry and prime numbers. But he also taught that the oceans were connected, that Africa might be circumnavigated, and that India could be reached by sailing westwards from Spain. It was he who accurately deduced the length of the year and established the calendar that Julius Caesar appropriated; who posited that the Earth is round, and calculated its circumference based on the measured distance between Aswan and Alexandria; and who worked out the Earth's diameter to within an error of only eighty kilometres. Eratosthenes also gave a home to Eudoxus, Euclid's brightest pupil, who became the first, we are told, to teach the motions of the planets. His contemporaries at the Museum included Aristarchos of Samos (310–230 BC), who proposed a heliocentric basis for the solar system 1800 years before Copernicus; Hipparchus, who imported the 360–degree circular system from Babylonia, and amassed charts of stars and constellations; and Herophilus and Erasistratus, who pioneered the study of human anatomy, until their efforts were dimmed by protests against the dissection of bodies.[24] The Library's unrivalled access to Babylonian and Egyptian knowledge gave it a pivotal position in the civilised world.

This 'golden age' was not to last forever. After Eratosthenes, the torch of Pharos passed to Aristophanes of Byzantium (c237–180 BC), a capable grammarian (no relation to the dramatist), who introduced the use of accents in the Greek language, but who seems to have exerted less magnetism on scholars around him. After an indifferent period of twenty years, he was succeeded by the last recorded Librarian, Aristarchus of Samothrace, an eminent Homeric scholar, appointed in 175 BC during the reign of Ptolemy VII. But by that time, as a recent author has put it, Alexandrian scholarship had become dominated by literary criticism. As a centre of knowledge, it resembled the thin neck of a very large bottle – in protecting its precious contents, channelling and letting little new knowledge flow.[25]

If, during the Library's first three centuries, its early philosophers had delivered major theoretical advances in mathematics and natural knowledge, by the beginning of the Christian Era, it had become better known for custodial scholarship than for innovation. During the first century BCE, moreover, the Museum seems to have been eclipsed by the Library, and by the Library's emphasis upon the systematic study of Greek literature and the translation of non-Greek works. For this, the Library possessed unrivalled opportunities. The Library's collections may, for example, have included the Egyptian 'sacred records', from which Hecataeus of Abdera wrote the *Aegyptiaca*. But 'meddling with prose', a frequent charge levelled at the staff, was difficult to deflect. And in that reality, lay both the Library's strength and weakness.

At the time of the great fire of Alexandria in 48 BC – by legend, accidentally spread by soldiers of Julius Caesar clearing the wharves to block the fleet of Cleopatra's brother, Ptolemy XIV – Livy says the Library had over 400,000 scrolls. Of this fact we are not sure; nor are we certain what changes took place in the Library after Strabo the geographer, who lived in Alexandria between 25–20 BC, left hints about the Library in his writings. But reflection suggests that the community he knew was preoccupied not with independent study of an Archimedian kind, but with the enterprise of translation, summarisation, and philological purification that failed to transcend the Museum's early mandate.

In the words of a recent commentator, the Library 'forged a new way of seeing' on the part of the reader; its scholarship was attentive to style, to literature, to the readability of classical works.[26] On the other hand, its emphasis upon literary craftsmanship lent an overwhelming weight to a textual hegemony that discouraged the exploration of the 'new'.[27] By the beginning of the Common Era, Alexandria was a place where what could be known of Babylonian, Egyptian, Jewish and Greek thought was strenuously collected, codified, systematised, and contained. Alexandria became the foundation of the text-centred culture of the Western tradition. The disciplined life of collection and classification and an emphasis upon erudition were essential to academic professionalism. But the Library failed to maintain the quest for deeper knowledge that had distinguished its early philosophers. Where the written word conflicted with empirical observation, the life of books could prove misleading and obscure an understanding of the world. This was a lesson to be learned and later demonstrated by the natural philosophers of the Renaissance.

An illustration of this survives in the work of the second century CE, Claudius Ptolemaeus (thus Ptolemy – with no known relation to the royal family), the last great astronomer of ancient times. Ptolemy excelled in the highest Alexandrian tradition, albeit one in tension with his innovative predecessors. In his thirteen-volume *Almagest*, he systematised Alexandrian knowledge of astronomy and catalogued a thousand stars. But his elegant mathematics of epicycles – the system to which he gave his name – was put to the service of the geocentric cosmology derived from the texts of Aristotle, rather than to the service of observational astronomy. Like his monumental *Geography*, which codified what was known from all the known world, his astronomy remained influential in Europe until the 16th century; in both cases, they bore the mark of the Alexandrian editions produced by dedicated scholar-librarians, who worked systematically through the emendation and collation of classical texts. Perhaps their greatest achievement was to frame questions that would launch men in the direction of exploration, enquiry, and discovery.

* * * *

Today, the history of Alexandria's Library has a universal appeal. Much of this resides in the reverence scholars have for independent scholarship and fundamental research. It is well to remember, however, that for almost all its life, the cloister lay close to the palace. If it was an institute of advanced study, the Library was never an ivory tower. Its intellectuals were public intellectuals, and suffered the contrary imaginations of civil war. Its rituals were interrupted by political unrest, its scholarly debates, inflamed by visiting exiles. It was a tolerant academy, but within the limits of kingly patronage. Scholars of antiquity are amused when modernists credit Francis Bacon with inventing the phrase 'knowledge is power'. Bacon may have popularised the tocsin of the scientific revolution, but in Alexandria, eighteen hundred years earlier, the quest for universal knowledge had already inspired kingly enterprise. The impulse emerged again in the time of Nicholas V and Pius II, in the creation of a library at the centre of the imperial Vatican, and it has reappeared repeatedly in Western history. To attempt to control the diffusion of knowledge is a concept of Ptolemaic ambition – perhaps an achievement impossible until the age of the key-hole satellite and the World Wide Web. Yet, this was the Alexandrian project at its best, and most problematic.

Coupled with its history of princes and principalities, information and scholarship, Alexandria affords a composite model – part 'think tank', part graduate school; part observatory and part laboratory. But Alexandria the city was a place at the centre of trade in goods and peoples, as well as ideas. It was a religious site, and a site of religions, a place where all the gods were worshipped, where Jews, pagans and Christians debated theologies influenced by the Zoroastrianism of Persia, and the Buddhism and Hinduism of India. Neoplatonism, some say, was actually invented in Alexandria. But the tensions that gave it life and vitality, also threatened its survival. By the Roman period, following Caesar's conquest of Egypt, its conditions of existence were shaped by the vexations of overseas dominion, whilst its quotidian routines were distracted by riots between doctrinaires of many persuasions. Ultimately, the Library's fortunes rose and fell with those of Alexandria itself. By the second century, Rome became less dependent on Alexandrian grain, and less interested in Alexandrian scholarship. The prosperity of the city declined, and so did the reputation of the Library. Its librarians were thereafter less well known; its scholars – with significant exceptions – less distinguished, or at least, less well known to posterity. Eventually, the word 'Alexandrian' became a metonym for the craft of 'editing', for the practice of consolidating and correcting scholarship rather than creating it – critical, custodial, preoccupied with the purity of old forms, rather than pursuing the new. Its rivals in Pergamon and elsewhere rose in status and celebrity and contested its leadership.

It is not clear what damage was caused to the Library, or what remained of the Museum, when Caracalla sacked of the city in the third century AD; nor how much damage was caused by the mob incited by the Emperor Theodosius and the patriarch Theophilus, who encouraged dictators in trying to eradicate ideas by burning books, notably those of the Serapeion, in 391 AD. The last famous figure associated with the Library was Theon, the mathematician, better known as father of the martyred Hypatia, whose independent studies of geometry and musicology convinced leading Christians that she was a heretic.[28] What remained of the prosperity of Alexandria, and of the Library, fell prey to rivalries between patriarchs, and to the conquest of the Arabs in 641 AD. [29]

In that year, the 20th year of the *hejira*, the Emir Amrou Ibn el-As took the city. It is said, the Library he found was not the place it had been. There seemed few works that Arabs, learned in optics and astronomy, versed in mathematics and geography, found interesting. Its holdings had become chiefly patristic writings, sacred literature, and that crawling with errors, for Greek had become increasingly foreign to their readers. Famously, when asked what to do with the books in the Library, the Caliph Omar sent the reply:

If the content of the books is in accordance with the book of Allah, we may do without them, for in that case, the book of Allah more than suffices. If, on the other hand, they contain matter not in accordance with the book of Allah there can be no need to preserve them. Proceed, then, and destroy them.

What books were found, were distributed to the public baths, and used to feed the stoves that kept the public warm. It is said that it took six months to burn the mass of words. Only Aristotle's books, it is said, escaped.[30]

* * * *

The story of the Arab burning of the Library is legend; it may also be history.[31] If true, it would be a tragedy of suitably Greek proportions. It has been suggested that only the Great Library burned in 48 BC, and that the Museum and Sarapeion survived until the edict of Theodosius in 391 S.C. By one influential account, the Arabs bear no blame for its destruction at all.[32] Whatever the case, in the prolonged moment of its loss, which may have lasted four centuries, we locate an important part of the European past. The vanishing Library spelled the end of one way of learning, and the beginning of the new. In the Library's reconstruction – an act both historical and literary and, in contemporary Alexandria, in actual fact – we gain a better understanding of that part of our heritage that is Hellenic, and of other traditions which, blended in the alembic of Alexandria, informed the modern European mind. To rediscover some of these forgotten passages, and renew acquaintance with forgotten legacies, is the goal of the following essays.

In the first, Dan Potts, an archaeologist of the Middle East, reminds us that the Library of Alexandria was neither an isolated manifestation of librarianship in the ancient world, nor a precocious example of archival praxis. Archives are found with the first appearance of writing at the site of Uruk in southern Mesopotamia c3400 BC. The archiving of cuneiform economic texts continued into the Roman/Parthian era, while the scholarly curation of canonical literary texts began by c2500 BC. Among the most famous libraries of Near Eastern antiquity was that of Assurbanipal at Nineveh, containing thousands of tablets, many of them brought from other sites. Professor Potts' essay underlines the historical significance of Alexandria by reviewing the essential points of its ancient Near Eastern antecedents.

In the second essay, linguist and traveller Wendy Brazil explores what it was that drew scholars and statesmen from all parts of the world to Alexandria, and goes in search of the attractions of the city and its famous visitors. In the third paper, classicist Robert Barnes describes what ancient sources tell us about the library, its books, its librarians, its scholarly work, and its eventual destruction. He also discusses Luciano Canfora's best-selling book, The *Vanished Library*, and considers the author's claim that, as all public libraries in Alexandria were destroyed, we owe the survival of ancient literature entirely to private collectors.

On a different tangent, one requiring the skills of a literary investigator as well as of a classicist, R. Godfrey Tanner, the distinguished Aristotelian scholar, unravels the complex history that accompanied the arrival of Aristotle's major scientific works in Alexandria. His attempts to solve the puzzle surrounding those works that Ptolemy took, and those that reached the Library around 40 BC, are the stuff of detective drama. In the sixth essay, John Vallance, a teacher of classics and medical historian, challenges the received view that Alexandria dominated the medical world of medical scholarship, and suggests there is little evidence that doctors (or medical philosophers) enjoyed royal patronage at Alexandria, or even that medical studies were part of the research programme of the Museum. His essay works through case studies to argue that the existence of the Library enabled earlier work in medical theory to be studied in entirely new ways, but that it also contributed to the rise of one of the most practical and anti-theoretical of all the ancient medical sects.

A similar interest in the relationship between theory and practice underlies the essay by Richard Green, ancient historian and theatre historian, who uses his expert knowledge of 4th century Paphos, the Ptolemaic capital of Cyprus, to demonstrate the cultural and stylistic legacy left by Alexandria. The University of Sydney's excavations at Paphos, now under way for three seasons, are drawn upon to deduce an Alexandrian form, which bears close similarities to the classic Roman theatre. In the next paper, a set of Hellenistic influences which came to dominate Western life from the first century BC until the end of antiquity are explored for their bearing upon Roman higher education and the book trade by Samuel Lieu, classicist and specialist in the history of Manichaeism.

Towards the end of the volume, Patricia Johnson, former assistant curator and conservator of the Nicholson Museum at the University of Sydney, weighs the contribution of Alexandria to the Mystery Schools of the Mediterranean, and in particular, to the rise of Neoplatonism, with which Alexandria is often associated. In the concluding essay, medievalist John O. Ward looks beyond the flames that consumed the Alexandrian Library, to the monasteries celebrated by Umberto Eco, and explores the significance for medieval Europe of the disappearance of the Alexandrian library, and the fabric of ancient learning. He considers what of Alexandria's literary legacy survived into Carolingian times, and asks how different the European medieval world might have been had the Library not been destroyed. As it was, only one medieval library approached Alexandria in nature and scope, and that was the library which forms the subject of Umberto Eco's *Name of the Rose*. Yet, this Library never existed and is fundamentally different from all medieval libraries for which we have evidence. Dr Ward takes up this paradox in a survey of the scope and function of the medieval library, and concludes by exploring why Eco should have chosen to invent a medieval library that more resembled the Alexandrian Library, than the actual libraries of the period he set out to portray.

Taken together, these essays comprise an introduction to fresh work along a wide spectrum of literary and historical scholarship, much of it stimulated by what can call an Alexandrian impulse. They represent a confluence of research in archaeology, linguistics, the history of philosophy, the history of medicine, and the history of travel, within a tradition that refuses to accept that Alexandria must forever remain lost beyond retrieval, in legend and myth. The ancient Library may have vanished, but its critical spirit endures.

NOTES

*   *Acknowledgements*: I should like to express my warm thanks to those colleagues who have contributed to this book, and commented upon this Introduction.

1.   For a popular survey of the Library, its history and its mythology, see John Marlowe, *The Golden Age of Alexandria: From its Foundation by Alexander the Great in 331 BC to its Capture by the Arabs in 642 AD* (London: Gollancz/ Trinity Press, 1971), and the useful, if not definitive, synthesis by Mostafa El-Abbadi, *Life and Fate of the Ancient Library of Alexandria* (Paris: UNESCO/ Mouflon, 1990, 2nd ed. 1992). For an account of the Library's place in scholarship and bibliography, see Rudolf Blum, *Kallimachos: The Alexandrian Library and the Origins of Bibliography* (Madison: University of Wisconsin, 1991), a translation by H.H. Wellisch of *Kallimachos unde die Literaturverzeichnung bei den Griechen* (1991) and also F. Wormald and

C.E. Wright (eds), *The English Library before 1700* (London: Athlone Press, 1958).

2. J. R. Hamilton, *Alexander the Great* (London: Hutchinson University Library, 1973), 149.

3. For the history of Alexandria in classical scholarship, see F. Leo, *Die grie-chische-römische Biographie* (Leipzig, 1901), and the more recent H. Blanck, *Das Buch in der Antike* (Munchen: C.H. Beck, 1991); there is also a useful article on 'Das alexandrinische Mouseion', in *Pauly-Wissowas Realencyclo-padie der classischen Altertumswissenschaft*, 16.1. cols 801–21. Scholarship on the Library's influence and disappearance has remained conjectural. For decades, most was owed to the work of a few pioneering scholars, among whom was (Sir) Harold Idris Bell. See, for example, his *Egypt from Alexander the Great to the Arab Conquest: A Study in the Diffusion and Decay of Hellenism.* Gregynog Lectures for 1946 (Oxford: Clarendon Press, 1948).

4. For introductory reading, see Emer D. Johnson, *History of Libraries in the Western World* (Metuchen, N.J.: Scarcrow Press, 1970, 3rd ed., 1976); Edward A. Parsons, *The Alexandrian Library: Glory of the Hellenic World: Its Rise, Antiquities and Destruction* (New York: Elsevier, 1952).

5. Luciano Canfora, *La Biblioteca Scomparasa* (Palermo, 1986), trans. Martin Ryle as *The Vanished Library: A Wonder of the Ancient World* (Berkeley: University of California Press, 1989; London: Hutchinson Radius, 1989; Vintage, 1991).

6. P.M. Fraser, *Ptolemaic Alexandria* (Oxford: Oxford University Press, 1973), 3 vols; Edwyn Bevan, *The House of Ptolemy: A History of Egypt under the Ptole-maic Dynasty* (London, 1927; reprint Chicago: Argonaut,1968).

7. Michel Foucault, 'Of Other Spaces', *Diacritics*, 16 (1), (Spring 1968), 22–27. The site of the Library is much debated. For attempts to locate it, see Evaristo Breccia, *Alexandria ad Aegyptum: A Guide to the Ancient and Modern Town, and to its Graeco-Roman Museum* (Bergamo: Institutio Italiano d'Arti Grafichi, 1922). A most readable modern account is E.M. Forster's *Alexan-dria: A History and a Guide* (Garden City: Doubleday, 1961; 3rd ed. 1982), which should be read in conjunction with G.L. Steen (ed.), *Alexandria, the Site and the History* (New York: New York University Press, 1993). Recent work by Judith McKenzie of the University of Sydney promises to throw new light on the subject. See her 'Alexandria and the Origins of Baroque Architecture', in *Alexandria and Alexandrianism* (Malibu: J. Paul Getty Museum, 1996), 109–125.

8. Lionel Casson, *Travel in the Ancient World* (London: George Allen and Unwin, 1974), 240; John A Brinkman, 'Mesopotamian Chronology of the Historical Period', in A. Leo Oppenheim, *Ancient Mesopotamia: Portrait of a Dead Civilization* (Chicago:University of Chicago Press, 2nd ed. 1977), 335–348; Nissen, Hans J. *The Early History of the Ancient Near East, 9000–2000 BC* (Chicago: University of Chicago Press, 1988); Benjamin R. Foster, *Before the Muses: An Anthology of Akkadian Literature* (Bethesda: CDL Press, 1993), 2 vols; Jeremy A. Black and W. J. Tait, 'Archives and Libraries in the Ancient Near East', in Jack M. Sasson (ed.), *Civilizations of the Ancient Near East* (New York: Scribners, 1995), IV, 2197–2209.

9. H.J. de Vleeschauwer, 'Afterword: Origins of the Mouseion of Alexandria', in H. Curtis Wright, *The Oral Antecedents of Greek Librarianship* (Provo, Utah: Brigham Young University Press, 1977), 176–180. This essay first appeared in Conrad H. Rawski (ed.), *Toward a Theory of Librarianship: Papers in Honor of Jesse Hawk Shera* (Metuchen, NJ: Scarcrow Press, 1973).

10. Bruno Latour, *Science in Action* (Milton Keynes: Open University Press, 1987).
11. Max Cary, *A History of the Greek World from 323 to 146 BC* (New York: Barnes and Noble, 1963).
12. El-Abbadi, *op. cit.* 86.
13. El-Abbadi, *op. cit.* 87.
14. See T. Heath (1896).
15. See Harold Idris Bell, *Cults and Creeds in Graeco-Roman Egypt* (Liverpool: Liverpool University Press, 1957); for the association of Alexandria with the history of religious cults, see R.T. Wallis, *Neoplatonism* (London: Gerald Duckworth, 1972) and David Fideler (ed.), *Alexandria, Journal of the Western Cosmological Traditions* (Grand Rapids: Phanes Press, 1991).
16. El-Abbadi, *op. cit.* 93.
17. Galen, *Commentary on Hippocrates Epidemics* III, XVIIA.606K. I am indebted to John Vallance for this reference.
18. Blum, *Kallimachos, op. cit.* 95 ff.
19. El-Abbadi, *op. cit.* 91; Alan Rowe, *Discovery of the Famous Temple and Enclosure of Serapis at Alexandria* (Caïre: Institut français d'archéologie orientale, 1946); Alan Rowe, 'A Contribution to the Archaeology of the Western Desert, IV: The Great Serapeum of Alexandria', *Bulletin of the John Rylands Library*, 39, (1956–57), 485–520.
20. El-Abbadi, *op. cit.* 93–94; C.O. Brink, 'Callimachus and Aristotle', *Classical Quarterly*, 40 (1946), 11–26.
21. See Raymond Irwin, 'Callimachus and the Alexandrian Library', in *The English Library: Sources and History* (London: George Allen & Unwin, 1966), 24–41; Peter Bing, *The Well-read Muse: Present and Past in Callimachus and the Hellenistic Poets* (Göttingen: Vandenhoeck & Ruprecht, 1988); Rudolf Pfeiffer (ed.), *Callimachus* (Oxford: Clarendon Press, 1949–1953); F.J. Witty, 'The Other *Pinakes* and Reference Works of Callimachus', *Library Quarterly*, 43, (1973), 237–244; and Aristoxenos D. Skiadas (ed.), *Kallimachos* (Darmstadt: Wissenschaftliche Buchgesellschaft, 1975).
22. H.L. Pinner, *The World of Books in Classical Antiquity* (Leiden: A.S.Sijthoff, 1948), 12–21; E.G. Turner, 'L'Érudition Alexandrine et les Papyrus', *Chronique d'Égypte*, 37 (1962), 135–152; M.A. Hussein, *Origins of the Book: Egypt's Contribution to the Development of the Book from Papyrus to Codex* (Greenwich, Conn.: New York Graphic Society, 1972).
23. Archimedes addressed his discoveries to mathematicians known to have lived in Alexandria. For introductions to his life and work, see Marshall Claggett, 'Archimedes', Dictionary of Scientific Biography (New York: Scribers, 1970), vol 1, 213–231; and Michael Authier, 'Archimedes: The Scientist's Canon,' in Michel Serres (ed.), *A History of Scientific Thought: Elements of a History of Science* (London: Blackwells, 1995), 124–160.
24. See G.E.R. Lloyd, 'A Note on Erasistratus of Ceos', *Journal of Hellenic Studies*, 95 (1975), 172–5.
25. Michael Ryan, reviewing Marc Baratin and Christian Jacob (eds), *Le Pouvoir des Bibliothèques* (Paris: Albin Michel, 1996).
26. Christian Jacob, in *Le Pouvoir des Bibliothèques* (Paris: Albin Michel, 1996).
27. See, for example, James J. O'Hara, *True Names: Vergil and the Alexandrian Tradition of Etymological Wordplay* (Ann Arbor: University of Michigan Press, 1996); Rudolf Pfeiffer, *History of Classical Scholarship from the Beginnings to the End of the Hellenistic Age* (Oxford: Clarendon Press, 1968).
28. See Maria Dzielska, *Hypatia of Alexandria* (Cambridge, Mass.: Harvard University Press, 1995).

29. Alfred J. Butler, *The Arab Conquest of Egypt* (Oxford: Clarendon Press,1902; 2nd ed., P.M. Fraser, 1978).
30. See Canfora, *op. cit.* 98.
31. Mohamed Awad, 'A Note on the Alleged Destruction of the Alexandria Library by the Arabs', *Journal of World History*, 8 (1964), 213–214.
32. El-Abbadi, *op. cit.* 145–179.

Part I.

Alexandria in History and Myth

Chapter 1

Before Alexandria: Libraries in the Ancient Near East

D.T. Potts

INTRODUCTION

Between 1849 and 1854 Austen Henry Layard and Hormuzd Rassam recovered roughly 30,000 cuneiform tablets, and fragments thereof,[1] at the Assyrian site of Nineveh in northern Iraq, most in the great mound of Kuyunjik.[2] Since then, most scholars have followed M. Jastrow[3] and A.L. Oppenheim[4] in identifying the late Assyrian king Asurbanipal (668–627 BC) as the assembler of 'what has every right to be called the first systematically collected library in the ancient Near East'.[5] In fact, Jastrow and Oppenheim were certainly wrong, not only because Assurbanipal's predecessor Senncherib (688–681 BC) had a library of his own in the Southwest Palace, or 'Palace without Rival' as it was known,[6] at Nineveh,[7] but more fundamentally because of mounting evidence attesting to the existence of libraries throughout Mesopotamia long before the mid-7th century BC. The purpose of this short communication is merely to provide a sketch of some of the most pertinent evidence now available for the earliest history of libraries in the ancient world.[8]

1. THE ORIGINS OF ARCHIVAL BEHAVIOUR

I shall take as my starting point the thesis that, in order to speak about libraries, we must first have evidence of the curation and storage of texts, and in order to speak of texts, we must of course have evidence of writing. In spite of much work in recent decades throughout the length and breadth of Western Asia, the fact remains that the so-called 'Archaic texts' found at Warka, the ancient city of Uruk in southern Iraq, and known since the beginning of this century,[9] are still the oldest written documents found anywhere in the world. Their absolute date is a subject of dispute, exacerbated by the dearth of radiocarbon dates from Uruk as well as from other, contemporary sites which have yielded examples of so-called Uruk IV and III tablets, but we shall not be far off in assigning them a broad time range of c. 3400 to 3000 BC.[10] In spite of much investigation elsewhere, it still seems true to say that writing was invented, not broadly in southern Mesopotamia, but very specifically at the site of Uruk, prompting one Sumerologist to speak of 'an' inventor, *literatus Sumericus Urukeus*, rather than a vague cohort of anonymous early scribes.[11] As many scholars have emphasised in recent years,[12] with an estimated size of over 200 ha. by the late fourth millennium BC, Uruk surpassed all other early urban centres in the region in areal extent and most probably population concentration, and it was here that the pre-conditions for the emergence of writing were most clearly in evidence. The fiction that all land belonged to the gods; that men and women should work that land on the deity's behalf; and that the deity's 'house', in our terms, his temple, but more realistically his *oikos* or household, should be managed by his servants – i.e., a priesthood – created not only social stratification but also generated a massive agricultural sector and a redistributive economy. It was here, in the nexus between production and redistribution in the form of rations to household employees, that the need for arithmetic and algebraic calculation and for the storage of information arose and that the *modus operandi*, in the form of writing, was invented.[13]

Writing was devised, purely and simply, as a solution to an account-technical problem, not for the perpetuation of myths, epics, hymns, historical records, or royal propaganda. All of this followed, but it was not in the minds of writing's inventor(s). What did accompany the earliest economic texts immediately, i.e. in the very first phase of writing's development, were lexical texts, word lists containing terms belonging to discrete semantic domains – titles and professions, names of metal objects, ceramic vessels, textiles, cities, trees, plants, cattle, swine, birds, fish, etc. Along with mathematical reckoning, these lexical lists were undoubtedly the backbone of early scribal education.

With this new technology came, it seems, an associated development of what we may call 'archival behaviour'. The vast majority of the c. 4500 Archaic texts from Uruk were found abandoned in lots, in secondary or even tertiary context (e.g. used as fill beneath new buildings) outside of the temples and other structures which make up the Eanna complex, the great temple household of Inanna, the city goddess of Uruk.[14] What is evident is that they had been discarded some time, perhaps a century or more, after having been written. As Veenhof has noted, 'Normally, old records no longer needed by the administration were thrown away in due time or put to secondary use, as building material... etc'.[15] The important point here, however, is that, for an unspecified period of time which probably exceeded several generations, texts at Uruk were curated or archived, in spite of the fact that the economic texts among them were certainly no longer current. Thus, in tandem with the birth of writing in the Near East we observe the birth of an archival, curatorial attitude towards written texts.

2. THE MECHANICS OF ARCHIVING

Because the early Uruk texts were found in secondary or tertiary contexts, we have no idea how they may originally have been stored. Our first information of this sort comes from the mid-third millennium BC. That tablets were being systematically stored by this time is demonstrated by the so-called 'tablet house' at Fara, ancient Shuruppak, and room L. 2769 in royal palace G at Tell Mardikh, ancient Ebla, in Syria, each of which dates to c. 2600–2400 BC. The combination of economic, administrative records and 'school texts', e.g. lexical lists and didactic, practice tablets (some of which contain literary fragments) in the tablet collections from the sites just mentioned more or less mirrors the situation which obtained in the late fourth millennium, suggesting that scribal education went hand in hand with ongoing, daily administration and that the former activity required the conservation of certain types of texts which could be studied and copied by scribal students. This didactic requirement was perhaps, as much as bookkeeping convention, responsible for the archiving of texts right from the beginning of Mesopotamian history. But physically a separation of the two operations – information storage and writing – can be observed at Ebla, where room L. 2769 represents the true archive room in which texts were stored and consulted,[16] while the adjoining L. 2875 seems to have been the *scriptorium* where scribes sat on low benches running around the walls of the room and wrote new texts.[17]

The ancient Mesopotamian archival room is obviously of interest for the history of the library in general. Clandestine excavations by local Arabs at Tello came upon mud brick benches, c. 50 cm. wide, both against the walls and in the middle of rooms in the 'archival building', on which up to six rows of tablets from the reigns of Shulgi (2094–2047 BC) and Amar-Sin (2046–2038 BC) were arranged in what appeared to be chronological order. Traces of wooden shelving are known from a number of sites including Ur in southern Mesopotamia; Ebla in Syria; and Kültepe and Boghazköy in Turkey. The largest tablets in L. 2769 at Ebla stood in rows on shelves (collapsed of course),[18] so that they could be quickly scanned like file cards by anyone needing to search for a particular text, while at Nippur tablets stood like books on a shelf. A honeycomb of 'pigeonholes' consisting of 25–30 cm. square niches, each c. 40–50 cm. deep, were found in the wall of the 'library room' of the Nabû temple at Khorsabad, ancient Dur-Sharrukin, in Assyria, each holding tablets of a specific genre, while a similar arrangement was used in Room 61 of Sennacherib's palace at Nineveh for holding papyrus documents. 'Brick boxes', sometimes described as ancient 'filing cabinets', were discovered in the Northwest Palace at Nimrud and this device, along with wooden boxes, woven baskets, and leather bags, served to hold tablets which were in use or during transport.[19] Small dockets, functioning as labels, have been found with the formula, '**gigipisan.dub.ba...i.[in.]gál**', meaning 'tablet basket/coffer which contains...', followed by the name of one or more officials and a date. The fact that many such dockets are perforated suggests that they were affixed to their respective containers with a cord.[20] In other cases, the upper edge of a tablet was often inscribed so that, when the tablets were standing like file cards, one could read a date, sometimes a summary of the transaction recorded, and occasionally the name of the scribe responsible. At Mari in Syria, small tablets marked with a red ochre stripe seem to represent economic texts, the contents of which had been noted and entered into a larger, summary ledger text.[21]

Another archival device which should be mentioned is an intrinsic one, namely tablet shape. As Veenhof has noted, tablets are known in a wide variety of shapes, ranging from the round agricultural texts of the Ur III period (2100–2000 BC) at Tello, to the small tablets used for daily economic transactions and the long, multi-columned tablets used for lexical lists. Tablet genre could thus be communicated by tablet shape, and tablets belonging to separate genres could thereby be sorted and stored separately.

These few remarks suffice to demonstrate that the physical organisation of tablet collections and their curation were well developed in Mesopotamia long before the time of Assurbanipal. But how do we move from archives to libraries?

3. THE RAISON D'ÊTRE AND COMPOSITION OF THE ANCIENT MESOPOTAMIAN LIBRARY

Thus far I have spoken only of official, temple and palace archives, and have not even mentioned so-called 'private archives' representing, for the most part, texts recording commercial transactions, real estate purchases, etc. of an individual and/or his family, sometimes over several generations, which resulted in the physical concentration of tablets within a house. Beginning in the second millennium BC, examples of private archives become too numerous to even begin to summarise here,[22] but neither these nor the official archives discussed earlier can be said to constitute 'libraries' in the modern sense of the term. For Oppenheim, the salient feature of Assurbanipal's library was the fact that its contents were representative of the sum total of the learned tradition of ancient Mesopotamia, whereas most of the archives just described have been collections of economic texts with an admixture of lexical and school texts deemed necessary by the scribes who wrote the administrative tablets.

Vital to an understanding of both Oppenheim's and the ancients' point of view is the notion of 'the stream of tradition – that is, what can loosely be termed the corpus of literary texts maintained, controlled, and carefully kept alive by a tradition served by successive generations of learned and well-trained scribes'.[23] This tradition of copying texts and thereby transmitting the tradition can be traced right back to the late fourth millennium BC, for duplicates of some of the earliest lexical lists from Uruk are known in copied form from other Mesopotamian sites some two to three thousand years later.[24] And it is to this same propensity to copy, re-copy, preserve and transmit that we owe our knowledge of most Mesopotamian literature and scholarly lore.

Ernst Weidner was perhaps the first to stress that, notwithstanding the c. 30,000 tablets and fragments recovered in excavation, the actual number of tablets in Assurbanipal's library was probably more on the order of 5000, not counting multiple copies of the same composition.[25] Oppenheim later arrived at a more conservative estimate of about 1500 'manuscripts', but Simo Parpola has recently called attention to three fragmentary administrative texts from Nineveh which 'record acquisitions or accessions to the palace libraries of Nineveh' amounting to c. 2000 tablets and 300 writing-boards.[26] Given that this was a single, 'major acquisition to the library', the total number of manuscripts may indeed have been close to Weidner's estimated 5000.

For Oppenheim, the Nineveh library was 'representative' of the Mesopotamian learned tradition. The question is, what did it contain?[27] Like most libraries, its collections were heterogeneous. Oppenheim made a rough attempt at giving a breakdown of its contents based on the 25,357 tablets and fragments which had been published or, in most cases, catalogued with their contents noted in a one-line summary, by the 1950's.[28] Listed in order of frequency, these are as follows: omen texts, c. 300; lexical (generally bilingual, Sumerian and Akkadian) texts, c. 100; 'cycles of conjurations for cathartic and apotropaic purposes', in addition to fables and proverbs, c. 100 texts; epic literature, e.g. Gilgamesh, Atrahasis, Erra, Etana, Anzu, Adapa, etc.[29], c. 35–40 texts.[30] Although he was somewhat loathe to do so, Oppenheim estimated that, as far as the number of lines on these texts went, 'the sum total would leave the Rigveda (about the size of the Illiad) and the Homeric epics, as well as the Old and the New Testaments (which surpass the epics only slightly as to the number of verses), far behind, and would probably reach, if not exceed in bulk, even the size of the Mahabharata with its 190,000 verses'.[31]

If we examine in greater detail the remarkable catalogues to which Parpola has drawn attention, then we find the presence of no fewer than 31 different text genres (which includes all varieties of omen texts), 17 of which are only attested by a single exemplar. The most common texts recorded are listed below (> = 'minimum of'):

haruspical omens[32]	> 135 writing boards
astrological omens	> 107 tablets, 6 boards
terrestrial omens	> 79 tablets, 1 board
medical recipes	> 6 tablets, 24 boards
dream omens	> 22 tablets
teratological omens[33]	> 10 tablets, 10 boards
exorcists' lore	> 18 tablets, 1 board
epics, myths	> 10 tablets

Oppenheim had already estimated that the *belles-lettres* for which Meso-potamia is today famous, whether the Flood myth (*Atrahasis*) or the Epic of Gilgamesh, constituted a numerically insignificant portion of the holdings in Assurbanipal's library. The new evidence adduced by Parpola confirms this, for here we find that an obsession with predicting the future and divining the most propitious moment for a particular act – be it for an individual or a whole nation – was of overriding concern. As Parpola writes, this is, in the main, 'professional literature of experts in Mesopotamian scientific and religious lore'.[34] These 'chief scholar-experts' (*rab ummâni*) were amongst the highest officials at the royal court, some even achieving a kind of immortal fame as sages which propelled them into the realm of myth. As Oppenheim has noted, 'The scholar-scribes' special but not exclusive concern is with divination: by interpreting ominous signs and features they predict the future for the king, the country, and private citizens. This they do on the basis of elab-orate textbooks. Such compendia on which many generations of scholars had worked constitute the largest body of organised text collec-tions coming from Mesopotamia'.[35] Thus, it is the textbooks of the 'chief scholar-experts' just described which constitute the overwhelming majority of manuscripts found in Assurbanipal's library.

4. LIBRARY ACQUISITION POLICIES

Although the tradition of copying was the primary mechanism in ancient Mesopotamia for the transmission of knowledge, there is another aspect to Assurbanipal's library which must be mentioned – namely, collecting.

Not all of the texts from Nineveh were written there. As William Hallo has stressed, even at the level of the individual scribe, 'the methods of the scribal schools may have encouraged their graduates to construct and maintain small libraries of their own'.[36] That tablets were indeed collected from other sources is shown by the provenience of some of the tablets acquired at Assurbanipal's library. Two came from Tabni, the scribe of the Assyrian crown prince's chief eunuch; eighteen texts, including a composition called 'Rope of Heaven', six tablets of exorcist's lore, and five lexical texts were acquired from Assurbanipal's brother, Ashshur-mukin-pale'a; and by far the bulk from Assyrian exorcists, scribes and priests. Parpola's conclusion is that these were 'donations made by the owners themselves' during their lifetimes.[37] Apart from this single acquisition, we know that the original core of Assurbanipal's library was the tablet collection of the priest Nabû-zuqup-kênu of Nimrud, dating to the late 8th/early 7th century BC, which Assurbanipal had brought to Nineveh.[38]

Because of the fact that some of the texts in Assurbanipal's library are dated (e.g. to 670, 665 and 655 BC), as are two of the three library acquisition catalogues under discussion (in one case to 28 January 647 BC, in another to 26 March 647 BC), we can say with confidence that a library such as this one took decades to be accumulated. It is important to note, moreover, that Assurbanipal collected tablets the way certain despots, in time of war, have collected art. The infusion of Babylonian texts recorded in the acquisitions catalogue occurred some five months after Assurbanipal had crushed his rebellious brother, Shamash-shum-ukin, who had broken with his brother and challenged Assyrian authority in Babylonia. As Parpola notes, Assurbanipal probably took advantage of the situation to increase his library's holdings by confiscating tablets at will. The fact that ten writing boards with extispicy texts were acquired from Bit-Ibâ is particularly telling, for this was a southern Babylonian (Chaldaean) 'house' (similar in some respects to a tribe, claiming descent from an eponymous ancestor) which had been at war with Assyria. An anonymous Assyrian letter, attributed by Weidner and Parpola to Assurbanipal, which was addressed to Shadunu, governor of Borsippa, explicitly orders 'the confiscation of all kinds of literary works both from temple and private libraries for inclusion in the Ninevite libraries'.[39] This unique document is worthy of quotation in full:

Word of the king to Shadunu: I am well, be of good cheer.
On the day when you receive my tablet, you shall take with you Shuma, the son of Shum-ukin, Bel-etir his brother, Apla, the son of Arkat-ilani, and the expert from Borsippa whom you know; and you shall bring forth (?) all the tablets that are in their houses (as well as)

those deposited in Ezida [the main temple of Borsippa's city god, Nabu]. You shall collect the tablets (which are recited on) the royal shores of the rivers during the days of the month of Nisan, the stone amulet (which is worn) on the river during the month of Tishri, (the tablet) of the ordeal by water, the stone amulet (which is worn) by the river for reckoning the day (?) "the four stone amulets (which are placed) at the head and foot of the royal bed," "the weapon of *eru* wood at the head of the royal bed" (and the tablet bearing) the incantation, "May Ea and Marduk complete wisdom". You shall search for and send me (the tablets of) the series "Battle", as many as are available, together with the tablet "Their blood" (and) the remaining ones, all that are available; (also the tablets): "In the battle the spear (?) shall not come near a man", "To rest in the wilderness (and) again to sleep (in the palace", (as well as) rituals, prayers, stone inscriptions and whatever is useful to royalty (such as) expiation (texts) for (the use of) cities, to ward off the (evil) eye at a time of panic, and whatever (else) is required in the palace, all that is available, and (also) rare tablets of which no copies (?) exist in Assyria. I have (already) written to the temple overseer (?) and to the chief magistrate (that) you are to place (the tablets) in your storage house (and that) no one shall withhold any tablet from you. And in case you should see some tablet or ritual which I have not mentioned to you (and) which is suitable for the palace, examine it, take possession of it, and send it to me'.[40]

Weidner was perhaps the first to emphasise the fact that, judging both by the clay of which they are made and by the orthography of the writing, many of the texts in Assurbanipal's library can be identified as genuine Babylonian texts, not copies of Babylonian texts.[41] This is confirmed by the acquisitions catalogue. Thus, one acquisition entry reads as follows: '1 one-column tablet, anti-witchcraft, Mushezib-Nabû, son of Nabû-shum-ishkun, the scribe of the king of Babylon', while another records, '2 (of) lamentations, 1 (of) the Dream Book, in all 125 tablets, Arrabu, an exorcist from Nippur'.[42] The sources of these two lots – Babylon and Nippur – lay far to the south of Nineveh in the heart of Babylonia.

Similarly, many tablets belonging to the astrological series *Enûma Anu Enlil* from the tablet collection of Nabû-zuqup-kênu of Nimrud, whose career as a senior scribe under Sargon II (721–705 BC) and Sennacherib (704–681 BC) spanned at least thirty-three years between 716 and 683 BC,[43] contain a subscript identifying his texts as copies of originals from Babylon, Borsippa, Uruk, and Kish.[44] One wonders how the originals were acquired. Nabû-zuqup-kênu was explicit in stating that he made his copies at Nimrud, not in Babylonia, but whether the texts reached there as booty we cannot say.

5. THE UNIQUENESS OF ASSURBANIPAL'S LIBRARY RECONSIDERED

By now it should be clear that, in view of everything just said, Assurbanipal's library was not unique. Nor was it, as Oppenheim once claimed, the first systematically collected library in the ancient world. The acquisitions catalogue published by Parpola attributes hundreds of tablets to individual donors – 435 to Nabû-x ... , 342 to Nabû-apal-iddin; 188 to Nabû-nadin-apli, etc. Whether these were confiscated or donated is of no consequence. What matters is that this information demonstrates the existence of numerous, well-stocked private libraries in the Neo-Assyrian period which were not simply collections of family bills and receipts. Nor was this a situation unique to Nineveh or to Assurbanipal, who prided himself on being a learned man and said of himself, 'The hidden treasure, the complete art of the written tablet, have I examined in the houses of heaven and earth, it has been delivered up to me among all experts'.[45]

The core of Assurbanipal's library was a collection put together by a priest at Nimrud in the late 8th/early 7 century BC, but there is another Assyrian example which pre-dates Assurbanipal by nearly 600 years. In 1904 the German excavators at Assur discovered a library in the temple of the city god Ashur,[46] the composition of which demonstrates conclusively that there was absolutely nothing unique about Assurbanipal's undertaking. The collection can be attributed to two of Assurbanipal's greatest predecessors on the throne of Assyria – Tukulti-Ninurta I (1243–1207 BC) and Tiglath-Pileser I (1114–1076 BC) – both of whom campaigned vigorously against Babylonia during their careers.

Given what we know of the evolution of Assyrian political power and learned tradition, it is understandable that each monarch, like Assurbanipal many centuries later, had a voracious appetite for Babylonian texts, for these were seen as the most sophisticated examples of wisdom and learning yet achieved in the ancient Near East. Tablets dating back to the reign of Hammurabi of Babylon (1792–1750 BC) were acquired by these two Middle Assyrian kings, although the bulk of their plundered Babylonian tablets date to the period of Kassite domination in Babylonia, which lasted from c. 1600 to 1155 BC. As with Assurbanipal's library, we can identify a wide range of text genres in the Ashur temple collection, including legal texts (e.g. Hammurabi's famous law code), omens of all sorts, medical texts, lexical texts (e.g. the bilingual list of god names AN = *Anum*), literary texts (e.g. so-called 'disputations', such as the 'Disputation between the Date-Palm and the Tamarisk'), and compendia of royal Assyrian edicts issued by no fewer than nine different kings.[47] The colophons on the texts actually written at Assur give us the name of a handful of scribes, including three sons of one Ninurta-uballitsu, who bore the title *tupshar sharri* or the 'king's scribe', who were particularly engaged in copying exemplars for deposit in the library.

As Weidner stressed, it is not only the fact that the 'right' selection of works were represented here which justifies calling the Ashur temple collection a library, rather it is also the unambiguous evidence of cataloguing procedures which adds weight to the use of the term. By this I mean that individual texts had begun to be assigned to canonical 'series' (e.g. **Lugal-e**; SIG_7.ALAM = *nabnitu*; DIRI = *watru; ana ittishu*), the names of which were written as a subscript on individual tablets assigned to that series. In one case, a tablet belonging to a particular omen series has the number '15' in a subscript, presumably identifying it as one of a set of tablets belonging to that series. Moreover, true catalogues of the Ashur temple collection were compiled in multiple copies, such as a catalogue of all the hymns, carefully indexed by their first lines or 'incipits', as was the norm in Assyria and Babylonia going right back to the early second millennium BC.[48]

Similar catalogues were found in Assurbanipal's library,[49] as were tags bearing the names of individual text series, such as the astrological series Enûma Anu Enlil,[50] which perhaps hung over shelves of tablets. Comments can be found on some of the omen texts from Nineveh, such as 'these (three omens) are from the series', clearly indicating that the omens had been classified. On the other hand, care was also taken to segregate non-canonical texts from those properly assigned to a series. Thus, we read in one case, 'this (is) not canonical', 'this (omen) is not from the ,series, it is not canonical' or 'this omen is not from the series, but from the mouth of a teacher'.[51]

If the Ashur temple library confirms the existence of sophisticated libraries in Assyria prior to the time of Assurbanipal, the Babylonian provenience of many of the tablets in both the Nineveh and Ashur libraries leaves us in no doubt as to the existence of libraries in Babylonia. Undoubtedly one of the most exciting discoveries of the last decade in Mesopotamian archaeology was that of 'a complete Neo-Babylonian temple library with the tablets in situ on the shelves' which a team of Iraqi archaeologists from the University of Baghdad made in January 1986 at the important site of Sippar in central Iraq.[52] The excavations took place in a subsidiary temple of the main temple to the sun-god Shamash, known as the **é-babbar** or 'white house'. Although previously investigated in the late 19th and early 20th centuries by Hormuzd Rassam, on behalf of the British Museum, and Vincent Scheil, for the Louvre, the Iraqi team discovered a previously untouched room. The situation has been described as follows:

> Northeast of the courtyard A lies a large room (not on Rassam's plan) with a long narrow room running southwest-northeast

between it and the É-babbar. The library is in a small room leading off this long room at its southwest end ... On entering the library, whose walls are preserved up to 1.5 m or more ... one finds oneself in a small room about 1.5 m wide and 1 m deep ... In the two walls to left and right (of the doorway), and the back wall ... are a series of niches built out from the mud-brick walls. The niches are c. 17 cm high and c. 30 cm wide, arranged in rows one above the other. In each of the two side walls are four ranks of niches, and in the back wall six. There are three levels of niches completely preserved; and a fourth above them, probably the top one, damaged at the left side but preserved at the right and back ... . Thus it is reckoned that there were originally 56 niches in all ... . Each niche is c. 70 cm deep; and shelves and partitions are mud-brick, but reeds are plastered inside as an upper lining ... . In these the tablets were stacked on their long sides like books, two or three rows deep, up to 60 per niche. Counting from the left, niches 1, 2 and 3 of the top level (here third from bottom), and 2 of the second level, have been cleared so far [1987], yielding 182 tablets and fragments, including some from the uppermost (fourth) level ... . It is estimated that more than 2000 tablets were stored in the library'.[53]

The fact that an adjacent room had a floor made of bricks stamped with the name of Nabonidus (555–539 BC), last king of the Neo-Babylonian dynasty, and that the latest economic text found in the library dates to the first year of the Achaemenid Persian emperor Cambyses (529 BC), is probably an indication that, however early the library's origins may be, the form in which it was found dates to the late 6th century BC. Tablets hailing from Agade, Babylon and Nippur – all sites in Babylonia – were present along with originals from Sippar. One of the oldest texts is a list of temple property in the Nippur area dating to the seventh year of Adad-apla-iddina, 1061 BC. In comparison with the Assyrian libraries discussed previously, the Sippar collection seems to have an unusually high proportion of literary and historical texts, but this may not be an anomaly, rather an indication that individual libraries differed in their make-up.

Finally, it should be pointed out that true libraries were not restricted to Mesopotamia proper. Forty tablet catalogues (including fragments), like those of the Assur and Nineveh libraries discussed earlier, have been found of Hittite texts at the Hittite capital Bogazköy in Turkey,[54] attesting to the existence there of a curated corpus of texts. Excavations at Sultantepe, ancient Huziririna, near Harran in southeastern Turkey, have also revealed a library from the 8th century BC belonging to one Qurdi-Nergal.[55]

CONCLUSION

Despite the undeniable impact of the discovery of Assurbanipal's library in the last century, discoveries of the subsequent 140 years have necessitated a revision in our thinking about libraries and their origins in the ancient Near East. While Assurbanipal may have been amongst the most zealous collectors of manuscripts the world has yet known, his bibliophile interests grew out of a much more ancient tradition which can be traced throughout Mesopotamia, Syria, Anatolia and, one suspects, most of the 'cuneiformised' Near East. That archival behaviour emerged concurrently with the origins of writing in the fourth millennium BC is not a matter for doubt. Thus, a good two and half to three thousand years of archival, curatorial, registrational behaviour can be documented in the Tigris-Euphrates river valley by the time we arrive at what was undeniably a monument of scholarly accumulation, the library of Assurbanipal. It is against this background of manuscript curation, collation and cataloguing that one must view subsequent developments in the field of ancient library development, of which the Alexandrian case is undoubtedly the most well-known.

NOTES

*   Note the following abbreviation: *CAL* = Klaas R. Veenhof (ed.), *Cuneiform Archives and Libraries* (Leiden: Uitgaven van het Nederlands Historisch-Archaeologisch Instituut te Istanbul 57, 1986).

1.   For the figure I follow Simo Parpola, 'Assyrian Library Records', *Journal of Near Eastern Studies*, 42 (1983), 6.

2.   Simo Parpola, 'The Royal Archives of Nineveh', *CAL*, 227.

3.   Morris Jastrow, 'Did the Babylonian temples have libraries?' *Journal of the American Oriental Society*, 27 (1906), 165.

4.   A. Leo Oppenheim, *Ancient Mesopotamia: Portrait of a Dead Civilization* (Chicago: Univ. of Chicago Press, 1977, 2nd ed.), 15.

5.   Dates used for Mesopotamian monarchs in this paper follow John A. Brinkman, 'Mesopotamian Chronology of the Historical Period' in Oppenheim, *op. cit.* 335–348.

6.   Sylvie Lackenbacher, *Le Palais sans Rival: Le récit de construction en Assyrie* (Paris: Éditions la Découverte, 1990).

7.   Simo Parpola, 'The Royal Archives of Nineveh', *CAL*, 232. Cf. Julian Reade, 'Archaeology and the Kuyunjik Archives', *CAL*, 218ff.

8.   For some previous reviews of the topic, see inter alia A.A. Kampman, 'Archieven en bibliotheken in het Oude Nabije Oosten', *Handelingen van het Zesde Wetenschappelijk Vlaamsch Congres voor Boek- en Bibliotheekwezen, Gent 31. Maart 1940* (Schoten-Antwerp, 1941), which was unfortunately unavailable to me; Mogens Weitemeyer, 'Archive and Library Technique in Ancient Mesopotamia', *Libri*, 6 (1956), 217–238; or Jeremy A. Black and W. J. Tait, 'Archives and Libraries in the Ancient Near East', in Jack M. Sasson (ed.), *Civilizations of the Ancient Near East* (New York: Scribners, 1995), IV, 2197–2209.

9. Adam Falkenstein, *Archaische Texte aus Uruk* (Leipzig: Ausgrabungen der Deutschen Forschungsgemeinschaft in Uruk-Warka 2, 1936). Cf. now Margaret W. Green and Hans J. Nissen, *Zeichenliste der archaischen Texte aus Uruk* (Berlin: Ausgrabungen der Deutschen Forschungsgemeinschaft in Uruk-Warka 11, 1987); Robert K. Englund and Hans J. Nissen, *Die lexikalischen Listen der archaischen Texte aus Uruk* (Berlin: Ausgrabungen der Deutschen Forschungsgemeinschaft in Uruk-Warka 13, 1993); Robert K. Englund, *Archaic Administrative Texts from Uruk: The Early Campaigns* (Berlin: Ausgrabungen der Deutschen Forschungsgemeinschaft in Uruk-Warka 15, 1994).

10. E.g. at Jamdat Nasr, for which see Robert K. Englund and Jean-Pierre Grégoire, *The Proto-Cuneiform Texts from Jemdet Nasr I: Copies, Transliterations and Glossary* (Berlin: Materialien zur frühen Schriftzeugnissen des Vorderen Orients 1, 1991).

11. Marvin A. Powell, 'Three Problems in the History of Cuneiform Writing: Origins, Direction of Script, Literacy', *Visible Language*, 15 (1981), 422.

12. e.g. Margaret W. Green, 'The Construction and the Implementation of the Cuneiform Writing System', *Visible Language*, 15 (1981), 367. Cf. Hans J. Nissen, *The Early History of the Ancient Near East, 9000–2000 B.C.* (Chicago: University of Chicago Press, 1988); Daniel T. Potts, *Mesopotamian Civilization: The Material Foundations* (London & Ithaca: Athlone and Cornell University Press, 1997).

13. Hans J. Nissen, Peter Damerow and Robert K. Englund, *Frühe Schrift und Techniken der Wirtschaftsverwaltung im alten Vorderen Orient* (Berlin: Franzbecher, 1990).

14. Hans J. Nissen, 'The Development of Writing and of Glyptic Art', in Uwe Finkbeiner and Wolfgang Röllig (eds.), *Ǧamdat Naṣr: Period or Regional Style?* (Wiesbaden: Tübinger Atlas des Vorderen Orients Beiheft B 62, 1986), 317–319.

15. Klaas R. Veenhof, 'Cuneiform Archives: An Introduction', *CAL*, 7.

16. Paolo Matthiae, 'The Archives of the Royal Palace G of Ebla: Distribution and Arrangement of the Tablets according to the Archaeological Evidence', *CAL*, 66.

17. Klaas R. Veenhof, 'Cuneiform Archives: An Introduction', *CAL*, 6.

18. Paolo Matthiae, 'The Archives of the Royal Palace G of Ebla: Distribution and Arrangement of the Tablets according to the Archaeological Evidence', *CAL*, 59, 62–63.
    Klaas R. Veenhof, 'Cuneiform Archives: An Introduction', *CAL*, 13.

20. Cf. N. Schneider, 'Die Urkundenbehälter von Ur III und ihre archivalische Systematik', *Orientalia*, 9 (1940), 4ff.

21. Dominique Charpin, 'Une pratique administrative méconnue', *MARI*, 3 (1984), 258.

22. e.g. Horst Klengel, 'Altbabylonische Privatarchive Babylons', *CAL*, 106–111; Dominique Charpin, 'Transmission des titres de propriété et constitution des archives privées en Babylonie ancienne', *CAL*, 121–140; Ran Zadok, 'Archives from Nippur in the first millennium B.C.', *CAL*, 278–288. The examples are endless.

23. Oppenheim, *op. cit.* 13.

24. Hans J. Nissen, 'Bemerkungen zur Listenliteratur Vorderasiens im 3. Jahrtausend', in Luigi Cagni (ed.), *La Lingua di Ebla* (Naples: Istituto Universitario Orientale, Seminario di Studi Asiatici Series Minor 14, 1981), 99–108.

25. Ernst Weidner, 'Die Bibliothek Tiglatpilesers I.', *Archiv für Orientforschung*, 16 (1952/3), 198.

26. Simo Parpola, 'Assyrian Library Records', *Journal of Near Eastern Studies*, 42 (1983), 4.

27. In addition to Parpola's study cited above, see also Stephen J. Lieberman, 'Canonical and official cuneiform texts: Towards an understanding of Assurbanipal's personal tablet collection', in Tzvi Abusch, John Huehnergard and Piotr Steinkeller, eds, *Lingering over words: Studies in ancient Near Eastern literature in honor of William L. Moran* (Atlanta: Scholars Press, 1990), 305–336 for a detailed analysis of the composition of Assurbanipal's collection.

28. Since then roughly 5000 more, generally small fragments have begun to be catalogued by W.G. Lambert. Cf. Simo Parpola, 'Assyrian Library Records', *Journal of Near Eastern Studies*, 42 (1983), 6, n. 12.

29. For reliable, recent translations of the 'classic' literature of ancient Mesopotamia, see Stephanie Dalley, *Myths from Mesopotamia* (Oxford: OUP, 1989), or Benjamin R. Foster, *Before the Muses: An Anthology of Akkadian Literature* (Bethesda: CDL Press, 1993), 2 vols.

30. Oppenheim, *op. cit.* 17.

31. Idem. 17–18.

32. i.e., those concerned with divination by means of the examination of an animal liver.

33. i.e., those concerned with divination by means of the examination of often malformed human or animal foetuses and newborns.

34. Simo Parpola, 'Assyrian Library Records', *Journal of Near Eastern Studies*, 42 (1983), 6.

35. A. Leo Oppenheim, 'The Position of the Intellectual in Mesopotamian Society', *Daedalus*, 104 (2), (1975), 41.

36. William W. Hallo, 'New Viewpoints on Cuneiform Literature', *Israel Exploration Journal*, 12 (1962), 22.

37. Simo Parpola, 'Assyrian Library Records', *Journal of Near Eastern Studies*, 42 (1983), 10.

38. Ernst Weidner, 'Die astrologische Serie Enûma Anu Enlil', *Archiv für Orientforschung*, 14 (1941/44), 178; Hermann Hunger, 'Neues von Nabû-zukupkena', *Zeitschrift für Assyriologie*, 62 (1972), 99.

39. Simo Parpola, 'Assyrian Library Records', *Journal of Near Eastern Studies*, 42 (1983), 11.

40. Robert H. Pfeiffer, *State Letters of Assyria* (New Haven: American Oriental Series 6, 1935), 179–180, no. 256.

41. Ernst Weidner, 'Die Bibliothek Tiglatpilesers I.', *Archiv für Orientforschung*, 16 (1952/3), 198.

42. F.M. Fales and J.N. Postgate, *Imperial Administrative Records, Pt. I. Palace and Temple Administration* [= State Archives of Assyria VII] (Helsinki: Helsinki University Press, 1992), 63–64.

43. Albert Schott, 'Das Werden der babylonisch-assyrischen Positions-Astronomie und einige seiner Bedingungen', *Zeitschrift der Deutschen Morgenländischen Gesellschaft*, 88 (1934), 325.

44. Ernst Weidner, 'Die astrologische Serie Enûma Anu Enlil', *Archiv für Orientforschung*, 14 (1941–44), 176–177.

45. Arthur Ungnad, 'Lexikalisches', *Zeitschrift für Assyriologie* 31 (1917/18), 43. Assurbanipal was hardly the first Mesopotamian monarch to boast of his intelligence. A hymn to Shulgi (2094–2047 B.C.), second king of the Third Dynasty of Ur (2100–2000 B.C.), says, 'Since my (very) youth I belonged in the edubba [scribal school], (and) on the tablets of Sumer and Akkad I learnt the art of the scribe. Of the young, none could write tablets like me;

people frequented the place of learning (to acquire) the scribal art, and striving and toiling went through their course in all the science of numbers. (As for me) goddess Nidaba, fair faced Nidaba, with a generous hand, provided me with intelligence and wisdom: whatever the teacher brought forward, I let nothing go by!' See Giorgio R. Castellino, *Two Šulgi Hymns* (BC) (Rome: Studi Semitici 42, 1972), 31–33.

46. Arndt Haller, *Die Heiligtümer des Gottes Assur und der Sin-Šamaš-Tempel in Assur* (Berlin: Wissenschaftliche Veröffentlichungen der Deutschen-Orient Gesellschaft 67, 1955). For a detailed analysis of the findspots of all the archives and libraries discovered by the German expedition to Assur, see Olaf Pedersén, *Archives and Libraries in the City of Assur I–II* (Uppsala: Studia Semitica Upsaliensia 6, 1985–86).
47. Ernst Weidner, 'Die Bibliothek Tiglatpilesers I.', *Archiv für Orientforschung* 16 (1952/3), 200–201.
48. Samuel Noah Kramer, 'The oldest literary catalogue', *Bulletin of the American Schools of Oriental Research* 88 (1942), 10–19.
49. Wilfred G. Lambert, 'Ancestors, authors, and canonicity', *Journal of Cuneiform Studies*, 11 (1957), 1–14; 'A catalogue of texts and authors', *Journal of Cuneiform Studies*, 16 (1962), 59–77; 'A late Assyrian catalogue of literary and scholarly texts', in Barry L. Eichler, ed., *Kramer Anniversary Volume: Cuneiform studies in honor of Samuel Noah Kramer* (Neukirchen-Vluyn: Neukirchener Verlag, 1976), 313–318.
50. Ernst Weidner, 'Die astrologische Serie Enûma Anu Enlil', *Archiv für Orientforschung* 14 (1941–44), 179.
51. Idem. 180.
52. F.N.H. Al-Rawi, 'Tablets from the Sippar Library I. The "Weidner" Chronicle: A Supposititious Royal Letter Concerning a Vision', *Iraq*, 52 (1990), 1.
53. Anonymous, 'Sippar (Abu Habba)', *Iraq*, 49 (1987), 248–249. Cf. Jeremy A. Black and W.J. Tait, 'Archives and Libraries in the Ancient Near East', in Jack M. Sasson (ed.), *Civilizations of the Ancient Near East* IV (New York: Scribners, 1995), 2207.
54. Heinrich Otten, 'Archive und Bibliotheken in Hattuša', *CAL*, 186ff.
55. Oliver R. Gurney and J.J. Finkelstein, *The Sultantepe Tablets*, I (London, 1957), and O.R. Gurney and P. Hulin, *The Sultantepe Tablets*, II (London, 1964).

Postscript

Since the chapter was written, the following monograph has appeared: Olaf Pedersén, *Archives and Libraries in the Ancient Near East 1500–300 BC* (Bethesda: CDL Press, 1998).

Chapter 2

Alexandria: The Umbilicus of the Ancient World

Wendy Brazil

νῆσος ἔπειτά τις ἔστι πολυκλύστω ἐνὶ πόντω
Αἰγύπτου προπάροιθε, Φάρον δέ ἑ κικλήσκουσι,
τόσσον ἄνευθ᾽ ὅσσον τε πανημερίη γλαφυρὴ νηῦς
ἤνυσεν, ἣ λιγὺς οὖρος ἐπιπνείῃσιν ὄπισθεν
ἐν δὲ λιμὴν ἐύορμος, ὅθεν τ᾽ ἀαπὸ νῆας ἐίσας
ἐς πόντον βάλλουσιν, ἀφυσσάμενοι μέλαν ὕδωρ

Now there is an island in the storm-ridden sea in front of the River Aegyptos, and men call it Pharos, as far away as a hollow ship sails in a whole day when a shrill fair wind blows upon it from behind. Therein is a harbour with goodly anchorage, from whence men launch their well-balanced ships into the open sea, after drawing black water.[1]

This is the place where Menelaus, King of Sparta, was detained for twenty days because he had not paid appropriate dues to the gods. This is the place which is so described by Homer in the Fourth Book of the Odyssey at least 2,800 years ago.

This is the place which has ever haunted my imagination and the imagination of countless others who came here for anchorage and fresh water from the very deep inland Lake of Mareotis. This is the place where a conqueror paused and considered it a goodly site for a great city. This is the place where a dynasty of kings ruled for nearly 300 years from 323 BC to 31 BC. This is the place where scholars gathered from all over the known world to teach, to learn, to dispute, to create the greatest library in the ancient world. This is the place where men of power came to seek funds from generous monarchs to enhance their power, or having lost their power they came here for refuge. This is also the place which other men of power came to destroy.

This, then, is the place which has taken me on a fantastic voyage of discovery. I had no notion where this voyage of discovery would take me, who would take me there, whom I would meet once I was there, and what I would find. I have been with Lawrence Durrell through his Alexandria – the Alexandria of Justine, Balthazar, Mountolive and Clea. I have also been with Strabo, the geographer and traveller, who lived at the time chronology turned its heel from BC into AD, and I have been with any other ancient writer who took the time and space in their writings to sketch any part of the city.

With Strabo's *Geography*[2] in hand (and with an occasional glimpse into the future city as Lawrence Durrell knew it)[3] I now go to Alexandria. I am bound to go to Alexandria from anywhere in the known world of this first century of the new era. I might come from Illyria, Macedonia, Thrace, Syracuse in Sicily, Massilia (Marseilles), Boeotia, Thessaly, Crete or Melita (Malta), and it could take me two weeks or more to get there. The most frequent ships to Alexandria are tramps making stops on the way to unload and then waiting to pick up another cargo. I could be forced to change ships many times *en route*. Since I have been well advised of the most convenient, the quickest and the surest way to get to Alexandria, I first head for a major port and find a ship which is going directly to Alexandria. I have taken my ship from Piraeus, the port below Athens; it is summer and the Etesian winds are blowing from the north and I reach Pelusium on the easternmost mouth of the River Nile in six days.

My ship sails westward from there, skirting the outlets of the great River Nile, until we reach the Canobic Mouth. From here it is a distance of one hundred and fifty stades (30 kilometres) to the Island of Pharos.

Pharos is an oblong shaped island very close to the mainland and forming a very convenient harbour for mainland Alexandria with two entrances, just as it was described in the Homeric epic 800 years ago.

In the time of the great King Alexander the shape of the Alexandrian mainland was probably rather like the top of a bull's head with two straight peninsular horns jutting into the open sea just beyond the two ends of the Island.

The eastern end of the Island of Pharos is closest to the mainland and to its opposite promontory which is called Lochias. The proximity of these two ends makes the eastern entrance to the harbour very narrow. At this extremity of the Island, there is a rock washed all around by the sea. As I approach Alexandria from the East, the very first thing I see from the ship is the enormous white marble tower which is built on this rock and houses at its top the famous light which can be seen for an astonishing number of whatever measures you may choose – 300 stades, 10 parasangs, 30,000 *passus* (Roman paces), 35 miles or 60 kilometres.

Strabo[4] tells me that the tower was an offering made by Sostratus of Cnidus, a friend of the first two kings of Alexandria called Ptolemy and it bears an inscription which reads: 'Sostratus of Cnidus, son of Dexiphanes, on behalf of mariners, to the Divine Saviours'. These 'Divine Saviours' are thought to be either King Ptolemy I and Queen Berenice or the fabled twin guardians of the sea, the Dioscuri, Castor and Pollux; I am inclined to agree with many others and favour the latter. Pliny the Elder[5] wrote in his vast book of trivial information about the natural world that the tower cost 800 talents and 'the use of this watch-tower is to show light as a lantern, and give direction in the night season for ships to enter the harbour and so avoid sand bars and reefs'.[6] Gaius Julius Caesar in his jottings on the Civil War[7] describes it as a tower of great height and a work of marvellous construction.

We rolled past the site of the ancient Pharos whose shattered fragments still choke the shallows. Toby Mannering, I remembered, had once wanted to start a curio trade by selling fragments of the Pharos as paperweights. Scobie was to break them up with a hammer for him and he was to deliver them to retailers all over the world. Why had the scheme foundered? I could not remember.[8]

When I am safely on land, I will make an offering to Poseidon and to the Dioscuri on behalf of any or all who had the foresight to establish this towering edifice, for reefs and shallows abound in these waters and we need a lofty and conspicuous landmark to enable our *gubernator* (pilot) to direct a true and safe course into the narrow entrance of the harbour.

Even if I had come from the West where the gap between the Island of Pharos and the mainland is wider, navigation through that entrance into the harbour would still be difficult, because there, too, are dangerous shoals to be negotiated. Perhaps that is why the Harbour at that end is called Eunostus, the Harbour of the Successful Return. But today I am coming from the East into the Great Harbour.[9] While the *gubernator* steers his way safely through the narrow entrance into the harbour I have time to reflect upon the founder of his eponymous city. Alexander, the great conqueror, in travelling over most of the then-known world came to Egypt in 332 BC. He went to Memphis and then sailed downstream towards the sea to Canobus. He sailed around Lake Mareotis and came ashore on the stretch of land between the Lake and the sea and it struck him that the position was favourable for founding a city there and that such a city would prosper.[10] According to Pausanias, a small town already existed there with the name Rhakotis, which survived as the name of the western end of the new city.[11]

In his lifetime, the great king was to pause at many a place and decide that it was a goodly site for a city, but this city of Alexandria in Egypt was destined to be the greatest of them all. Both Plutarch[12] and Arrian[13] record his enthusiasm for this particular site and his eagerness to mark out a plan of the city. There was either no chalk at all or insufficient to hand to complete the outline of the foundations, but one of the builders had the happy thought of collecting flour from the soldiers and marking the lines with flour wherever Alexander led the way. Alexander laid out the streets with considerable care and skill by selecting the right angle of the streets which stretched from the sea harbour to the lake to coincide exactly with the direction of the Etesian winds, which blow across a great expanse of sea, so that the winds would be able to pass between the buildings of the future city and provide its inhabitants with cool air in the summer, a moderate climate and good health.[14]

The same Etesian wind which has brought us so swiftly to Egypt blows from the sea over Alexandria and makes the summer here very pleasant, just as Alexander foresaw when he carefully planned his right angles for the city grid. Alexandria at the turning point between BC and AD is a most salubrious and delightful city. The land is washed on all sides by water – on the north by the Sea:

> But here, at least, in Alexandria, the sea-breaths save the populace from the tideless weight of summer nothingness, creeping over the bar among the ships, to flutter the striped awnings of the cafés upon the Grande Corniche.[15]

– and on the south by Lake Mareotis which is filled by many canals from the River Nile which bring not only fresh water, but also imports of food and other goods from other parts of Egypt. At the beginning of summer, in particular, the Nile waters fill the Lake to its brim, so that there are no marshes on the edge to corrupt the air.

> Mareotis turns lemon-mauve and its muddy flanks are starred by sheets of radiant anemones, growing through the quickened plaster-mud of the shore.[16]

While Alexander was absorbed in the task of demarcating his city, Plutarch[17] tells us that an infinite number of great birds of several kinds, rising like a black cloud out of the river and the lake devoured every morsel of the flour that had been used in setting out the lines.

> Ancient lands, in all their prehistoric intactness: lake-solitudes hardly brushed by the hurrying feet of the centuries where the unin-terrupted pedigrees of pelican and ibis and heron evolve their slow destinies in complete seclusion. ... A landscape devoid of songbirds yet full of owls, hoopoes, and kingfishers hunting by day, pluming themselves on the banks of the tawny waterways.[18]

The king at first took this to be an unfavourable omen, but the sooth-sayers assured him that it was a sign that his new city would prosper in all things, but especially in the fruits of the earth, and that it would be a provider of food for many nations. Alexander commanded the builders to proceed.[19]

But now our ship is being moored right at the steps of the shore because the harbour is deep enough to allow even the largest ship to moor alongside the embankment at the water's very edge. Since our cargo includes bundles of books, we will be allowed to dock in the Royal Harbour which has been dug and shaped by the hand of man. As we sail close along the edge of the promontory which is called Lochias, I can see the royal palace and the groves and an extraordinary number of lodges painted in a variety of colours.

On our right is a small island, which was also once the private property of the Kings of Egypt. It is called Antirrhodos, because it was regarded as a rival to the Island of Rhodes. On this island is another royal dwelling and a small harbour for the private use of the royal family alone.

I have stepped ashore and mounted the steps which take me onto the southern end of the Promontory of Lochias. I pass through the Gate of the Moon to walk along one of the two extremely broad avenues which form the axes for the city grid. All the streets here are broad enough for horses and chariots, but I am at the sea end of the Boulevard Argeus, which is at the very least thirty metres in width.

A short walk brings me to the point where this street intersects with the Meson Pedion. Straight ahead of me is the Gate of the Sun which is the entry to the city from the Lake Harbour at the top end of Lake Mareotis. Looking to my left I can see the Canobic Gate, and to the right at the far end of this magnificent boulevard I can just glimpse the Western Gate.

As I stand at this junction, I gaze in awe at the magnificent buildings all around me – 'building upon building' as Homer would say.[20] And so it is, for all the buildings are connected one with another and even at the water's edge buildings seem to rise straight out of the harbour. If I were to turn left and pass through the Canobic Gate I would come to the Hippodrome and beyond that to the newer city of Nicopolis which was founded by Octavian in recognition of his victory over Mark Antony. All that will have to wait for another day, for I have chosen to turn right and walk down the Meson Pedion towards the West.

On my left I very soon come to the Paneium, the sanctuary of Pan. The Paneium is a man-made hill, fashioned into the shape of a fir cone; it resembles a natural rocky hill and is ascended by a spiral road.

So it was with a sense of familiarity that I walked beside Justine through the twisted warren of streets which crown the fort of Kom El

Dick, trying with one half of my mind to visualize how it must have looked when it was a Park sacred to Pan, the whole brown soft hillock carved into a pine-cone.[21]

I climb up the spiral road to the very top and from here I can see the whole of the city in every direction. Strabo[22] tells me that the outline of the city is like the chlamys which I had pinned around me on the ship for extra warmth on the open sea. The long sides of the chlamys are washed by the two waters – the Sea and Lake Mareotis. The short sides of the chlamys are the two ends of the isthmus pinched in on one side by the sea and on the other by the lake. Others might have a more vivid imagination than I, but I have some difficulty with discerning the shape of the chlamys, which is also attested by Plutarch in his biography of Alexander:[23] Alexander took in a large compass of land in a semicircular figure, thus giving it something of the form of a chlamys.

Philo (Philo Judaeus), a Graeco-Jewish philosopher, who was born in Alexandria in 15 BC tells us that the city was divided into five sections, which were designated as Alpha, Beta, Gamma, Delta and Epsilon.[24] Beta was the area to the north and included the palaces, the Museum, and the Sema; Delta was towards the East and was known as the Jewish quarter, but the boundaries of Alpha, Gamma and Epsilon are not exactly known.

Alexandria is a city of sects – and the shallowest inquiry would have revealed to him the existence of other groups akin to the one concerned with the hermetic philosophy which Balthazar addressed: Steinerites, Christian Scientists, Ouspenskyists, Adventists.[25]

From the vantage point of the summit of the Paneium I can see the city spread out around me much as it appears on the map at the beginning of this book unlike

the great sprawling jellyfish which is Alexandria today.[26]

The city teems with public buildings and temples and sacred sites. Some of these buildings are now over three hundred years old and have fallen into neglect, but when I have descended the Paneium and continue once more along the Meson Pedion, I come next to Strabo's favourite building in Alexandria. This is the bastion of Hellenistic physical and intellectual education especially for the Hellenistic young, the Gymnasium, with its breathtaking porticoes that are more than a stade or about 200 metres in length (a stade = 200 metres).

From here I cross the thirty-metre wide Meson Pedion and come to the Mausoleum or the Sema, the enclosure which contains the burial places of the thirteen Kings of the name Ptolemy of Alexandria – and Alexander himself. I have been told that the guardian of the Mausoleum will be able to regale me with all the differing accounts of the disposal of the sacred body of the great Alexander.

One story relates that Perdiccas, the chief successor of Alexander's empire, was escorting the body of Alexander from Babylon to Egypt, in the hope and desire of taking control of that country as well. But Ptolemy Soter (Ptolemy I) stopped him and took the body away from him; later when Perdiccas was barricaded by Ptolemy on a desert island near Memphis, he was killed by his own soldiers who transfixed him with their long Macedonian pikes or sarissai.[27]

Another story has it that Phillip Arrhidaeus, half-brother to Alexander, spent two years in making elaborate preparations for the removal of Alexander's body, but Ptolemy Soter travelled to Syria to meet Arrhidaeus and from there took the body back to Egypt for burial. From 323 BC Arrhidaeus was the recognised King of Macedon jointly with Alexander Aegos (Alexander IV), but in 317 he and his wife, Eurydice, were put to death by the command of Olympias, the mother of Alexander the Great, still living and still wielding great power through the posthumous glory of her son.[28]

Yet another story has the body buried by Ptolemy Soter at Memphis and it was Ptolemy Philadelphus (Ptolemy II) who transferred it to its present resting place in Alexandria.

Whichever Ptolemy brought the body to Alexandria, it was finally installed in a *temenos*, a sacred precinct of a size and construction worthy of Alexander's glory.[29] The body of Alexander is still here on view, but it no longer lies in its original golden sarcophagus, for the gold was plundered by the Ptolemy who was called both 'Cocces' (the Scarlet) and 'Pareisactus' (the Usurper) (who is thought to be Ptolemy XI). Strabo says that his plunder proved unprofitable to him.[30] It seems that the gods themselves ordained that Alexander should lie in glory at the centre of his most famous city.

The present sarcophagus is made of some transparent material – alabaster or glass – and the body lies there with a broken nose, for when Octavian, the future Emperor Augustus of Rome was in Alexandria, he asked to see the body. He not only saw the body but he also touched it, whereupon a piece of the nose broke off.[31]

As she speaks I am thinking of the founders of the city, of the soldier-god in his glass coffin, the youthful body lapped in silver, riding down the river towards his tomb.[32]

As I continue westwards I come now to the very building which I and every scholar who comes to Alexandria have long desired to see. This is the Museum which houses the Great Library and here is the Exedra, where tomorrow I will come to observe the philosophers, the rhetoricians and the other scholars take their seats to engage in intellectual debate and disputation.

> He saw the Mouseion [Museum], for example, with its sulky, heavily-subsidized artists working to a mental fashion-plate of its founders: and later among the solitaries and wise men the philosopher, patiently wishing the world into a special private state useless to anyone but himself – for at each stage of development each man resumes the whole universe and makes it suitable to his own inner nature: while each thinker, each thought fecundates the whole universe anew.[33]

The Museum has a public walk, a park and a zoo, and the large building into which I can see a dilatory scholar disappearing to partake of his meal in the common dining-hall, for the scholars hold all their property in common. They also have their own priest who has charge over the Museum. Today he is appointed by the Emperor in Rome, but formerly he was appointed by the Kings.

I now take one of the side streets which leads back towards the Great Harbour and I walk through the Forum with the Caesarium on my left. Philo was particularly fond of the Caesarium, begun by Cleopatra in honour of Mark Antony and completed by Octavian in honour of himself:

> For there is elsewhere no precinct like this temple, situated on an elevation facing the harbours renowned for their excellent moorage; it is huge and conspicuous, decorated on an unparalleled scale with dedicated offerings, surrounded by a girdle of pictures and statues in silver and gold, forming a precinct of enormous breadth, embellished with porticoes, libraries, chambers, groves, gateways, broad walks and courts and everything adorned with all the beauty that the most lavish expenditure could provide.[34]

On my right is the Theatre which one reaches by a covered gallery which runs between the water garden known as the Maeander and the wrestling arena.[35] Before me is the Poseidium situated on a piece of the foreshore shaped like an elbow. Here I will seek entry to the Temple of Poseidon to make suitable obeisance in gratitude for a safe arrival and offer up prayers for a passage home free from storms and pirates.

To this elbow Mark Antony added a mole projecting still further into the Great Harbour. After he was defeated at the Battle of Actium and deserted by all his friends, he had a royal retreat built on the extremity which he called Timonium. Here he planned to live the life of a Timon of Athens, the celebrated misanthrope, who hated all men because he believed that he had been wronged and treated with ingratitude. Timon's tomb bears an inscription,[36] which I translate from the Greek:

Here lie I, having burst my soul
Laid low by the heavy hand of fate.
Seek not to know my name.
May all of you accursed be
And meet a cursed fate.

This must be Timonium ... . When Antony came back defeated from Actium – where Cleopatra fled with her fleet in panic and tore open his battle-line, leaving him at the mercy of Octavianus; when he came back after that unaccountable failure of nerve, when there was nothing for them to do but to wait for the certain death which would follow upon Octavian's arrival – he built himself a cell on an islet. It was named after a famous recluse and misanthrope – perhaps a philosopher? – called Timon. And here he must have spent his leisure – here, going over the whole thing again and again in his mind. That woman with the extraordinary spells she was able to cast. His life in ruins! And then the passing of the God, and all that, bidding him to say good-bye to her, to Alexandria – a whole world![37]

But now it is time to turn back towards the west for I have much business to transact if I am to pursue my passion for book trading and I need to locate the warehouses in the Emporium and all the ship moorings. Right at the edge of the Harbour stretch the Neoria, the shipyards, which extend as far as the Heptastadium, which is a narrow causeway resting on piles driven into the sea-bed. This man made land bridge is seven stadia (1,400 metres) in length (hence the name Heptastadium) and divides the natural harbour into two separate harbours, the Great Harbour and the Eunostos, and provides easy access to the Island of Pharos.

I am indebted to Julius Caesar[38] for the information that the Heptastadium was built by the early Kings of Alexandria to join the Island of Pharos to the mainland. Ships are still able to pass from one harbour to another through two breaks at either end of the Heptastadium which are covered by bridges to allow vehicles and pedestrians to have free access between the Island and the mainland. If I were to cross over to the Island I would find a large village almost the size of a town. But I have been warned that it would be wiser to stay on the mainland. Even ships are careful to avoid the island because the inhabitants of Pharos, like pirates, are in the habit of plundering vessels which move out of their direct course through carelessness or bad weather. When Caesar came to Alexandria he took the precaution of stationing troops on the Island to ensure the safe arrival of his supplies and reinforcements.

I pass quickly along the shore of the Eunostus Harbour as far as the nearest edge of another artificial harbour, called the Cibotus. This harbour is linked by a navigable canal to Lake Mareotis. Around the Cibotus there are more ship-moorings (Neoria) which I need to examine, although books mostly come to Alexandria from lands to the north and are usually unloaded in the Great Harbour near the Museum.

> You can for one moment look down into one corner of the harbour. Framed by the coloured domes there lay feluccas and lateen-rig giassas, wine-caiques, schooners, and brigantines of every shape and size, from all over the Levant. An anthology of masts and spars and haunting Aegean eyes; of names and rigs and destinations. They lay there coupled to their reflections with the sunlight on them in a deep-water trance.[39]

It is time to turn my back on the sea harbours and walk towards the south along the eastern bank of the canal through the suburb of Rhakotis, which is built on the original town that was already here when Alexander came here to establish his new city. It is here that most of the native-born non-Greek Alexandrians live.

> They were drifting, Melissa and he, across the shallow blood-red water of Mareotis, in each other's arms, towards the rabble of mud-huts where once Rhakotis stood.[40]

I have once more crossed the Meson Pedion and am heading towards the Serapium. On the other side of the canal there is only a small part of the city and beyond that there is Necropolis, the city of the dead, with its gardens and groves and its 'catagogae', which are wayside stations fitted up for the embalming of corpses.

> The cemetery was completely deserted in the sunshine. Capodistra had certainly spared no expense to make his grave imposing and had achieved a fearsome vulgarity of decoration which was almost mind-wounding. Such cherubs and scrolls, such floral wreaths. On the slab was engraved the ironic text: 'Not lost, but gone before'. Balthazar chuckled affectionately as he placed his flowers upon the grave and said 'Happy Birthday' to it.[41]

Now I have come to the precinct of the Serapis, a god who was begotten by a committee and turned into the tutelary deity of this very

Greek city in an alien land. Within the Serapium resides the overflow from the Great Library. This ancillary library is becoming an active centre of learning in its own right since the Roman prefects have been governing this city.

Within the vicinity of the Serapium, there is the site for a future structure, which Strabo cannot mention, as it was possibly erected in the third century AD in honour of Diocletian, but which is commonly called 'Pompey's Pillar'.

The Cabal met at this time in what resembled a disused curator's wooden hut, built against the red earth walls of an embankment, very near to Pompey's Pillar.[42]

Beside the Temple precinct there is a stadium dedicated to the invented god, but dusk is drawing on and it is time to find a lodging place in the hope of meeting other travellers and spending a long night in talk.

I am here in the *umbilicus* of the world, and what I have been exploring is the mystical and seductive magnetism of Alexandria. I wanted to know who went there, why they went there and what they did when they were there.

We know that Ptolemy Soter, son of Lagus, went there to establish the city which had been marked out by Alexander and to rule over the area that was then known as Egypt. Very soon the city became the focal point for scholars and refugees of the Greek and Judaic world. In the latter half of the second century BC the Romans began to be attracted to this famed city of Alexandria. Roman merchants settled there. Roman Senators made tours of inspection up the River Nile and took in the sights of Alexandria on the way. Eminent Romans went to Alexandria in the first century BC for a variety of reasons, mostly to do with war – they went there to raise money for more wars; they went there for refuge when the battle and the day was lost; they went there in a pursuit of a conquered enemy.

In 87 BC Lucius Licinius Lucullus, a Roman general, serving under the Fortunate and all-powerful Lucius Cornelius Sulla, was sent into Libya and Egypt to procure shipping. On the way to Egypt he was hard pressed by pirates who were rife in the Mediterranean until Gnaeus Pompeius Magnus (Pompey the Great) later eradicated them in the astonishing short space of three months. Lucullus narrowly escaped with his life and his ship, but was still able to make a magnificent entry into Alexandria. The whole of the Alexandrian fleet met him in full array, and the young Ptolemy showed him great kindness. He was appointed a lodging, presumably in one of the painted residences which I saw as I passed by the Promontory of Lochias, and he was given dining rights in the palace, an honour which had never before been accorded to a foreign commander. Ptolemy also gave Lucullus extravagant presents, which Lucullus refused. He desired nothing from the king beyond his immediate needs for ships and crews.

Lucullus was urgently needed by Sulla so he had little time for sightseeing, but one hopes that he had time, at least, to see the Great Library and the Sarapium. When he finally retired in Rome, his own library won considerable renown, for it contained very many fine manuscripts. The doors were always open and the walks and the reading-rooms were free to all Greeks, whose delight it was, says Plutarch,[43] to leave their other occupations and hasten thither as if to the habitation of the Muses, and there to walk about and divert one another. His house became a Greek *prytaneum*, a house of intellectual hospitality and entertainment for visitors to Rome.

When it was time for Lucullus to leave Alexandria, Ptolemy sent a convoy of ships with him as far as Cyprus and parted with him with much ceremony and gave him a precious emerald set in gold. Lucullus at first tried to refuse such a valuable gift, but when the king showed him his own likeness cut upon it, he accepted for fear of offending his royal patron and jeopardising the safe passage which had been accorded to him.[44]

A number of Romans became involved during the fifties (BC) in assisting or promising to assist Ptolemy Auletes to regain his kingdom after a palace coup. In 59 this Ptolemy promised or actually paid 6,000 talents to Pompey and Julius Caesar in return for recognition by Rome of his rights to the sovereignty of Egypt.[45] In the following year he was deposed by the Alexandrians and went to Rome himself to seek assistance for his restoration; specifically he asked for Pompey to lead whatever forces were needed to achieve his request.

It was not entirely the fault of Pompey that this request was not granted. The Roman Senate resisted the proposal because it would have given unprecedented powers to Pompey, and the memories of the overweening power of the dictators, Marius and Sulla, were still fresh in the minds of Senators. After protracted negotiations, the task was given to a friend of Marcus Tullius Cicero, the great Roman orator, a certain Publius Lentulus Spinther, who was about to be proconsul of Cilicia.[46] But the mission was abandoned when a flash of lightning struck a statue of Jupiter in Rome. The custodians of the sacred Sibylline books, which were consulted in times of dire crisis, fortuitously came across an oracle which forbade the restoration of an Egyptian king 'with a multitude', which was interpreted to mean 'an armed force'.[47] Ptolemy's request to the Senate for armed forces was refused.

In the end, Ptolemy regained his kingdom with the help of a different Roman, one Aulus Gabinius, the governor of Syria, to whom he paid 10,000 talents. In the year 55, Gabinius brought his troops into Alexandria, won the day, and restored Ptolemy to power. Ptolemy was grateful, Rome was not. Gabinius was banished by the Roman Senate for invading Egypt without its authority and for undertaking a war which was forbidden by the Sibylline books.

Ptolemy XI left a will invoking the assistance of Rome to ensure that the kingdom of Egypt be divided between his eldest daughter, Cleopatra VII, and his eldest son, Ptolemy XII. When Ptolemy died in 51, the kingdom was seized by Ptolemy XII and his usurpation was tolerated but not formally recognised by Rome.

By the time Pompey headed for Alexandria, he was a refugee, a defeated general and a man who was perceived as not having honoured his commitment to Ptolemy XI. When the day was lost for Pompey at Pharsalus on the 9th August 48 BC, he fled with four friends on horseback to Larissa. From Larissa he fled to the sea, where he embarked in a small boat. He met a ship by chance which took him on to Mitylene where he joined his wife, Cornelia, and they embarked with four triremes which had come to him from Rhodes and Tyre. He then mulled over several possible plans and discussed them with his friends. In the end, they all agreed on going to Egypt, which was nearby and was still a great kingdom, prosperous and powerful in ships, provisions and money.[48]

So Pompey set sail for Egypt. Cleopatra had been ousted by her brother and was collecting an army in Syria. Ptolemy was camped with his army near Pelusium awaiting her invasion. Pompey sailed to Pelusium and stopped his ship there when he saw the large army on the shore. He sent a message to the King to tell of his arrival and to remind him of the friendship between himself and Ptolemy's father.

Young Ptolemy, then aged 13, took counsel with his senior advisers, Achillas who commanded the army, Pothinus a eunuch in charge of the treasury, and Theodotus, a rhetorician of Chios and tutor to Ptolemy. It was Theodotus who offered the suggestion that they should lay a trap for Pompey and kill him in order to curry favour with Caesar who was hard on Pompey's keel: 'Dead men do not bite'. The suggestion was adopted.

A small skiff was sent to bring Pompey ashore. The reason given for the smallness of the boat was the shallowness of the sea. Some of the King's attendants came in the skiff, among them a Roman, who had previously served under Pompey; his name was Sempronius according to the Roman historian, Appian,[49] or Septimius according to others.[50] At the same time the whole army was marshalled along the shore as if to do honour to Pompey, and the King was conspicuous in the midst of them by his purple robe.

Pompey was suspicious: an army marshalled on the shore, a very small boat to escort him with neither King nor any high dignitary on board – this was not the reception he had imagined. The Roman gave his hand to Pompey in the name of the King and directed him to take passage in the boat to meet the young monarch in friendship on the shore.

I think of Cornelia, the wife of Pompey, who stayed on board the trireme and would have been in an agony of fear and apprehension for her husband. She would have watched him prepare to step into the skiff. She would have heard her husband quoting Sophocles as he entered the small boat: 'Whosoever has dealings with a ruler, is that man's slave, even if he goes to him as a free man'.[51] She would have watched the boat move away towards the shore. No-one in the boat spoke and the silence must have been eerie; the tension must have extreme. Cornelia would have sensed that her husband was becoming more nervous. Since the silence was so intense and any sound carries clearly over water she would have heard him say to the Roman who was standing alone in the boat: 'Don't I know you, comrade?'. She would have seen the Roman nod without speaking. She would then have seen Pompey turn away and the Roman move behind him to give him the first stab and then others in the boat stabbed him as well.

Cornelia and her friends at once let out a dreadful cry and lifting their hands to heaven, they invoked the gods to avenge such a violation of faith. But they also set sail very swiftly to avert further danger to themselves, since they could not now save Pompey.

Only the head of Pompey went to Alexandria, for the body was stripped and dumped naked on the shore; the head was taken to Alexandria as a trophy for Caesar in expectation of a large reward. The remainder of the body was buried on the shore near Pelusium.[52]

Four days later Gaius Julius Caesar arrived in Alexandria. As soon as he learned that Pompey was making for Egypt after the Battle of Pharsalus, Caesar sailed first to Rhodes. His army was following behind, but Caesar was not willing to wait and embarked with such troops as there were on the triremes of Cassius and a certain Rhodian. He was in desperate haste to catch up with Pompey not necessarily to kill him, but to prevent him from occupying Egypt and building up sufficient resources to regain power.[53]

He let nobody else know of his exact destination. He set sail toward evening, telling the other pilots to steer by the torch of his ship by night and by his signal in the daytime; after they had proceeded a long way from the land, he then ordered his pilot to steer for Alexandria.

He reached Alexandria four days after the death of Pompey. The accounts vary but it seems most likely that he did not venture ashore until he was shown the head and the signet ring of Pompey.[54] These caused him real or feigned distress, for it was said that he could not bear to look at the head and ordered it to be buried in a small plot of ground near the city which was dedicated to Nemesis;[55] or, as others said, he wept bitterly at the sight of the head, called him fellow countryman and son-in-law and recounted happier times they had spent together; he reproached the murderers and commanded that the head should be adorned, properly prepared and buried.[56]

The Roman historian, Dio Cassius, has his own interpretation of Caesar's thoughts and actions at the time: Caesar, he says, had from the outset been very eager for dominion. He had always hated Pompey as his antagonist and rival, and he had brought on the war with Pompey for no other purpose than to secure his rival's destruction and his own supremacy. He had hurried to Egypt with no other intention than to overthrow Pompey completely if he should still be alive. Therefore, he pretended to mourn his death and made a show of vexation over his murder.[57]

When Caesar finally disembarked in Alexandria he incurred the wrath of the palace royal guard when his lictors marched in front of him carrying the *fasces*, the symbol of his office, which was regarded as a serious slur on the dignity of the King. However, this disturbance was quelled and Caesar made his escape into the palace.[58] For several days afterwards, however, there were frequent riots wherever there were crowds and several soldiers were killed.[59] Some of Caesar's soldiers also had their weapons confiscated and some of them put out to sea again until the rest of Caesar's ships with the whole army had reached port.[60]

In the meantime Caesar pretended to be on holiday. He received visitors and treated them in a friendly and gracious manner. He went sight-seeing in the city. He admired its beauty. He listened to some of the lectures in the Exedra and stood among the crowd. Gradually he was gaining the good will and esteem of the Alexandrians as one who had no military designs against them.[61]

As soon as his army arrived by sea, Caesar had Pothinus and Achillas executed for their crime against Pompey. Theodotus escaped, but was later crucified by one of the future conspirators against Caesar, Gaius Cassius Longinus, who found the disgraced rhetorician wandering in Asia.[62]

The Alexandrians rebelled against Caesar for these unauthorised acts upon their own people and so began the Alexandrian War. Caesar had some narrow escapes during a war which was being fought very much to his disadvantage in a hostile city against citizens who were defending their King. There was the famous swim when he lost his garments which were weighing him down, but saved his papers and even kept them dry by holding them aloft in his left hand as he swam. The Alexandrians took his clothing and hung it as a trophy to commemorate a victory in this particular rout.[63]

And there was the famous fire resulting in the destruction of the docks and storehouses of grain and other buildings. Dio Cassius says that the Great Library was burned as well,[64] but Caesar himself says in his account of the Civil War that he burned all the vessels in the harbour which had come to support Pompey plus 22 warships which had usually been on guard at Alexandria. He said that he did this because he could not protect so wide an area as the harbour with his small number of troops. This fire apparently spread to the warehouses and the cargo on the wharves, which would most certainly have included many bales of books.[65] Aulus Gellius[66] says that all the books acquired or copied in Egypt under the kings of the name of Ptolemy (which he estimated as numbering approximately 700,000) were burned during the first Roman war with Alexandria in 48 BC, not intentionally nor by anyone's order, but accidentally by the auxiliary soldiers. But it is generally believed that only a part of the Library's holdings were burned at that time, and that these losses were made good in part by Marcus Antonius in 41 BC.

Despite the unfavourable odds, Caesar won the Alexandrian War after nine months of fighting during the year 47. He fought the last battle against the young King on the banks of the Nile, in which he won a decisive victory.

In the meantime he had met the sister, Cleopatra. While she was in exile she had sent word to Caesar and asked to be allowed to plead her case for sovereignty in person. Permission was granted and she entered the city by night without her brother's knowledge and went into Caesar's quarters in the palace. Plutarch has the story of her arrival in the bed roll.[67] He says that she came to Alexandria in a small boat with one attendant, Apollodorus of Sicily, and landed near the palace at dusk. She was at a loss how to get into the palace unnoticed, until she thought of lying at length inside a bedroll. Apollodorus tied up the bedding and carried it on his back through the gates to Caesar's apartment.

Dio Cassius[68] says that she was a woman of surpassing beauty and at that time she was in the prime of her youth. She also possessed a delightful voice and used the full force of her feminine charm to cast a spell upon everyone she met. With Caesar it also worked. He succumbed to her skill and her charms and before dawn he sent for Ptolemy and tried to reconcile the pair, but the young King was outraged at the sight of his sister in the palace and all Caesar's attempts to achieve a constitutional solution to the dispute ended in war and the death of Ptolemy.

At the end of the war Caesar established Cleopatra and her other brother as joint sovereigns of Egypt. He felt that it was safer at the present time to preserve Egypt as a kingdom rather than turn it into a Roman province. Sovereigns who were beholden to him personally would be easier to manage than a headstrong governor who could use the wealth of Egypt to mount a revolution against the power of Rome.[69]

Nevertheless, he was reluctant to make Cleopatra sole ruler for two reasons: he was afraid that the Alexandrians might rebel again under a woman alone as a sovereign; he also feared that the Romans might be angry with his establishment of a woman as the sole sovereign of Egypt, especially the woman with whom he had been consorting for many months. Therefore he ordered Cleopatra to marry her brother and nominally consigned the kingdom to them both. In reality, Cleopatra was the supreme ruler, since her husband/brother was still a child. Sharing the rule was a pretence; Cleopatra ruled alone and spent her time in Caesar's company.[70]

Caesar was in no great hurry to depart from Alexandria. There was much to enjoy in the city now that the war was over and Cleopatra was excellent company. Together they went on a sight seeing trip up the Nile with 400 ships before Caesar returned to Rome and to his eventual death. In George Bernard Shaw's play of *Caesar and Cleopatra*, Caesar comforts the queen at the time of his departure by telling her that he will send her a man, 'Roman from head to heel and Roman of the noblest; brisk and fresh, strong and young, hoping in the morning, fighting in the day, and revelling in the evening'.[71]

And so it came to pass in the course of time that Mark Antony came to Alexandria for the second time. He had already been there once before when he was serving as a *magister equitum* (Master of the Horse) under Gabinius during the restoration of Cleopatra's father. Appian says that Antony was very susceptible to women and that he had fallen in love with Cleopatra at first sight when she was still a very young child.[72]

They met again in Cilicia. Antony and Octavian had finally routed the murderers of Caesar at the battle at Philippi in 42 BC. Octavian returned to Italy, while Antony went on a tour of the eastern provinces and Cleopatra came to meet him in Cilicia. The initial reception of the Queen by Antony was distinctly frosty. He blamed her for not supporting Octavian and himself in avenging the death of Caesar. But she was equal to the jibes of Antony and catalogued a list of things that she had done as well as things that she had not done to help their cause. By the end of the interview Antony was struck by her wit as well as her beauty, and Appian says that he became her captive swain as though he were a young man, although he was then forty years of age.[73]

As winter approached Antony distributed his army in winter quarters in the Eastern provinces and went to Alexandria at the invitation of the Queen. On his arrival, Cleopatra gave him a magnificent reception, and he spent the winter in dalliance and a process of de-Romanization. He put off the Roman dress and his insignia of office. He wore the square-cut garment of the Greeks instead of the toga and joined the white-shoe brigade of the Athenian *gymnasiarchs* and the Alexandrian priests. There was even a Greek name for this particular style of shoe:

the *phaikas* or *phaikasion*. Did he do this because he was in a foreign jurisdiction, or because he was in a city ruled by a sovereign or because he regarded his wintering in Alexandria as a festive occasion? Whatever his motive, Antony abandoned any pretence of participating in public matters. He went out only to the temples, the schools and the discussions of the learned, and spent most of his time with Greeks, and with Cleopatra.

> A drunken whore walks in a dark street at night, shedding snatches of song like petals. Was it in this that Antony heard the heartnumbing strains of the great music which persuaded him to surrender for ever to the city he loved?[74]

At the end of the winter Antony left Alexandria, but was to return again. He conquered Armenia in 34 and made King Artavasdes a prisoner and sent him and his wife and his children and a great mass of booty ahead of him into Alexandria in a triumphal procession.[75] He himself drove into the city upon a chariot, and came before Cleopatra seated in the midst of her people on a gilded chair on a platform plated with silver. He presented to Cleopatra all the spoils and the defeated royal family which he had taken prisoner and bound in chains of gold.[76]

The feasting and the festivities began again. Antony sat in the assembly with Cleopatra and her children as his side. In his address to the people of Alexandria he commanded that Cleopatra should be called Queen of Kings.[77] His headquarters was now called a *basileion*, a palace; he wore an Oriental dagger at his belt; he let himself be seen in public on a gilded chair; he posed with Cleopatra for painted portraits and statues.[78]

He bestowed one lasting benefit on Alexandria. He stole the library of Pergamum, containing 200,000 volumes, as a gift to Cleopatra in reparation for the books which were lost in the fires of Caesar's Alexandrian War.

Meanwhile in Rome, the Romans were becoming greatly alarmed at the doings of Antony and Cleopatra. They were almost paranoid at the thought of a Roman assuming the title of *rex* and the role of a monarch. They had already killed Caesar when he toyed with the idea of exchanging the title of *dictator* for *rex*. Now they were afraid that Antony would eventually bestow their own city on Cleopatra and transfer the seat of power to Alexandria.[79] I, with Shakespeare's Polonius (whom I anticipate by 1600 years), often swear on a certainty: 'And it must surely follow, as the night the day';[80] but the Romans were appalled to learn that Cleopatra had begun to swear to a certainty with the words: 'As surely as I shall one day dispense justice on the Roman Capitol'.[81]

The Battle of Actium was inevitable. Antony lost the day to Octavian and followed Cleopatra back to Alexandria where he eventually died in her arms.

I thought suddenly of the dying Antony in the poem of Cavafy – a poem he had never read, would never read. Sirens whooped suddenly from the harbour like planets in pain. Then once more I heard this gnome singing softly of chagrin and bonheur ... How different from the great heart-sundering choir that Antony heard – the rich poignance of strings and voices which in the dark street welled up – Alexandria's last bequest to those who are her exemplars. Each man goes out to his own music.[82]

Octavian came to Alexandria in pursuit of Antony. Antony died clumsily and conveniently by his own hand. Precautions were taken to ensure that Cleopatra should remain alive to be the glittering trophy in the glorious triumph of Octavian back in Rome. But Cleopatra would not be slave or vassal to anyone; she would be mistress of her own death either by the bite of an asp or the prick of a poisoned pin.[83] Octavian did everything he possibly could to resuscitate her with drugs and the aid of the Psylli, that extraordinary tribe of males who are propagated from one another and have the power to suck out the poison of any reptile and prevent the death of a victim if they are summoned to use their powers before the victim dies. But the Psylli were too late; Cleopatra was already dead.

Octavian accorded an honourable burial to the lovers. He had the bodies embalmed and they were buried in the same tomb in a mausoleum which Cleopatra and Antony had begun and which was finished by the express order of Octavian.[84]

This, then, was the terminus of the three hundred year dynasty of Kings descended from Ptolemy Soter, son of Lagos. Octavian spared the city and none of the people perished. He removed to Rome all the portable royal treasures which Cleopatra had collected in the palace, but it was claimed that he kept nothing for his own personal use except one calyx made of murrhine glass.

The Romans took vast sums of money away from Alexandria, but without violence. Heavy fines were exacted from every man in Alexandria who was charged with any misdemeanour. All the rest of the populace paid a levy to the value of two-thirds of their property. Out of this hoard, all the troops of Octavian received all the back-pay that was owing to them, and those who were with Octavian in Alexandria received an additional thousand sesterces on condition of not plundering the city.[85]

Before he left the city, Octavian also had his soldiers dredge the canals into which the Nile overflowed for they had become choked with mud through years of neglect. He also founded a new city close to Alexandria to celebrate his victory over Antony – the city which he named Nicopolis. At the end of my tour of the city I had come to the Serapium and the nearby stadium. These places were glossed over by Strabo because he said that they were almost abandoned on account of the construction of the newer buildings at Nicopolis, where there was in his time an amphitheatre and a stadium and the quinquennial games were celebrated there, presumably rather than at Alexandria.[86]

> Beloved Alexandria ... Capitally, what is this city of ours? What is resumed in the word Alexandria? In a flash my mind's eye shows me a thousand dust-tormented streets. Flies and beggars own it today – and those who enjoy an intermediate existence between either.[87]

Octavian came to Alexandria, saw the centre of learning, conquered Antony and Cleopatra and left to return to Rome and deliberate with great care on the choice of a title for his supreme office. He took the name Augustus, he adopted the title of *princeps*, an acceptable Republican appellation, but he secured *imperium* for life with the right to be called *imperator*, and so became the First Emperor of Rome and the Roman world, including the city of Alexandria.

Roman Prefects (*praefecti*) came to administer the city in place of the great dynasty of rulers. Other Romans of renown will come to this city: the great Nero Claudius Germanicus Caesar (Germanicus) in a time of famine and Titus Flavius Sabinus Vespasianus (the future Emperor Vespasian) who will heal the sick here, but be despised by the people. And there will be many others, but none will again reveal the potency and magic of this city until there is a poet and a novelist, a Cavafy and a Durrell.

And with the poet I will

Turn to the open window and look down
To drink past all deceiving
[My] last dark rapture from the mystical throng
And say farewell, farewell to Alexandria leaving.[88]

for I have walked the streets of Alexandria with Strabo, I have burned Caesar's boats, I have bought my books, I have fallen in love with a city which I have never seen. I have haunted the great library through the few existing records. I have mourned the future loss to the world of so many valuable books, for here in the great library reside the writings of the greatest Greek, Roman and Jewish authors, each carefully rolled around its *umbilicus*, and I, too, have come to the end of my scroll.

ohe, iam satis est, ohe, libelle!
iam peruenimus usque ad umbilicos.[89]
Aha! it is enough, little book! I have come all the way through to the end rods, the 'umbilici'!

NOTES

1. Homer, *Odysseia (Odyssey)*, IV, 354–359. (London: Heinemann, 1919: The Loeb Classical Library) The 'black water' would be drawn from Lake Mareotis, a fresh water lake fed by tributaries of the Nile; the lake was so deep in the summer that the bed was invisible, hence 'black water'. Homer is the name attributed to the author or authors of the two great Greek epics, *Iliados (The Iliad)* and *Odysseia (The Odyssey)*, which probably date from some time between c. 810 and 730 BC.

2. Strabo, Greek historian and geographer, a native of Amasia in Pontus, was born in 64 or 63 BC and died in AD 21 or later. He travelled widely throughout the known world and stayed for some time in the city of Alexandria during his visit to Egypt. His major work, *Geographikon (Geography)*, has survived intact, except for the seventh book, of which only the epitome exists; the seventeenth book deals with Egypt and Africa.

3. Lawrence Durrell, poet and novelist, was born in India in 1912 He spent some years in Alexandria as Foreign Service Press Officer and Press Attaché. He wrote four novels which are known collectively as the Alexandria Quartet: *Justine* (London: Faber and Faber, 1957); *Balthazar* (London: Faber and Faber, 1958); *Mountolive* (London: Faber and Faber, 1958); and *Clea* (London: Faber and Faber, 1960).

4. Strabo, *Geography*, XVII. 1. 6. (London: Heinemann, 1917–1932: The Loeb Classical Library).

5. Pliny the Elder (Gaius Plinius Secundus Maior), Roman author, was born probably at Comum (Como) in Gallia Transpadana (Transpadane Gaul) in about AD 23 and died in 79. Although he was a diligent scholar and prolific writer, only his Historia Naturalis (Natural History) has survived. The fifth book contains a description of Africa, and the thirty-sixth book treats of marble and stone for building.

6. Pliny, *Natural History*, XXXVI. 18. (London: Heinemann, 1949–1963: The Loeb Classical Library).

7. Caesar, *De Bello Ciuile (Civil War)*, III. 112. (Oxford: Oxford University Press, 1901, London, Heinemann, 1914: The Loeb Classical Library): 'Pharus est in insula turris magna altitudine, mirificis operibus exstructa'. Gaius Julius Caesar was born in 102 or 100 BC. After defeating Gnaeus Pompeius Magnus (Pompey the Great) at Pharsalus, he was for a time in Alexandria settling the question of the succession between Cleopatra and her brothers (the Alexandrian War) before returning to Rome where he was killed as a result of a conspiracy in 44 BC. He was the author of many works of which only his war memoirs have survived: *De Bello Gallico (The Gallic War)* and *De Bello Civile (The Civil War)*.

8. Lawrence Durrell, *Clea*, 211.

9. This harbour does not appear to have a special name, being merely referred to as μέας λιμήν, 'big harbour' by Strabo, *Geography*, XVII. 1. 6 and 1. 9.

10. Arrian, *Anabasis of Alexander*, III. 1. 5. (London: Heinemann, 1929–1933: The Loeb Classical Library).

Arrian, Greek historian and philosopher, was born at Nicomedia in Bithynia in about AD 96 and died at an advanced age during the reign of Marcus Aurelius (161–180). His most important work was this history of the expeditions of Alexander.

11. Pausanias, *Periegegesis of Greece (Description of Greece)*, V. 21. 9. (London: Heinemann, 1918–1935: The Loeb Classical Library).

Pausanias, Greek traveller and topographer, was possibly born in Lydia and flourished in the time of Antoninus Pius and Marcus Aurelius, i.e. the period from AD 138 to 180.

12. Plutarch, *Lives: Alexander*, 26. (London: Heinemann, 1847–1920: The Loeb Classical Library).

Plutarch, Greek miscellaneous writer, philosopher, moralist and biographer, was born at Chaeronea in Boeotia in about AD 46. He wrote *Bioi Paralleloi (Parallel Lives)* of eminent Greeks and Romans, forty-six of which were arranged in pairs for comparison (e.g. Alexander the Great and Julius Caesar) and four are separate lives.

13. Arrian, *Anabasis of Alexander*, III. 1. 5.

14. Diodorus, *Bibliotheca Historica (Historical Library)*, XVII. 52. (London, Heinemann, 1933–1967: The Loeb Classical Library).

Diodorus Siculus, Greek historian, was a native of Agyrium in Sicily. He was a contemporary of Gaius Julius Caesar and Augustus and lived to at least 21 BC. During his life he travelled through much of Europe, Asia and Egypt, collecting material for his great work; between 60 and 30 BC, he wrote the *Historical Library* as a set of annals covering a period from the remotest ages to the beginning of Caesar's campaigns in Gallia in 58 BC. Only Books I–V and XI–XX and some fragments have survived. The earlier set of extant Books (I–V) recounts the mythical history of Egypt, Assyria, Ethiopia and Greece, and the later books (XI–XX) cover the years 480–302 BC.

15. Durrell, *Balthazar*, 11. The Grande Corniche stretches around the shoreline of the Eastern Harbour (the ancient Great Harbour); the shoreline has extended further into the harbour as a result of centuries of silting. The 'pleasantness of the air by the continuous breezes which arise both from the lake which debouches into the sea and from the sea hard by' is confirmed by Philo Judaeus, *De Vita Contemplatiua (On the Contemplative Life, or Suppliants)*, 23. (London: Heinemann, 1929–1962: The Loeb Classical Library).

16. Durrell, *Justine*, 40.

17. Plutarch, *Lives: Alexander*, 26.

18. Durrell, *Clea*, 40.

19. Plutarch, *Lives: Alexander*, 26.

20. Homer, *Odyssey*, XVII. 266: ἐξ ἑτέρων ἕτερ᾽ ἐστίν in reference to the palace of Odysseus, but quoted by Strabo, *Geography*, XVII. 1. 8. Here it may refer to the fact that many of the Ptolemaic buildings may have been built on the foundations of earlier Egyptian structures, which appears to be borne out by the recent archaeological discoveries of large blocks of stone found at the bottom of the harbour.

21. Durrell, *Justine*, 88.

22. Strabo, *Geography*, XVII. 1. 8.

23. Plutarch, *Lives: Alexander*, 26.

24. Philo, *in Flaccum (Against Flaccus)*, VIII. 55.

Philo Judaeus, a Graeco-Jewish philosopher, was born in Alexandria in about 20 BC. Jews had settled in Alexandria soon after the establishment of the city and had access to the Museum and the Library. Philo's main interest as a scholar was in the study of Greek philosophy, especially the work of Plato. His works in Greek include expositions of portions of the Torah, and ethical, historical and political writings.

25. Durrell, *Balthazar*, 24.
26. Durrell, *Balthazar*, 127.
27. Diodorus, *Historical Library*, XVIII. 33ff.; Strabo, *Geography*, XVII. 1. 8.
28. Diodorus, *Historical Library*, XVIII. 26–28ff.
29. Diodorus, *Historical Library*, XVIII. 28.
30. Strabo, *Geography*, XVII. 1. 8.
31. Cassius Dio Cocceianus (Dio Cassius), *Romaike Historia (Roman History*, LI. 16. (London: Heinemann, 1914–1955: The Loeb Classical Library).
    Dio Cassius, born in about 155 in Nicaea in Bithynia, wrote a history of Rome from landing of Aeneas on the coast of Italy to 229 AD. *Romaike Historia (Roman History)* comprised 80 books divided into decades. Books XXXVII-LIV have survived intact and large sections of LV–LX have also survived; these books cover the period from 68 BC to 47 AD. Only fragments remain of books I–XXXVI and LXI–LXXX. An inexpert abridgement of books XXXV–LXXX was made by Xiplilinus in the 11th century AD.
32. Durrell, *Justine*, 34.
33. Durrell, *Justine*, 156.
34. Philo, *Legatio ad Gaium (Delegation to Gaius Caligula)*, XXII. 151.
    Philo spent all his life in Alexandria, except for one journey to Rome at the head of a Jewish delegation (AD 39–40) to ask the Roman emperor, Caligula, for exemption from the obligation of emperor worship.
35. Polybius, *Pragmateia (Universal History)*, XV. 30. (London: Heinemann, 1954: The Loeb Classical Library
    Polybius was a Greek historian, born in Megalopolis, Arcadia, in c.204 BC, but was taken to Rome as a hostage in 168. His historical work. of which the first five books and some fragments are extant, covered the period from 221 to 144 BC. In 181, Polybius was selected to serve on an embassy to Egypt, but the audition was cancelled because of the sudden death of King Ptolemy VI Eupator. He eventually made a visit to Alexandria at a much later period in his life .
36. Quoted in Plutarch, *Lives: Antony*, 70.:
    ἐνθάδ᾽ ἀπορρήξας ψυχὴν βαρυδαίμονα
    κεῖμαι τοῖνομα δ᾽ οὐ πεύσεσθε, κακοὶ δὲ κακῶς ἀπόλοισθε.
37. Durrell, *Clea*, 196–7.
38. Caesar, *Civil War*, III. 112.
39. Durrell, *Clea*, 29.
40. Durrell, *Justine*, 96.
41. Durrell, *Clea*, 170.
42. Durrell, *Justine*, 88.
43. Plutarch, *Lives: Lucullus*, XLII.
44. Plutarch, *Lives: Lucullus*, II-III.
45. Gaius Tranquillus Suetonius, *Diuus Iulius (Life of Julius Caesar)*, 54. (London: Heinemann, 1913–1914: The Loeb Classical Library).
    Suetonius, a Roman historian and scholar, was born about 70 AD. His most famous work was *De Vita Caesarum (The Lives of the Caesars)*, which is a set of biographies of the twelve rulers of Rome from Gaius Julius Caesar to Domitian.

46. Marcus Tullius Cicero, *epistulae ad familiares (Letters to family and friends)*, I. i. 7 (London, Heinemann, 1928–1952: The Loeb Classical Library; Oxford: Oxford University Press, 1952–1956); *epistulae AD Quintum fratrem (Letters to Quintus, his brother)*, II. ii. 3 (Oxford: Oxford University Press, 1956); Dio Cassius, XXXIX. xii. 16.
Cicero was a famous orator, lawyer and politician in Rome. He was born in Arpinum, Italy, in 106 BC and was killed in the proscriptions of 43 BC at the behest of Mark Antony. He was a prolific letter writer and many of his letters and speeches have survived.

47. *The Cambridge Ancient History: Volume IX: The Roman Republic 133–44 BC*, edited by S. A. Cook, R. E. Adcock, and M. P. Charlesworth. (London: Cambridge University Press, 1932), 531.

48. Appian, *Rhomaika (Roman History)*, II. 83. (London: Heinemann, 1912– 1913: The Loeb Classical Library).
Appian was a Greek historian of Alexandria, who lived about the middle of the second century AD. He pursued a career as an advocate in Rome until he secured the post of imperial procurator in Egypt. His history of Rome in twenty-four books extends from the earliest development of the Roman Empire to the time of Trajan. His work was divided into special periods and regions rather than a chronological ordering of events. Books 13 to 21 dealt with the Civil Wars from the time of Marius to the Battle of Actium; Books 18 to 21 were also called *Aigyptiaka (Egyptian Affairs)*. Books 13 to 17 have survived in entirety, but only fragments of the other books remain.

49. Appian, *Roman History*, II. 84.

50. Caesar, Plutarch, Florus and Dio Cassius.

51. Lines from an unknown play. Sophocles, *Tragoediae septem*: Fragment 54. (Oxford: Oxford University Press, 1800, volume II, 273):
ὅς τις δὲ πρὸς τύραννον ἐμπορεύεται,
κείνου' ὅτι δοῦλος, κἂν ἐλεύθερος μόλῃ.

52. Appian, *Rhomaika (Roman History)*, II. 85–86.

53. Dio Cassius, *Roman History*, XLII. 6.

54. Dio Cassius, *Roman History*, XLII. 7.

55. Appian, *Roman History*, II. 90.

56. Dio Cassius, *Roman History*, XLII. 8.

57. Dio Cassius, *Roman History*, XLL. 8.

58. Caesar, *Civil War*, III. 106; Dio Cassius, *Roman History*, XLII. 7.

59. Caesar, Civil War, II. 106.

60. Dio Cassius, *Roman History*, XLII. 7.

61. Appian, *Roman History*, II. 89.

62. Appian, *Roman History*, II. 90; or, according to Plutarch, *Lives: Pompey*, LXXX. 6, he was killed at the order of Marcus Brutus Junius, also a future conspirator against Caesar.

63. Dio Cassius, *Roman History*, XLII. 40. 4.

64. Dio Cassius, *Roman History*, XLII. 38.

65. Caesar, *Civil War*, III. 111.

66. Aulus Gellius, *Noctes Atticae (Attic Nights)*, VIII. xvii. 3. (London: Heinemann, 1927–1928: The Loeb Classical Library).
Aulus Gellius was born in Rome in c. 123 AD and died in 165. He spent most of his life in Rome except for a period of time in Athens to study philosophy; while he was there he wrote *Attic Nights*, which is a conglomerate of anecdote, linguistic theory, historical trivia, argument and opinion.

67. Plutarch, *Lives: Caesar*, XLIX.
68. Dio Cassius, *Roman History*, XLII. 34.
69. Suetonius, *Life of Julius Caesar*, XXXV.
70. Dio Cassius, *Roman History*, XLII. 44.
71. George Bernard Shaw, *Three Plays for Puritans: Caesar and Cleopatra*, Act IV (London: Constable, 1901).
72. Appian, *Roman History*, V. 8.
73. Appian, *Roman History*, V. 8.
74. Durrell, *Justine*, 12.
75. Artavasdes was detained in Alexandria until he was put to death at the order of Cleopatra in 30 BC.
76. Dio Cassius, *Roman History*, XLIX. 40.
77. Dio Cassius, *Roman History*, XLIX. 41.
78. Dio Cassius, *Roman History*, L. 5.
79. Dio Cassius, *Roman History*, L. 4.
80. William Shakespeare, *Hamlet*, I. 3. 79. (London: Oxford University Press, 1928)
81. Dio Cassius, *Roman History*, L. 5.
82. Durrell, *Justine*, 99.
83. Dio Cassius, *Roman History*, LI. 14.
84. Suetonius, *Diuus Augustus (Life of Octauius Augustus Caesar)*, XVII. 4. 5.
85. Dio Cassius, *Roman History*, LI. 18.
86. Strabo, *Geography*, XVII. i. 10.
87. Durrell, *Justine*, 11.
88. C. P. Cavafy, *The God Abandons Antony*, translated by Lawrence Durrell, *Justine*, 222.
89. Martial, *epigrammata (Epigrams)*, IV. 89 (Oxford: Oxford University Press, 1903).
    Marcus Valerius Martialis (Martial), was born at Bilbilis, Spain, in c. 40 AD, was a popular Roman poet whose epigrams were published in twelve books; he was famous for his wit, his acerbic pen and his felicity of language.

Chapter 3

Cloistered Bookworms in the Chicken-Coop of the Muses: The Ancient Library of Alexandria

Robert Barnes

INTRODUCTION

Books have been collected since the invention of writing in the Middle East about 5000 years ago. In the temples of ancient Egypt, priests preserved both small collections of texts relating to their sacred duties, and larger collections in special rooms or buildings known as the 'house of life', which also seem to have been used as schools for future priests and public officials. In Mesopotamia, the remains of several royal libraries have been discovered, including most notably that of Ashurbanipal, King of Assyria in the seventh century BC, much of which was removed to the British Museum in the nineteenth century. This collection clearly represented an attempt to gather earlier Babylonian and Assyrian literature as it was known at Ashurbanipal's date, and may therefore rank as the first known 'national', if not universal, library.

In the Greek world, the first libraries were those of the sixth century BC tyrants Pisistratus of Athens and Polycrates of Samos. Athenaeus, an Egyptian Greek literary scholar of about AD 200, mentions among well-known earlier libraries those of 'Polycrates of Samos, Pisistratus the tyrant of Athens, Eucleides, also an Athenian, Nicocrates of Cyprus, the kings of Pergamum, Euripides the poet, Aristotle the philosopher, Theophrastus, and Neleus, who preserved the books of these last two'.[1] Strabo, a historian and geographer at the turn of the Christian era, claims that Aristotle was 'the first man of whom I know to have collected books and to have taught the kings of Egypt how to arrange a library'.[2]

FOUNDING

After the death of Alexander the Great in 323 BC, his generals, known as the *diadochoi*, or successors, fought among themselves for fragments of his empire. One of the most successful was the Macedonian Ptolemy, son of Lagus, who declared himself king of Egypt, as Ptolemy I Soter, in 304, and thereby founded the Ptolemaic dynasty, with its capital at Alexandria. The dynasty lasted until the death of Cleopatra in 30 BC, at which point Egypt became a Roman province.

Ptolemy I Soter had considerable intellectual interests, and himself wrote what seems to have been the best of the early lives of Alexander the Great (which survives only through the use made of it in other works). He also tried to attract Greek intellectuals to Egypt, of which the best-known was Demetrius of Phaleron, an Aristotelian philosopher and politician from Athens. Others included the poet Philitas of Cos, the grammarian Zenodotus of Ephesus and another Aristotelian philosopher Strabo, who became the tutor of Ptolemy's son and heir Ptolemy II Philadelphus. Under the latter and his successors, many other scholars, scientists and poets came to Alexandria.

Diogenes Laertius, who in the third century AD wrote a collection of lives of the Greek philosophers, records: 'Hermippus says that, after the death of Cassander, he [Demetrius], fearing Antigonus, came to Ptolemy Soter. There he spent a considerable time and advised Ptolemy, among other things, to pass on his kingship to his children by Eurydice. Ptolemy did not agree to this, but gave the crown to his son by Berenice [i.e. Ptolemy Philadelphus], who, after Ptolemy's death, decided to keep Demetrius a prisoner in the country until a decision was made about him. There he lived, with crushed spirits, and was somehow bitten by an asp on the hand and so died'.[3]

Demetrius also seems to have played a leading role in creating, or at least providing ideas for, the celebrated Museum in Alexandria. This foundation evidently carried further the concept of a combined school and research institute which Aristotle had created with his Lyceum at Athens. We know little about the precise organisation of the Museum, but can assume that it was well funded at least in its early days, that it was so named because it included a shrine to the Muses who were supposed to inspire it, and that it was close to the royal palace in the Brucheion quarter of Alexandria. We do hear of dinners and symposia, often attended by the king, at which scientific, philosophical and literary problems were discussed. Although we know little of the Museum's activities, there is no reason to doubt that it contributed much to the scientific and literary research for which Alexandria was to be famous. It also gave rise to malicious comment from outside Alexandria. Timon of Phlius, sceptical philosopher and satirist of the period, remarked: 'In populous Egypt many cloistered bookworms are fed, arguing endlessly in the chicken-coop of the Muses'.[4]

Strabo records, evidently on the basis of personal knowledge: 'The Museum also is part of the royal palaces. It has a covered walk, an *exedra* [i.e., a hall with seats for discussion] and a large house, in which is the common dining-room of the learned men who share in the Museum. This association has its property in common, and also a priest in charge of the Museum, who was formerly appointed by the kings, but now by Caesar'.[5] Royal patronage was, in fact, critical for the Museum. The earlier Ptolemies, who were all intellectual men, seem to have kept up its funding, but in the second century BC, the dynasty had to meet increasing resistance from the native (i.e., non-Greek) population of Egypt, as well as threats from outside, and its support for research declined.

Ptolemy I also founded the cult of Serapis, a synthetic deity (essentially a combination of the ancient Egyptian gods Osiris and Apis), who was to play an important part in Ptolemaic dynastic propaganda. He, or his son Philadelphus, may already have begun work on Serapis' great sanctuary, the Serapeum, at Rhakotis in the southwestern part of Alexandria, although, as noted below, this was essentially the creation of Philadelphus' son, Ptolemy III Euergetes. The Serapeum was to be the site of a second library in Alexandria, variously described as the 'external' or 'daughter' library, which seems in fact to have outlived the main library.

The museum presumably possessed some books from the beginning, but curiously enough we do not know for certain whether it was the first or the second Ptolemy who made the decision to expand these into a universal library. Most sources suggest it was the second, Ptolemy Philadelphus. The *Letter of Aristeas*, a Jewish writing of perhaps about 100 BC, has the following story.

> When Demetrius of Phaleron was put in charge of the king's library he was lavished with resources with a view to collecting, if possible, all the books in the world; and by making purchases and copies he carried out the king's intention as far as he could. When he was asked, in my presence, how many thousands of books were there, he said: 'more than 200,000, my king; and I will try in a short time to fill up the number to 500,000. I have been told that that the laws of the Jews also deserve to be copied and to be part of your library.' 'What is there to prevent you from doing this?', the King replied. 'Everything necessary is at your disposal.' Demetrius said: 'A translation is required; in the country of the Jews they use their own characters, just as the Egyptians use their own arrangement of letters and have their own language. They are supposed to use Syrian, but that is not so, but rather a different mode of writing.' When he learned these details the king ordered a letter to be written to the High Priest of the Jews, so that the aforementioned plans could be completed.[6]

This letter, whose essential purpose is to explain the origin of the Septuagint, or Greek translation of the Hebrew scriptures, and to defend its accuracy, gives what must be a garbled version of events. It elsewhere claims that the king in question was Ptolemy Philadelphus, but as we know that this king's first action on succession was to remove Demetrius of Phaleron, then Demetrius cannot have been his first librarian. However, the letter may still be of some value in indicating Demetrius' part in creating the Museum under Ptolemy Soter, and in showing the scope of the library as envisaged by Ptolemy's successor Philadelphus.

HOW MANY BOOKS, AND WHERE DID THEY COME FROM?

Some of our most important information about the library is provided by John Tzetzes, a Byzantine scholar of the twelfth century AD, in the prologue to his commentary on three plays of Aristophanes. We do not know exactly where Tzetzes obtained this information, but it was presumably from Alexandrian commentaries on Aristophanes or other classical authors. *Inter alia* Tzetzes tells us the following.

> This King Ptolemy [Philadelphus], of whom I have spoken, had a truly philosophical and divine soul, and was a lover of everything noble, in sight, deed and word. Through Demetrius of Phaleron [as with the *Letter of Aristeas* this must be a mistake] and other advisors he collected books from everywhere at royal expense and housed them in two libraries. Of these the external library had 42,800 books; the internal library of the court and palace had 400,000 mixed books and 90,000 single, unmixed books, as Callimachus, who was a young man of the court, records; after the editing of the books he compiled his *Pinakes* of them.[7]

There has been much discussion of Tzetzes' distinction between 'mixed' and 'single, unmixed' books in the library, but it seems most likely that 'mixed' simply means that these rolls contained more than one work, and 'single, unmixed' that the others contained single works, or parts of single works. (Incidentally, throughout this essay, 'book' is to be understood as synonymous with 'roll'; the codex only became a normal format for books some way into the Christian period.)

The figures given by Tzetzes for the size of the libraries have also been discussed. We do not know the source of his information, and in any case, numbers in Greek manuscripts are notoriously liable to be corrupted. However, one confirmation that his figures could be of the right order of magnitude is that the library at Pergamon, which Mark Antony may have offered to Cleopatra, is said to have contained 200,000 books. It is possible that the main Alexandrian library had reached 700,000 books by the first century BC. That, at least, is the figure mentioned by the second century AD literary scholar Aulus Gellius, in connection with the supposed burning of the library in 48/7 BC.[8]

What is less clear is how many 'titles', in our sense, such figures really indicate, given that the library certainly held many duplicate copies of certain Greek authors, and that some of these copies probably filled a number of rolls. It has been suggested that the total number of titles in the library at the time to which Tzetzes refers may been about 70,000, with a maximum of 100,000 reached in the first century BC. We have no way of knowing what proportion of Greek literature to these times such figures represent, but given the limited literacy of all ancient societies, and the scarcity and cost of books, the figures seem impressive.

Galen, the famous Greek doctor of the second century AD, includes several stories about the library in his writings. When explaining how a copy of the *Epidemics* (a work of the Hippocratic medical corpus), which had once belonged to Mnemon of Sidon, reached the library, he claims that Ptolemy III Euergetes ordered that all ships which came to the harbour of Alexandria be searched for books. The books were to be copied, the copies given back to the owners, and the originals placed in the library with a label 'from the ships'.[9] Second, the same Ptolemy borrowed from Athens the official copies of the three tragedians, Aeschylus, Sophocles and Euripides, after paying a deposit of fifteen talents. He then kept the official texts and returned copies only, thus forfeiting his deposit.[10] Third, Galen refers to competition between the kings of Pergamon and Alexandria in bidding for old books, which inflated the prices and led to forgeries being made.[11] Finally, Galen claims that the Alexandrians did not place new acquisitions immediately in the libraries, but placed them first in warehouses, all heaped together.[12]

The first of these stories raises the question of how the books were labelled when they were acquired. From Galen, and other evidence, it seems that the labels may have indicated where and how the copies were acquired, and even the name of the previous owner. When the books reached the library, further information may have been added, in particular as a result of any editorial activity on the text . This can now only be traced in the scholia, or textual notes, in the medieval manuscripts of many classical authors. The scholia to Homer and Aristophanes, for example, regularly refer to editions made by Alexandrian librarians, and those to Homer to manuscripts from different parts of the Greek world, e.g. Chios, Argos and Sinope (on the Black Sea). Such references may well go back to the labels of copies in the Alexandrian library. We can also assume that Alexandrian editorial activity helped to standardise not only the text, but also the format, of classical texts throughout the Greek world.

One much debated question is whether the library acquired part or all of the collection of Aristotle's Lyceum, a point on which sources disagree. Athenaeus continues, in the passage quoted above: 'From Neleus our king Ptolemy, surnamed Philadelphus, bought them all [i.e. the books of Aristotle and Theophrastus] and transferred them, with those he had captured at Athens and Rhodes, to the beautiful city of Alexandria.'[13] However, Strabo gives a different account, which modern scholars are more inclined to accept. The story is worth quoting in full, as illustrating the dangers threatening private libraries in the ancient world.

From Scepsis came the Socratic philosophers Erastus and Coriscus and Neleus the son of Coriscus, a man who was a student of Aristotle, and inherited the library of Theophrasus, which included that of Aristotle. Aristotle at any rate bequeathed his library to Theophrastus, to whom he also left his school; and he is the first man I know of to have collected books and to have taught the kings of Egypt how to arrange a library. Theophrastus bequeathed it to Neleus, and Neleus took it to Scepsis and bequeathed it to his heirs, common people who kept the books locked and not carefully stored. When they discovered the zeal of the Attalid kings (who ruled the city) in searching for books to build up their library in Pergamon, they hid the books under the ground in a kind of pit. Much later, when the books had been damaged by damp and moths, their descendants sold them to Apellicon of Teos for a large amount of money, both the books of Aristotle and those of Theophrastus. Apellicon was a book-lover rather than a philosopher, and so, trying to restore the parts that were eaten through, he made new copies of the texts, filling up the gaps incorrectly, and published the books full of mistakes ... . Immediately after the death of Apellicon, Sulla, who had taken Athens, removed Apellicon's library to Rome and Tyrannio the grammarian, who loved Aristotle, got it into his hands by cultivating the librarian, as did certain booksellers who employed poor copyists and did not collate the texts.[14]

It seems from this account that Aristotle's library in fact eluded the Ptolemies, as it did the Attalids of Pergamon. There is no evidence that editorial work on the text of Aristotle was ever carried on in Alexandria, and Alexandrian scholarly standards seem to have been higher than those of the Roman booksellers Strabo mentions.

THE FOREIGN BOOKS

The library was essentially a collection of Greek literature, but there is evidence that it also included specially commissioned Greek translations of works in other languages. The *Letter of Aristeas* claims that the Hebrew scriptures (or at least the Pentateuch) were translated into Greek as part of this programme. Manetho, an Egyptian priest in Heliopolis, dedicated to Ptolemy Philadelphus a history of Egypt, in Greek, but drawn from Egyptian records, which may also have been part of such a programme. (The work survives in the form of quotations by Josephus, the Jewish historian, and by Christian writers). Pliny the Elder, the Roman encyclopedist of the first century AD, records that Hermippus, a student of Callimachus (see below), wrote a commentary on the verses of Zoroaster.[15] This story implies that these verses had been translated from Iranian into Greek, and were available in Alexandria.

Much larger claims were later made for these translations. George Syncellus (a Greek monk who died about AD 810) states in his *Chronographia*, or World Chronicle : 'When Ptolemy Lagus died of a thunderbolt his son Ptolemy Philadelphus inherited the kingdom of Egypt. He was a man wise and energetic in every respect, who collected the books of all the Greeks as well as of the Chaldaeans, Egyptians and Romans, having the foreign-language ones translated into Greek'.[16] Tzetzes similarly claims: 'When all the Greek books, and those of every foreign people, including the Hebrews, had been collected, then that generous king [Ptolemy Philadelphus], who was a river flowing with gold and pouring it out through seven mouths, had the foreign books translated into the Greek script and language by bilingual scholars who spoke Greek accurately. For example the Hebrew books were done by seventy-two Hebrew translators who were experts in both languages'.[17] However, despite these claims we may suspect that the works in the library translated from other languages were in fact comparatively few. The whole surviving body of ancient Greek and Latin literature includes only a handful of translations from one of these languages into the other, and translations from other languages may have been rarer still.

ARRANGEMENT AND CATALOGUING

In the absence of any certain knowledge of its site, the physical arrangement of the library is difficult to reconstruct, The few comparable sites excavated elsewhere in the Hellenistic world (e.g., at Pergamon) suggest that the library was essentially a store of books, which would have been read in nearby passages or colonnades. It was perhaps the Romans who invented the 'reading room' as the central feature of libraries (and then exported it back to the Greek world, as with the Library of Celsus in Ephesus). It is no doubt significant that Strabo, in his description of the museum buildings, does not mention a separate library building (or indeed, at this point, the library at all).

A similar conclusion may also be suggested by the Serapeum, or daughter library. The excavations of this site by Alan Rowe and others in the 1940s indicate that it was essentially a creation of Ptolemy III Euergetes, the son of Philadelphus.[18] At the southern end of the site are two long corridors, opening into small rooms, and in particular a row of 19 uniform rooms, each of about three by four metres. The excavators plausibly suggested that these rooms were used to shelve the rolls of the Serapeum library, and that the rolls were consulted in the corridors. However, in the Roman period the whole Serapeum site was considerably altered, and the library may at that stage have moved into the main temple buildings.

The division of books between the main and daughter libraries is not something on which we have much information. Tzetzes, as noted, seems to refer to the Serapeum library as the 'external library', which presumably implies that the 'internal' library in the Brucheion was not accessible except to scholars of the Museum. Epiphanius of Salamis, a Christian writer of the fourth century AD, says that the Septuagint (the Greek translation of the Bible) was placed in 'the first library' in the Brucheion, and adds: 'and still later another library was built in the Serapeum, smaller than the first, which was called the daughter of the first one'.[19] The 'still later' here probably refers to the fact that this library, like the main buildings in the Serapeum as a whole, was created by Ptolemy Philadelphus' son Euergetes. The rhetorician Aphthonius of Antioch, who must have visited the Serapeum in its last days in the fourth century AD, mentions the storerooms for books attached to the colonnades, and claims, perhaps exaggeratedly, that the books were open to all who desired to study, and attracted the whole city to master wisdom.[20]

We also have little precise information on the arrangement and cataloguing of the books. Tzetzes claims that, under the patronage of Ptolemy Philadelphus, 'Alexander of Aetolia edited the books of tragedy, Lycophron of Chalcis those of comedy, and Zenodotus of Ephesus those of Homer and the other poets'.[21] The 'editing' here presumably included some kind of grouping and cataloguing of the relevant authors' works, and may also have been extended to other genres of literature.

A closely related question is what part Callimachus, the Alexandrian poet, may have played in the library. Despite claims to the contrary there is in fact no evidence that he was ever 'librarian', and the

Oxyrhynchus Papyrus would seem to exclude him. However Callimachus was certainly the author of what seems to have been the first comprehensive bibliography of Greek literature, the *Pinakes*, and this work must have owed something to the collection then being assembled in the library. Its full title was *Pinakes (or Tables) of those who were eminent in every branch of learning, and what they wrote, in 120 volumes.* Quite possibly, however, it included works not, or not yet, in that collection, which Callimachus knew about from other sources.

Our scattered information about this work suggests that it included the main genres of Greek poetry, at least five genres of prose: history, rhetoric, philosophy, medicine and law, and a miscellaneous section.[22] Within the genres, authors may have been listed alphabetically, with a short biography, a bibliography of the author, also alphabetical, the opening words of each work, and an indication of the length of the work. However, even if we could be certain about how Callimachus arranged his bibliography, we could still not be sure that this reflected the arrangement of the Alexandrian library catalogue. We also do not know what format this catalogue took, how it listed duplicates and variants, or the answers to many other questions which modern library practice naturally raises. A few fragmentary book-lists from other parts of the ancient world are suggestive (e.g. about alphabetical listing of authors' names and titles), but not conclusive, on these matters.

THE LIBRARIANS

Although Callimachus was apparently never the librarian at Alexandria, we do know something of the men who were. One interesting, though rather garbled, source of information on them is a papyrus fragment, forming part of a school exercise of the second century AD, and published in 1914. The legible part of the text reads:

> Apollonius, the son of Sillus, of Alexandria, called the Rhodian, a friend of Callimachus; he was also the teacher of the first [actually of the third] king. He was succeeded by Eratosthenes, after whom came Aristophanes, son of Apelles, of Byzantium, and Aristarchus. Then Apollonius of Alexandria, called the Idograph, and after him Aristarchus, son of Aristarchus, of Alexandria, originally of Samothrace; he was also the teacher of the children of Philopator [actually Philometor]. After him came Cydas of the spearmen. Under the ninth king there flourished Ammonius and Zenodotus and Diocles and Apollodorus, who were grammarians.[23]

From other sources we can be fairly certain that this is a list of the Alexandrian librarians. These sources give several terms for 'librarian', and it is not clear exactly what duties the appointment involved. Some of the earlier librarians were, as in the papyrus, said to be tutors of the royal children, and possibly the offices were usually combined.

There is no space here to discuss the evidence for the librarians, or their exact order and dates, but a probable list of the early ones (which, it will be seen, differs from the list in the papyrus) is: Zenodotus, Apollonius of Rhodes, Eratosthenes, Aristophanes of Byzantium, Apollonius the Idograph (the exact meaning of the title in unclear, and it is possible that Apollonius of Rhodes is in fact being listed twice) and Aristarchus. Most of these were eminent literary scholars, who played a major part in establishing the text of several of the classical Greek authors, and most of them are listed, with further details (not always consistent with the above order) in a Byzantine encylopedia, the *Suda*, of about the 10th century AD.

The last named, Aristarchus, went into exile when Ptolemy VIII Euergetes II came to the throne in 145 BC. The later librarians were less distinguished men. The reference in the papyrus to 'Cydas of the spearmen' becoming librarian suggests that the Ptolemies were no longer concerned for the scholarly reputation of the library, or even hostile to it. They were very likely cutting its resources, along with their support for the museum as a whole.

WHEN WAS THE LIBRARY DESTROYED?

One of the most controversial questions about the library is how much of it may have been destroyed in the fighting between Julius Caesar and Cleopatra, on the one hand, and Ptolemy XIII on the other, for control of Alexandria in 48/7 BC. It is worth setting out the main ancient sources in some detail, with comments.

Seneca the Younger, the Stoic philosopher of the first century AD, condemns large libraries altogether: 'What is the point of countless books and libraries, whose titles the owner can barely read through in his lifetime? The sheer number of them burdens and does not instruct the one who wants to learn, and it is much better to entrust yourself to a few authors than to wander through many. 40,000 books were burnt at Alexandria. Let someone else praise this finest monument of royal wealth, as Livy did, who says that it was the outstanding achievement of the good taste and care of kings'.[24] This information is evidently based on Livy's History of Rome (the relevant section of which does not survive). It has been suggested that Seneca's figure should be changed to 400,000 books, but only to adjust it to Orosius' figure, which, as will be seen below, is itself not certain.

Plutarch's version of the story is: 'Being cut off he [Caesar] was forced to remove the danger by setting fire to the fleet, which, spreading from the docks, also destroyed the great library.'[25] This version would seem conclusive, but may nevertheless still be an assumption by Plutarch as to what exactly was destroyed. Dio Cassius, a historian of the early third century AD, writes: 'After this many battles took place between them [i.e. the forces of Caesar and Cleopatra and of Ptolemy XIII] by day and night, and many parts were set on fire, so that among other places the docks and the grain warehouses were burnt, and also the books, which were, they say, very many and excellent.'[26] It will be noted that Dio does not say how many books were burned, or what part of the library they represented. It is worth recalling here Galen's story, cited above, that the Alexandrians did not place new acquisitions immediately in the libraries, but they were first placed in warehouses. Dio might mean that it was only the books that happened to be in the warehouses in 48/7 BC which were destroyed.

Ammianus Marcellinus, a historian of the fourth century AD, states:

In addition there are [in Alexandria] temples with elevated roofs, among which the Serapeum stands out. Although it cannot be done justice with an inadequate description, it is so adorned with great columned halls, and statuary which seems almost alive, and a great number of other works, that, apart from the Capitolium, by which the venerable city of Rome claims eternal renown, nothing more magnificent can be seen in the whole world. In this temple were libraries beyond calculation, and the trustworthy testimony of ancient records agrees that 700,000 books, brought together by the unsleeping care of the Ptolemaic kings, were burned in the Alexandrian war, when the city was sacked under the dictator Caesar.[27]

Ammianus here clearly confuses the library of the Serapeum with the main library in the Brucheion district, which renders his whole story suspect. It is quite possible that he simply assumes that the whole library (his figure for which agrees with that of Aulus Gellius, already cited) was burned.

Finally, Orosius, a Christian chronicler of the fifth century AD, gives the following version: 'In the course of the battle the royal fleet, which happened to have been hauled onto the shore, was ordered to be set on fire, and that fire, when it had spread also to a part of the city, burned 400,000 books which happened to have been stored in a nearby building, a remarkable record of the zeal and efforts of our forebears, who had collected so many great works of human genius'.[28] This very late version of the story may not deserve credence. The figure stated for the number of books burned is not certain, and one manuscript reads '40,000', agreeing with Seneca as above. More significantly, for what it is worth, Orosius' version if anything may confirm the suspicion that it was only a warehouse of books which was destroyed.

Our judgement of these stories is clearly made more difficult by our not knowing the exact location of the museum or its library. If the library was destroyed, then the whole palace area must have been affected. However, Caesar himself states that at the time of the fire he was occupying one of the palaces.[29] His continuator in this account (probably Hirtius) says that Caesar was able to extend his occupation of the city, and explicitly states that Alexandria was almost safe from fire because the buildings did not use beams and wood.[30] Further, if the library was destroyed, we would expect enemies of Caesar, such as Cicero, to have mentioned the fact. Finally, Strabo, as already cited, gives an apparently eyewitness account of the museum which does not mention any destruction, although if there was destruction it must have occurred only twenty years or so before his visit to Alexandria.

Clearly, we cannot draw any certain conclusions from this partly contradictory information. It seems possible, however, if not likely, that it was only a warehouse of books, or some other comparatively small part of the library's collection, which was burned, and that this story was elaborated into the tradition that the whole library was destroyed.

A further, and equally suspect, tradition is that Mark Antony gave Cleopatra the library of Pergamon to compensate for the loss. Here our main source is Plutarch, who records that: 'Calvisius, who was an associate of Caesar, also made the following charges against Antony in his actions towards Cleopatra: He had offered to her the libraries from Pergamum, in which there were 200,000 books ...' . However, Plutarch continues: 'Calvisius was thought to have slanderously invented most of these charges'.[31] The Greek in the first passage is ambiguous, and could mean either 'offered' or 'bestowed'. In either case, Plutarch does not imply that the books were in fact ever dispatched to Alexandria, and he seems to doubt the whole story. We should probably do likewise.

We are told very little about the library (or whatever was left of it) in the Roman imperial period. Strabo, as cited above, recorded that in his own time (the age of Augustus) the emperor appointed the priest in charge of the museum at Alexandria, as the Ptolemies had done earlier. This might also imply some imperial patronage of the library. Suetonius, the early second century AD biographer of the emperors, records of Domitian that: 'At the beginning of his reign he neglected liberal studies, although he had arranged for the libraries [in the Porticus Octaviae in Rome], which were destroyed by fire, to be replaced at great expense, seeking everywhere for copies of books, and sending scholars to Alexandria to transcribe and correct them'.[32] This report indicates, if not imperial support for the Alexandrian library, then at least the reputation it still had for holding accurate copies of Greek literature.

The final destruction of the museum library probably occurred in AD 272. Ammianus Marcellinus records: 'But Alexandria itself was extended, not gradually, like other cities, but at its very beginning, to great dimensions, and for a long time was exhausted with internal disputes, until finally, after many years, when Aurelian was emperor, the civic quarrels escalated into deadly strife. Its walls were torn down and it lost the greater part of the area which was called the Brucheion, and which had long been the dwelling place of its most distinguished men'.[33]

The destruction of the Serapeum was to follow in AD 391, though our sources (mainly Christian chronicles of the period) do not directly record this, any more than they do the destruction of the main library in the Brucheion. In 391 the Christian patriarch of Alexandria, Theophilus, attempted to turn one of the temples of the city into a church. After a resistance from the pagan side, which led to street-fighting and much destruction, Theophilus obtained the approval of the emperor Theodosius I for closing all the temples, including the Serapeum. A number of pagan scholars and philosophers were forced to leave the city.

Orosius, who wrote in about 416, evidently after a visit to Alexandria, continues the passage cited above with the following much debated (and very obscure) remarks: 'Therefore, although there are still today book cases in the temples, which we have seen, whose spoliation reminds us that they have been emptied by the men of our age (which is certainly true), yet it would be more worthy to believe that other books had been acquired to vie with the concern for studies in earlier times, than to believe that there was some other library separate from the 400,000 books, which in this way escaped the latter's fate'.[34]

This has often been taken to refer to the destruction of the Serapeum library in 391. However, the passage has to be seen in the context of Orosius' belief (which may not be correct, as shown above) that the main Alexandrian library of 400,000 books had been destroyed in 48/7 BC. He is arguing that efforts have been made more recently to build up temple libraries in Alexandria, but seems to believe that there was in fact no other library contemporary with the main library which survived its fate, i.e., he does not know of the earlier history of the Serapeum library. At all events, he makes it clear that there was no large library surviving in Alexandria in his day.

DID THE ARABS BURN THE BOOKS?

It seems that both the Alexandrian libraries had been destroyed by the end of the fourth century AD. Despite this, there is a persistent tradition in modern times (although already debunked by Edward Gibbon),[35] that 'the library' was destroyed by the Arabs when they conquered the city in AD 642. The Arabic and other sources for this tradition were discussed at length in Alfred J. Butler in 1902,[36] and there is little new information to add to Butler's account.

The story first appears in Abu'l Faraj (an Arab historian of the thirteenth century AD), and is to the effect that an unfrocked Christian priest called John the Grammarian approached the Arab conqueror of Alexandria, 'Amr, and asked for 'the books of wisdom which are in the imperial treasuries', as these could be of no use to the Arabs. 'Amr wrote about this to the caliph Omar, who replied: 'Touching the books you mention, if what is written in them agrees with the Book of God, they are not required; if it disagrees, they are not desired. Destroy them therefore.' 'Amr ordered the books to be sent as fuel to the baths of Alexandria, and it took six months to use them up.

As Butler pointed out, there are many objections to accepting this tradition. The story first appears more than 500 years after the Arab conquest of Alexandria. John the Grammarian appears to be the Alexandrian philosopher John Philoponus, who must have been dead by the time of the conquest. It seems, as shown above, that both the Alexandrian libraries were destroyed by the end of the fourth century, and there is no mention of any library surviving at Alexandria in the Christian literature of the centuries following this date. It is also suspicious that the caliph Omar is recorded to have made the same remark about books found by the Arabs during their conquest of Iran. In short, the story is at best a testimony to the persistence of legends about the library long after it had in fact disappeared.

THE VANISHED LIBRARY

It is finally necessary to mention Luciano Canfora's bestseller about the Alexandrian library, *The Vanished Library*.[37] This account reads like a detective novel, and parts of it are pure fiction. Nevertheless it does pose real questions about the library, and makes interesting, and often convincing, attempts to answer them.

First, Canfora gives much space to earlier temples in Egypt which contained libraries, and in particular to the Ramesseum, or mortuary temple of Rameses II in Thebes. This building is known both from a description by Hecataeus of Abdera (about 300 BC, who attributes it to Ozymandias), as cited by the first century BC historian Diodorus Siculus (*Bibliotheca historica*, I.49.8), and from archaeological excavations. Canfora concludes, plausibly enough, that this temple did not contain a separate library building, but rather that its books were stored in the niches of colonnades or passageways. The Alexandrian library probably followed the same principle.

Canfora also discusses at length the supposed destruction of the main library in 48/7 BC, and concludes that only a small store near the harbour of Alexandria, of 40,000 books, was destroyed, leaving the main collection in the Brucheion intact. This means accepting the figure given by Seneca, and supposing that the historians who give larger figures mistakenly believed that the main collection was destroyed, and give whatever figure they thought constituted this collection. Canfora also believes that this main library was in fact destroyed in AD 272, along with the rest of the Brucheion district.

Finally, Canfora records the eventual destruction of all the great libraries of the ancient world, and concludes his book: 'The great concentrations of books, usually found in the centres of power, were the main victims of these destructive outbreaks, ruinous attacks, sackings and fires. The libraries of Byzantium proved no exception to the rule. In consequence, what has come down to us is derived not from the great centres but from the 'marginal' locations, such as convents, and from scattered private copies'.[38]

This is a sobering thought, which must ultimately call in question the wisdom of large concentrations of books, in ancient or modern times. Canfora might perhaps have recognised that the Alexandrian library, and others like it, did nevertheless have some permanent effect on the preservation of ancient literature, through their encouragement of scholarly research on the texts. Human efforts to bring all literature together may ultimately be doomed to frustration, but there is no doubt that large libraries contribute enormously to the advancement of knowledge while they exist and are maintained.

In the late twentieth century, the problems of large libraries have by no means been resolved. There has been much premature speculation that digital recording of texts will overcome all difficulties of collecting and storing them, and will make them available immediately to anyone, anywhere in the world. In fact the digitising of library holdings of printed texts has scarcely begun, and its costs, with present technology, would seem to limit it to a comparatively small selection of commonly used texts. Although most new books nowadays must be recorded somewhere in digital form, the economics of publishing discourage wide access to the books in that form. Above all, we simply do not know whether present technology will preserve texts even as efficiently as libraries of manuscript and printed books have done. The Alexandrian library may have preserved its books, without substantial loss, for up to 600 years. We should not be too confident that we will preserve our own literature for anything like as long.

CONCLUSION: LEGEND AND LEGACY

The Alexandrian library became a legend well within its own lifetime, and has remained one down to the present day. With the possible exception of Ashurbanipal's palace library, it represents the first attempt known to us to collect one literary heritage (in its case the Greek) comprehensively, and even foreign literature in summary form. It has continued to inspire, and perhaps delude, all later would-be creators of universal libraries.

It is noteworthy that the Athenian democracy (and for that matter the Roman republic) never created a public library. It was only the cultural pretensions of tyrants, kings and emperors which could conceive anything like a universal collection of books. It is no accident either that the Ptolemies restricted access to their library to the comparatively few scholars of the museum, who were all on the royal payroll. (The Serapeum, or 'external', library may well have been created only as an afterthought, and it never seems to have grown to anything like the size of the main library). The dangers inherent in such patronage inevitably followed: the Ptolemies eventually lost interest in scientific and literary pursuits (or at least were forced to spend most of their time defending themselves against internal and external enemies), the funds for the library dried up, and most of the scholars drifted away.

Even in modern democratic societies, where everyone pays lip-service to the need for 'information', the problem of how to fund libraries, and what sort of libraries to fund, remains unresolved. Even in the richest countries libraries are less and less able to afford the ever expanding tide of printed and (where it has to be paid for) electronic information. The result is ever more patchy and selective collections, which threaten the whole fabric of scholarly communication around the world, at the very moment when electronic links should in theory be making that communication effortless.

The Alexandrian library is important to us not least because it first raised these problems. Research libraries may well seem to outsiders, as the Alexandrian museum seemed to Timon, to cater only to cloistered bookworms arguing endlessly in the chicken-coop of the Muses, but human civilisation cannot survive without them.

NOTES

1. Athenaeus, *Deipnosophistae*, I.3; to this list we should probably add the library of Plato's Academy.
2. Strabo, *Geographia*, XIII.1.54, cited at greater length below.
3. Diogenes Laertius, *Vitae philosophorum*, V.77.
4. Timon, frg. 12 Diels.

5. Strabo, *Geographia*, 17.1.8.
6. *Letter of Aristeas to Philocrates*, 9–11.
7. Tzetzes, *Prooemium II*, Koster.
8. Again see further below; Aulus Gellius, *Noctes Atticae*, VII.17.3.
9. Galen, *Commentarius in Hippocratis Epidemias III*.
10. Galen, *ibid*; the exact status of these official copies at Athens has been much discussed.
11. Galen, *Commentarius in Hippocratis librum De natura hominis*, I.44; this must of course refer to the time after the foundation of the library by the Attalid kings in Pergamon, in the second century BC.
12. Galen, *Commentarius in Hippocratis Epidemias III*.
13. Athenaeus, *Deipnosophistae*, I.3.
14. Strabo, *Geographia*, 13.1.54.
15. Pliny, *Naturalis historia*, XXX.4.
16. Syncellus, *Chronographia*, I, 516, 3–10 Dindorf; Syncellus goes on to claim that Ptolemy collected 100,000 books in the libraries [sic] he had founded in Alexandria, but this number is inconsistent with Tzetzes' and other figures.
17. Tzetzes, *Prooemium II*, Koster.
18. Alan Rowe, *Discovery of the Famous Temple and Enclosure of Serapis at Alexandria* (Le Caïre: Institut français d'archéologie orientale, 1946); and : 'A Contribution to the Archaeology of the Western Desert, IV: The Great Serapeum of Alexandria', *Bulletin of the John Rylands Library*, 39 (1956–57), 485–520.
19. Epiphanius, *De mensuris et ponderibus*, 11.
20. Aphthonius, *Progymnasmata*, 12.
21. Tzetzes, *Prooemium II*, Koster.
22. Cf. especially Rudolf Blum, Kallimachos: *The Alexandrian Library and the Origins of Bibliography* (Madison WI: University of Wisconsin Press, 1991), although some of Blum's conclusions need to be treated with care.
23. *Oxyrhynchus Papyri*, 1241.
24. Seneca, *De tranquillitate animi*, IX.4–5.
25. Plutarch, *Caesar*, 49.
26. Dio Cassius, *Historiae romanae*, XLII.38.2.
27. Ammianus Marcellinus, *Historiae*, XXII.16.13–14.
28. Orosius, *Historiae adversum paganos*, VI.15.31.
29. Caesar, *De bello civili*, III.112.
30. *Bellum Alexandrinum*, 1.
31. Plutarch, *Antonius*, 58 9.
32. Suetonius, *Domitianus*, 20.
33. Ammianus Marcellinus, *Historiae*, XXII.16.15.
34. Orosius, *Historiae*, VI.15.32.
35. Edward Gibbon, *The Decline and Fall of the Roman Empire*, ch. 51.
36. Alfred J. Butler, *The Arab Conquest of Egypt*, Second Edition by P.M. Fraser (Oxford: Clarendon Press, 1978; original edition 1902), ch. 25.
37. Luciano Canfora, *The Vanished Library* (London: Hutchinson Radius, 1989).
38. Canfora, *op. cit.* 197.

Chapter 4

Aristotle's Works: The Possible Origins of the Alexandria Collection

R. G. Tanner

INTRODUCTION

Some of the most puzzling issues surrounding the Alexandria Library involve the source and content of the Library's holdings of Aristotle's works. The history of these works bears a close and intriguing relationship to the history of the library. The argument of this paper is that there are two sources for the transmission of Aristotle's work from the ancient to modern world. The first – what we may call the traditional view – holds that Aristotle's corpus was inherited entirely by Theophrastus, and subsequently buried, sold, and edited in Rome. Thence, in Roman times, copies made their way to the library. The second, the more controversial, but possibly more interesting view, argues that there is a collection of Aristotle's works which was derived from the works prepared at Mieza for the education of Alexander; and that these were either given by Alexander to Alexandria, or were subsequently stolen for the library by Ptolemy Soter.

These two, parallel accounts, present us with Aristotle's thought at two different stages in its chronological development. One phase we can describe as the 'educational stage', dealing with works intended for the education of Alexander, and embracing Aristotle's four so-called 'non-scientific' works on poetry, ethics, politics and rhetoric; the other can be described in terms of Aristotle's larger philosophical corpus.

We know that the great philosopher was engaged by Alexander's father, Philip II of Macedonia, to give his son an Athenian upper class Greek education in the Nymphaeum of Mieza. The choice was perhaps influenced by the fact that Nicomachus, Aristotle's late father, had been court physician to the previous king, as much as by Aristotle's eminent role as scholar and teacher in Plato's Academy until 347 BC.[1] Certainly, other eminent educationists were vying for the appointment; and the prominent Athenian orator and political thinker Isocrates, who had written letters of advice to Philip, may well have seemed the likely choice for this post.

However, it was Aristotle who received the invitation, and began teaching Alexander in 343 BC. when the prince was thirteen years old. It is still disputed whether Alexander was taught alone or with a class of Royal Pages. I believe it was a group education rather than private instruction, aimed at training a class of young companions loyal to Alexander and sharing his ideals in administering those Asiatic conquests his father meant to make. On the other hand, on the basis of a letter Alexander sent Aristotle, rebuking him for divulging his teaching to a wider public,[2] Trevor Saunders holds that the instruction was private[3]. This is a serious objection; but I hope to answer it later.

Ancient sources tell us that Aristotle wrote for the young prince two treatises, one *On Monarchy*, and a second, *On Colonies*.[4] He is also reputed earlier to have prepared for his pupil a especially edited text of Homer, which Alexander carried with him all his life.[5] Let us then consider the likely pattern of the Prince's education. Athens aimed at producing a good citizen capable of holding public office in his city republic, both in peace and war. This entailed *gymnastic* (or athletic prowess) and skill in handling weapons, both imparted by a trainer. However, tradition also required, as gentlemanly accomplishments, a grasp of *music*, a term covering the interests of all nine Muses. In practice, this meant skill in flute playing and the ability to explain the poets, especially Homer, and to recite them by heart – which one was taught by a *grammaticus*.[6] Armed with these skills, an upper class Athenian boy moved at fifteen or sixteen to the study of oratory and political wisdom (or practical *virtue*), taught by a *Sophist*, such as the great Protagoras. This was the kind of education Isocrates could have imparted splendidly. But, for a potential world ruler, Philip wanted his son to have more education about the nature of man and the world. Hence the choice of Aristotle, who had been writing on *Ethics* in 346 at Assos, and who was hard at work on natural history on the island of Lesbos when the appointment came.

The likely curriculum at Mieza may be presumed to have covered **Poetics**, with special reference to Homer; so much the text book of Greek morality, **Rhetoric** to give power to persuade, as well as **Ethics**, with reference to proper conduct for Kings and subjects, and Politics to help understanding of the role of government and its constitutional embodiments. Again, it would be reasonable to expect that the tone of these works would represent a 'Monarch's eye' rather than 'citizen's eye' view of their topics. Possibly, too, we have relics of some basic scientific teaching, for works like *De Anima* and *De Memoria* may well have been written for royal instruction and possibly revised later. Concerning research reported in *Historia Animalium*,[7] D'Arcy Thompson long ago drew attention to references made to places in Asia Minor and Lesbos, rather than Greece. So basic biology may have been included also.

When Aristotle left Mieza to return to Athens, ca. 334 BC, we may presume he took his treatises, lecture notes and papers, and continued to work on such topics in the what we today know as the recently discovered Lyceum site, behind the present Byzantine and Air Force Museums, between Leophoros Sophias and Leophoros Constantinou, and almost opposite the British Embassy compound. In essence, the body of treatises that was extant in Athens when Aristotle fled to Euboca after Alexander's death are the foundation of the current Aristotelian corpus.

I. THE FATE OF THE ARISTOTELIAN CORPUS

By the *Aristotelian Corpus* we mean the body of writings which came to Europe in Arabic versions, made in Syria and Baghdad under the 'Ummayyad' and 'Abbasid' Caliphates, from Greek originals by scholars who were largely Syriac-speaking Nestorian Christians, or learned Jews. Because of their importance for twelfth century debates – notably, between Christian thinkers, influenced by the writings of Averroes, the great Muslim philosopher who questioned the independent existence of the soul, and St. Thomas Aquinas, who affirmed it – Latin versions were made from the Arabic at that time. Later negotiations for Church reunion between Rome and Constantinople brought to Europe Greek scholars of Aristotle with some texts in Greek; and many more copies arrived after the fall of Constantinople to the Turks in AD 1453. Around AD 1300 Dante, in his *Convito*, described Aristotle as *lo maestro de la umana ragione* – 'the master of human reason',[8] so copies of his Greek text must have circulated widely in Europe, both in manuscript and, after the Renaissance, in print.

However, it is vital to know more about the actual character and content of the Aristotelian corpus that was transmitted in this way. Although ancient Greek and Roman authors praise the charm and style of Aristotle's dialogues, none of these were recovered in the Renaissance; and most of the voluminous body of Greek text appears to have been written either as lecture notes or as discussion papers for use in his philosophy school in the Lyceum at Athens between 334 and 323 BC. These include studies on metaphysics, physics, biology, meteorology and astronomy, as well as logic and argument. All these are called his 'scientific writings'. Then we have a body of works referred to as 'non-scientific'. These treat of poetry, oratory, ethics and politics – major elements in traditional Greek and Roman education. Scholars have agreed in pronouncing some of the writings to be works of the master's pupils – or his later philosophical school in Roman times, which was often called 'the Lyceum', members of which were called 'the Peripatetics'. Some of these works are still from time to time disputed. The great German scholar Bekker, whose landmark edition of 1831 still remains fundamental, put up a classification of genuine and spurious which is still widely accepted. Indeed, so great is Bekker's influence that to this day we refer to passages in Aristotle's Greek text by the page and line numbers in his edition.

Those texts most contested for their alleged genuineness are two 'non-scientific' texts, the ethical treatise entitled *Magna Moralia,* and the oratory handbook called *Rhetorica ad Alexandrum*. On the continent, Von Arnim and Jaeger defended the authenticity of *Magna Moralia,* as did Thomas Case in Oxford.[9] In addition, Case has also offered a very able defence of the *Rhetorica ad Alexandrum*.[10] Otherwise, we have to recognise that assuredly genuine works may contain later insertions. Further, apparently late *spuria,* though not from Aristotle, may well be from the hand of Theophrastus, his successor in the Lyceum, or else from Dicaearchus or Straton, his pupils. Unless demonstrably late, they cannot be assigned to the age of Andronicus, who worked on the corpus in Rome in 70 BC. Interesting speculations regarding the order of composition and the evolution of the Stagirite's thought may be studied in Jaeger's works and those of Düring, together with the recent work of Rist.[11]

At this point, we may wonder how the Lyceum collection came to be in Rome by 70 BC.

Strabo tells us that the works of Aristotle and Theophrastus were bequeathed by the latter to Neleus of Scepsis, who in 285 BC took them from Athens to his home at Scepsis in Asia Minor.[12] To nearby Assos Aristotle retired after Plato's death in 347, and there he lived until moving to the isle of Lesbos – not far from Theophrastus' home at Eresos – a few years before returning to Pella in 343 BC in order to become Alexander's tutor. Neleus' kinsfolk buried the books to protect them from the agents of King Attalus, who was seizing books by royal warrant to stock his Pergamene Library between 238 and 198 BC. This family then sold them to the Athenian bibliophile Apellicon about a century later, and he took them to his house in Athens. When Sulla took Athens in the Mithradatic War he seized them and sent the collection to Rome where Tyrannio and Andronicus edited them about 70 BC. Some works survived only in highly conjectural copies of damaged originals made by Apellicon, while the rest suffered from moths and damp. Plutarch echoes this account,[13] and both insist that after Neleus took away the collection, the Lyceum had copies of only a small part of the master's work, chiefly exoteric works. These were, in part, the dialogues now lost to us, rather than much of our surviving corpus of philosophical essays that were largely inspired by teaching in the Lyceum.

This received account seems too circumstantial for mere fabrication. If genuine, it may reflect a real concern inspired by Theophrastus when he visited Ptolemy Soter to advise about the Alexandria library. There, doubtless, he met Philadelphus and Arsinoe, and feared perhaps that they would intervene in Greece, occupy Athens, and seize the Lyceum collection for Alexandria. Soter died in 283, but Theophrastus died even earlier – about the time that the King's exiled son Ceraunos was received in Macedonia, rendering the allies of Macedon, like Athens, open to Ptolemaic revenge. The risk that this occasion could be used to invade Attica, and carry off the Lyceum library to Alexandria, would have been a natural concern at the time of Theophrastus' death.

If the tradition is true, most of the works in our corpus antedate 285 BC, and Straton would be the last contributor. However, apart from any contemporary gap-filling efforts by Andronicus to manufacture missing works in 70 BC, it is not unlikely that some other Peripatetics in the crisis of 262 BC fled to Scepsis from Athens, and deposited added contributions in that library. In short, if rightly set in context, the traditional explanation greatly elucidates the texts.

2. ANCIENT LISTS OF ARISTOTLE'S WORKS HELD IN ALEXANDRIA

In his *Lives of the Philosophers*, dating from AD 200, Diogenes Laertius gives us what he considers a full list of the works by Aristotle in the Library at Alexandria – so full, indeed, that a number of items are listed twice.[14] Presumably in such cases, the Library held two papyrus manuscript copies. Scholarly opinion holds that this index list was compiled about 200 BC by a scholar called Hermippus. At this time, the traditional account, as given above, relates that the works we inherited from the Middle Ages were hidden in a cellar or cave at Scepsis. However, very few of the titles given in Hermippus' list in Diogenes Laertius match up with those of our current body of texts. Bekker's table of contents lists 32 genuine works, seven pseudepigraphic, and ten deemed to combine genuine and spurious elements. By contrast, Diogenes lists 150 titles, while the Menagian fragment based on Hesychius gives much the same list, with additions bringing it up to 198 titles. In addition, we have some very garbled Greek, preserved in a thirteenth century Arabic work, purporting to offer us a list made in the second century AD by a Greek of Alexandria called 'Ptolemaeus the Philosopher'. Allegedly there were 1000 books, but this Ptolemy cites one hundred works, comprised in 550 books, or papyrus volume rolls, and 92 of them are listed in our text. These works include both those in our earlier two lists, and some which those lists do not mention, but which are in our present corpus of Aristotle published by Bekker.

The survival of these lists suggests that a large accretion of works, previously lacking, joined the Alexandria collection of Aristotle between 200 BC and AD 200. Further, they strongly implied that these works – for example, Ptolemaeus no. 10, *De lineis insecabilibus*, no. 17 *De motu (animalium)*, no. 20 *De spiritu*, no. 41 *De partibus animalium* – came from the Lyceum in Theophrastus' collection. However, the Hesychian list, which purports to follow Andronicus of Rhodes who edited the Scepsis material at Rome for Tyrannio, lists most of our Scepsis-derived corpus as well as the items listed by Hermippus.[15] This may suggest that copies of that corpus were sent from Rome to Alexandria between 70 and 45 BC, and that the list embraces both volumes already held by the Ptolemies in other copies, as well as the rediscovered materials from Scepsis. All this leaves open to debate the origins of the collection listed by Hermippus at Alexandria, whose titles Diogenes Laertius believed to be on the shelves about 200 BC.

Here, one should note John Rist's recent caveat: 'The gap between the composition of the texts and their appearance in Alexandria is still too big to be bridged. Few reliable inferences can be made from the lists in Alexandria to the books and notes Aristotle left when he died, let alone when he was actually writing'.[16] Despite this warning, I believe Plutarch gives us grounds for attempting an explanation. In the passage of the *Life of Alexander*, which Trevor Saunders saw as telling against class instruction at Mieza, there are interesting hints. We are told that Alexander wrote from Asia, objecting to the publication by his teacher, Aristotle, of 'acroamatic' discourses which he had attended – apart from the general classes in Ethics and Politics. In reply, Aristotle explained that they were both published and not published, because no untrained person could follow them, especially **Metaphysics**.[17] Now this excuse would be more convincing if the new publications had new distinct titles. So it is significant that, although some works held at Alexandria may seem to treat metaphysical questions, there is no work entitled *Metaphysics*. However, Alexander's objection may imply that he felt he held a kind of royal copyright on the Mieza material, because his father had paid Aristotle for his education; and that he could insist upon obtaining copies of all materials. Certainly, specific works like *Alexander on Colonies* and *On Monarchy* were almost certainly written at Mieza, especially for the prince's guidance.

Given the hypothesis which argues that the current corpus was sent to Scepsis to avoid the greed of the Ptolemies, and the tradition of its concealment there to escape the agents of the Attalids, it seems that the list of Hermippus represents those works which the Ptolemies in fact acquired. Whence did they come? The most likely answer is, the castle of Mieza where Aristotle taught Alexander. If there is any foundation to Alexander's letter rebuking Aristotle in Athens for publishing acroamatic doctrines, one must assume that Aristotle left his pupil copies of all the materials they discussed. In that event, it is likely that royal scribes copied all the books the teacher brought from Assos near Atarneus, and any other such notebooks or dialogues used in teaching at Mieza before Aristotle left for Athens.

On this view, we reach the conclusion that we have a list of the treatises, notes and dialogues that Aristotle took back from Pella to Athens, when he returned to open a school in the Lyceum in 335 BC. The 'mirror-image' royal copy remained at Mieza as the King's Library, but after the foundation of Alexandria in 332, it may well have been sent there in the King's lifetime, and thus became part of the core of the Ptolemaic collection. Then in the second century BC, Hermippus would have used this and catalogued it, together with other Peripatetic works since acquired for the Library.

If this was the basic body of research papers, dialogues and lecture notes that Aristotle brought to the Lyceum, it follows that in the next twelve years, some texts were re-worked to suit the resources available to him. There he met the need to compete with Plato's Academy over metaphysical and logical issues, as well as the task of teaching leading men of a democracy, rather than a prince and the royal pages. This would require him to reshape his teaching programmes in politics, ethics and rhetoric. Again, poetic theory would become more important than the detailed poetic studies used for the preliminary 'musical' instruction at Mieza – before the class was ready for the Aristotelian version of the Protagoran 'sophistic', concerning practical virtue and eloquence. Moreover, resources given by Alexander permitted Aristotle to expand the studies of animals he had begun at Assos and Mitylene.[18] Our current *Nicomachean Ethics* and the *Politics* may well represent a revision and expansion, both to link with more recent scientific and metaphysical work, and to conciliate moderate democrat opinion in Athens after the death of Callisthenes in 327, when the Conspiracy of the Pages damaged Aristotle's relations with Alexander.

If we accept the Strabo tradition, it would follow that most of the works represented a re-arrangement and editing by Theophrastus and Straton of texts largely combined from earlier short works of Aristotle and the Lyceum, large parts of which survived in the Alexandria Library in their earlier or shorter forms. Thus, though having very few of the works in our form, the original Lyceum corpus and Ptolemy's copy had a great deal of identical content under different formats.[19] What Apellicon gave us back, was Theophrastus and

Straton's Peripatetic *system* rather than better *ipsissima verba*. Then, by the time of Ptolemaeus in the second century, the 'system books' from Scepsis can feature equally with the earlier Mieza work in the Arabic records depending on his list.

The ancient list of Hermippus tells us much about the growth of the Peripatetic system, as well as giving reason to see the 'non-scientific' works as evolving out of Mieza instructions to Alexander and the Pages – works more in tune with Macchiavelli's *Prince*, than with the more 'constitutional' tone of his writings on Politics, Ethics and Oratory. The assumption that the core of all these began at Mieza would serve to further justify the Case-von Arnim view of the priority of the *Eudemian Ethics*, as dating between the dialogue *Protrepticus* and the *Nicomachean Ethics*, and the von Arnim claim that the *Magna Moralia* is the earliest ethical work.[20] In my view, this was brought from Assos and re-developed into the five books of the Eudemian, as distinct from the Nicomachean text, whilst the philosopher was in Macedonia. Similarly, Case's defence of the date of the *Rhetorica ad Alexandrum* to before Alexander's regency is only doubted because it treats 'inquiry', a matter not part of manuals of rhetoric until Hellenistic times. But if it was written to instruct a future king and ministers, then proper 'Privy Council' procedures are a necessary element even at this date. The argument for this view of the lists remains circumstantial, but it may be a useful approach to further examination of the Aristotle's legacy.

3. THE STRUCTURE OF THE NON-SCIENTIFIC WORKS

The inter-relationship between the various works in Aristotle's corpus has been brought to the attention of English readers by the recent works of Richard Sorabji and John Rist.[21] Let me begin by recalling that by *scientific* works, I mean those studies on metaphysics, physics, natural and medical phenomena, and language and logic. 'Non-scientific', in this sense – although not illogical or unmethodical – are the works on ethics, politics, rhetoric and poetry. These, of course, were primary elements in the Athenian curriculum used in teaching the youth at Mieza.

Although Jaeger is probably right to see Aristotle's teaching of poetics, rhetoric, ethics and politics as beginning to show its distinctive features at Assos from 347 BC,[22] this scheme of theory and instruction was probably developed during his stay in Macedonia between 343 and 336 BC, especially if a class of Royal Pages studied with the Prince at the Nympheum. It is interesting also, that at the outset of the 13 year old Alexander's education, Aristotle prepared a special text of Homer, for Philip wished his son to acquire the full culture of his Athenian foes.

Thus 'music' and 'gymnastic', involving skills of the *grammaticus*, would have been followed by a course in 'persuasion and practical virtue' such as Protagoras is found professing in Plato's dialogue of that name.

Teaching in the Nymphaeum at Mieza is unlikely to have been confined to one pupil. Alexander''s contemporary Royal Pages who later – as in the case of Hephaestion or Ptolemy – shared in his administration and conquests, are likely also to have shared his education. Thus, they would have been informed by the same views of Homer and poetry, the same skills of persuasion, and the same approach to morality and government as their future sovereign. Formal classes would have taken place, for which our present *Poetics*, *Rhetoric*, *Ethics* and *Politics* would have been composed. As A.A. Long observes of the *Ethics* in its present Lyceum-Apellicon Nicomachean version, all these works are full of happy poetical quotations illustrative of their argument. This is a teaching technique admirably suited for impressing notions on young men lately well grounded in the poets.

Regarding *Rhetoric*, Thomas Case's argument for dating the *Rhetorica ad Alexandrum* before 340 BC is compelling.[23] However, the preface is characteristic of a later age, and there may have been other meddling with the text by subsequent peripatetics. The presence of *exetasis* as a rhetorical form seems also third century.[24] But it is just possible that Aristotle invented it for the Mieza course, as well suited for a ruler of a violent society that sometimes used 'Star Chamber' methods.

In Diogenes' list, the *Ethics in 5* books may well be the original draft of *Eudemian Ethics* I-III and VII, probably deriving, as Jaeger holds, from Assos.[25] Further, Diogenes' *On Justice in 4 books* may represent part of the Mieza ethical and political coursework. After his return to Athens, advice for kings would have been removed, and the three books boiled down from it used to constitute V-VII in the Lyceum *Nicomachean Ethics*, which also constitute IV-VI of the present *Eudemian Ethics*. The reason for this may be, as von Arnim surmised, that the original text of the *Magna Moralia* was of early date, about 336 BC. Indeed, it is possible that if *Magna Moralia* may date from 443 BC; it could have been composed to show that Aristotle would impart sound views to Philip's son. When one studies the three books we would derive from the lost *On Justice* we find they are all most relevant to the ethics of a King. Thus EN V (= EE IV) discusses Justice itself, a prime royal function whether jurisdiction or fairness is needed. Then EN VI (= EE V) teaches intellectual *virtues* like wisdom, judgment and understanding – qualities again essential for a royal personage. Finally, EN VII (= EE VI) treats the incontinent appetites for pleasure wealth and power, which can undermine monarchy, as we have seen in both ancient and recent times.

When we look at the *Politics*, it seems reasonable to look for traces of the philosopher's Mieza teaching. At first glance there seems no relic of *Alexander on Colonies*. But when the form of an ideal city constitution is described in Book VII, we find odd features. Saunders noted its incompleteness and lack of connection with criticism of such states in Book II (Penguin edition, p.34). I find its mention of siting the city near a subject population (1330a25) and in a defensible site as suggestive of a Greek colony in Asia, while the elaborate rules for integrating the citizens also suggest it is to be peopled by settlers from different parts of Greece. This leads me to believe much of the book was cannibalised from *On Colonies*. Again, the incomplete study of education in the ideal city in Book VIII may suggest we have an unfinished extract from Diogenes Laertius' list item *On Paideia* from Hermippus' catalogue.

This leads one to wonder if Book III with its advocacy of good kingship was in fact a reworking of the Mieza study *On Monarchy*. Books IV-VI explaining Greek polis structures and ideas of citizenship, constitutional change, and devices for preserving convenient constitutions, all were probably worked up at the Lyceum. But their starting point may have been a draft of advice for a Macedonian King on controlling allied Greek client states. On the other hand Books I and II are clearly Lyceum work. The treatment of economic issues and links between household and state recall the fact that Dicaearchus was writing his *Livelihood of Greece* at the Lyceum and Book I may reflect his influence. Book II debunking other thinkers' Ideal States had an obvious role when Plato's *Republic* was still admired in the Academy whose dominance Aristotle had to challenge. Probably begun after Alexander had executed Aristotle's pupil Callisthenes, it marked the breach with the King perhaps by stressing its palatability to Athenian conservative moderates who tended to regard the new school as a foreign Macedonian implant.

I believe that the four works discussed – *Poetics, Rhetoric, Politics* and *Ethics* – are all texts which passed through a Mieza phase in their development. Further, I suspect that the extant *Rhetorica ad Alexandrum* and *Magna Moralia* are somewhat mangled survivors of that phase – if the latter did not begin earlier, in a first draft at Assos composed by 343 BC, perhaps to commend Aristotle to Philip II as a suitable moral instructor for Alexander.

CONCLUSION

Aristotle influenced the development of the Ptolemaic Library in Alexandria Museum even in death. It was his able pupil, Demetrius of

Phaleron, who organised the new Library for Ptolemy Soter, making Aristotle's arrangement at the Lyceum the model for the layout and cataloguing of this great collection and providing accommodation for scholars.

As to the Aristotelian corpus itself, this inquiry suggests that the papers from Mieza reposed in the Library at Alexandria after their capture by Ptolemy. For a King who knew how to steal his sovereign Alexander's body, such an annexation would not be difficult. But at the same time, the copies taken to the Lyceum were re-worked into a new modified corpus to educate republican Athens. This was to allow Aristotle to attempt to complete such projects as Rist detects in the *de Motu Animalium* – to give an insight into the whole pneumatic physical system of the universe.[26] At a later stage – after 70 BC – the revised and improved Lyceum works came to join their predecessors in the *scrinia* of the great Library, later to be listed with them by Ptolemy the philosopher in the 2nd century AD. Was he perchance the great astronomer and mathematician Ptolemy as well?

This inquiry also suggests that the non-scientific works that we now possess derived from works that were originally devised in Mieza to train the young Alexander for Kingship. When Aristotle went to Athens, with a set of all his papers from the Nymphaeum, he found it necessary to modify his teaching of Rhetoric, Politics and Ethics to suit life in a democracy, thus bringing into being our current treatises. However, it is likely that Alexander insisted on keeping copies of the Mieza papers, and these first found their way to Alexandria, perhaps by 300 BC, and thus figure in the ancient lists. Later, the present corpus – which had been hidden in Scepsis – came to light and joined the other volumes in the Museum between 70 and 40 BC. Unhappily, the Mieza papers have mostly perished, but probably differed from our current corpus more by title, emphasis and arrangement than in widely divergent doctrine. Had they survived, they would have helped us to chart Aristotle's voyage of development in doctrine. Without the ancient catalogues, we might not have known that they ever existed. Altogether, the Alexandrian experience should warn us of the risks we take – especially if we replace libraries with the Internet!

APPENDIX

The discussion of Ethics suggests that the old story about Aristotle naming the *Magna Moralia* to instruct his father Nicomachus, the royal physician; the *Eudemian Ethics*, to instruct his friend Eudemus of Cyprus; and the *Nicomachean Ethics*, to guide his son Nicomachus, needs attention.[27] As Aristotle's father died in his childhood, and as

Aristotle died when his son was but thirteen, these explanations seem false as they stand, but may conceal a truth. If the *Magna Moralia – pace* Kenny[28] – is earliest, as von Arnim believed, and if we can push it back to 343 BC, then it could well have been sent to King Philip, with a letter explaining that it represented the high ethical views which Aristotle learnt from his dead father, **Nicomachus**, the royal physician to Amyntas. If the later gossip about Aristotle's gluttony, drinking and sodomy is not all entire scandal, he may have needed to discredit the rumours if he were to seek the tutorship of Alexander.[29] Similarly, one could see the *Eudemian* named as a tribute to his dead friend Eudemus of Cyprus, and the *Nicomachean*, as theophrastus' tribute to his ward, his master's young son who fell in battle.[30]

NOTES

*   I agree with W.K.C.Guthrie, *A History of Greek Philosophy* (Cambridge: Cambridge University Press, 1981), vol. VI, 'Aristotle, an Encounter', 35–6, that Jaeger's theory is interesting but not essential. See Werner Jaeger, *Aristotle – Fundamentals of the History of his Development* (Oxford: Oxford University Press, 2nd ed., 1962), 119–21.

1.   Plutarch, *Alexander* 7, in C. Sinten (ed.) Plutarch, Vitae (Leipzig: Teubner, 1876–81), vol.III, 285–6.

2.   Ibid.

3.   Aristotle, *The Politics*, trans. T. A Sinclair, in T.J Saunders (ed.) (Harmondsworth: Penguin, 1981).

4.   Sir David Ross, *Aristotle* (London: Methuen, 1966), 4.

5.   Plutarch , *op. cit.* 8.

6.   On such feats of memory, see E.C Marchant (ed.), *Xenophontis Opera Omnia* (Oxford: Oxford University Press, 1942), vol.II.

7.   Guthrie, *op. cit.* 29–30.

8.   Dante, in E. Moore (ed.), *Tutte le Opere* (Oxford: Oxford University Press, 1897), 297.

9.   Thomas Case, 'Aristotle', *Encyclopedia Britannica* (Cambridge: Cambridge University Press, 1910), 11th edition, vol. II, 514; cf. H. Von Arnim, *Die Drei Aristotelischen Ethiken* (Wien: Akademie der Wissenschaften zu Wien,, 1924), Sitzurgberichte 202, Abh. 2, 146, as assessed by Ross, *op. cit.* 15.

10. Case, *op. cit.* 515–6.

11. See Jaeger, *op. cit.* 228–46; Ingemar Düring, *Aristoteles* (Heidelberg: Winter, 1966), passim; John M. Rist, *The Mind of Aristotle: A Study of Philosophical Growth* (Toronto: Phoenix, 1989), Suppl. Series XXV, 3–36.

12. August Meineke (ed.) *Geographica* (Leipzig: Teubner, 1866), XIII, i, 851–3.

13. *Sulla*, 26, C. Sinten (ed.), (Leipzig, Teubner, 1876–81), vol.II, 450. For a different and more recent view of the role of Andronicus, see H.Gottschalk in R. Sorjabi (ed.), *Aristotle Transformed* (London: Duckworth, 1990), 55–81.

14. H.S. Long (ed.), *Diogenes Laertius*, V, 21 (Oxford: Oxford University Press, 1964), vol. I.

15. Edward Zeller, *Outlines of Greek Philosophy* (London: Longmans, 1885), 172–3.

16. Rist, *op. cit.* 13.

17. Plutarch, *Alexander*, 7, C.Sinten (ed.), (Leipzig: Teubner, vol.III, 1876–81), 285–6.
18. Sir David Ross, *Aristotle* (London: Methuen, 1966), 6.
19. Ross, *op. cit.* 9.
20. von Arnim, *op. cit.* passim.
21. Sorabji, *op. cit.* 1–30; Rist, op. cit. 13–36.
22. Jaeger, *op. cit.* 45–6.
23. Case, *op. cit.* XI, II, 515.
24. Case, *op. cit.* XI, II, 515; cf Ross, op. cit. 16.
25. Jaeger, *op. cit.* 1966, 256.
26. Rist, *op. cit.* 246–252.
27. Porphyry, *Proleg.* 9, CAG IV. i, A. Busse (ed.), (Berlin, 1887); cf. Sir Alexander Grant, *Ethics of Aristotle* (London: Parker, 1857), 12, also in ed. 2, 32, 1874.
28. A. Kenny, *The Aristotelian Ethics* (Oxford: Oxford University Press, 1978); Guthrie, *op. cit.* 40–41.
29. See Andronicus fragment in Valentin Rose, *Aristotle's Fragmenta* (Stuttgart: Teubner, 1966), 10.
30. Thus Aristocles in Eusebius *Praep. Evsng.* XV, 793 c 2–7 (Gaisford, Oxford: 1843, vol. IV). However, Suidas' *Lexicon* part i (vol. II, ed. Gaisford & Bernhardy, 989–90 – Halle & Braunschweig, 1853) preserves a tradition that young Nicomachus became a philosopher himself and wrote six books on Ethics. This led several German scholars to maintain that these books constituted *EN* I–IV & VIII–IX, and that a later hand composed *EN* X subsequently. In his commentary Bernhardy finds the theory that Nicomachus was responsible for composing *EN* attractive. If true, I suspect it amounted to completing an unfinished work of Aristotle in collaboration with his guardian.

Part II.

Scholarship in the Alexandrian Manner

Chapter 5

Doctors in the Library: The Strange Tale of Apollonius the Bookworm and Other Stories

John Vallance

INTRODUCTION

The Library at Alexandria remains as much the stuff of legend as of hard evidence. The legend is, of course, a potent one, and many of the older standard accounts of Hellenistic science – mathematics, astronomy, geometry, meteorology and medicine stress (if sometimes rather vaguely) the positive influence of the early Alexandrian Ptolemies and the institutions they established on the development of research.[1] We tend to assume that the Great Library, from early on, *must* have contained the important, canonical works of Greek philosophy and medicine, and that local and visiting scholars *must* have had ready access to them.[2] Circumstantial evidence certainly supports this view. It seems that some scholars enjoyed patronage, tax free status, the right of residence in the royal quarter of Alexandria and that the Library and Museum were not linked to any particular philosophical school or doctrine.[3] The traditional view that the origins of liberal critical scholarship lie here, seems to be a reasonable one. Groups of scholars from the late fourth century BC onwards, were able to take meals together in the *Museion*, their association with one another reinforced by benign cultic affiliations, their gatherings presided over by priests. The result of all this, the story goes, is that it is no wonder that these Alexandrian institutions led to an extraordinary flowering of empirical scientific work, in which great individuals were able, for the first time, to liberate themselves from the epistemic shackles of the philosophers.[4]

However, this story needs some qualification. My subject here is medicine. I consider two cases which relate to work in medical theory and practice done in and around the Library and Museum in the first hundred years of their existence. It may well be true that the Library owed its intellectual origins to the research methods of Aristotle's

Lyceum, but a rather different view of Alexandrian intellectual culture will emerge here – one in which the influence of the Library and Museum can just as readily be associated with a shift away from the practical, autoptic investigation of nature which is characteristic of earlier Aristotelian science.

1. ALEXANDRIA, BOOKS AND THE HIPPOCRATIC TRADITION

Some preliminary points need not detain us long. Most ancient witnesses agree that the early Ptolemies (especially, perhaps, Ptolemy II, "Philadelphus" 308–246 BCE) were jealous patrons of the arts and sciences; prosopographical and biographical research indicates that many thinkers did make their way to Alexandria, and in some cases settled there.[5] As for medicine, as Herodotus had observed in the fifth century, Egypt teemed with physicians. Two centuries after his own visit, Greek doctors had arrived in strength, and the list of famous physicians who visited, or lived in Alexandria in the third and second centuries BC is so extensive that medicine in the period between Aristotle and Galen is often described as 'Alexandrian'.[6] Writing in the second century AD, Galen of Pergamon often refers to the quality of opportunities for both education and practice which had been enjoyed by Alexandrian doctors in the centuries before his own. Early Alexandria occupied the kind of status that Cos and Cnidos had earlier enjoyed among certain doctors.[7]

Linking practising doctors, and iatrosophists – as medical theorists came to be called – with the Library and *Museion* is rather more difficult. First there is a basic problem of evidence. No third century medical work survives intact until we reach the second century; we are reliant at every point upon fragments, quotations embedded in the work of later writers. A second problem relates to an incompatibility between what we know of the aims and structure of the *Museion*, and the character of medical education in Alexandria, which followed the standard Greek model of apprenticeship and was generally organised around individuals in private practice.

If we are correct in believing that the idea behind the establishment of such a centre of learning had its ultimate origins with the early Peripatetics – Strabo, for instance, suggests that Aristotle himself offered advice which influenced its establishment and early administration, and other sources implicate the peripatetic military man Demetrius of Phaleron[8] – it would be reasonable to suggest that research supported by the Royal Court might have proceeded along lines broadly similar to those advocated by the Lyceum. Aristotle and Theophrastus, for instance, spent much of their later lives gathering zoological and botanical data, and working out detailed taxonomies and aetiologies which might frame the presentation of this huge amount of empirical data. Constrained by the need to make a living, few practising doctors would have been able to pursue such a programme. In fact, it is difficult to find specific instances of any medical research demonstrably supported by the Royal Palace, let alone the Library or Museum, or to point to physicians whose work flourished under the direct patronage of the first Ptolemies.[9]

In medicine, the best known (probable) case of patronage is perhaps the only one. It relates to the anatomists Herophilus and Erasistratus. Herophilus (ca. 330–260 BC) came from Chalcedon, and spent much of his life working in Alexandria. Erasistratus of Ceos (ca. 315–240 BC) almost certainly worked there too.[10] They are linked, according to the Roman encyclopaedist A. Cornelius Celsus, by the fact that they pursued detailed anatomical researches into the human body by means of vivisecting the bodies of criminals supplied 'out of prison by the Kings'.[11] It is widely assumed – although Celsus does not make it explicit – that these experiments took place in Alexandria. The implication of Celsus' report – and it is an implication which has been widely embraced by modern scholars – is that at least some of this research was conducted under the patronage of the Court.

The Kings in question would have to be Ptolemy II (Philadelphus) 308–246 BC and Ptolemy III (Euergetes) (284–221 BC). These investigations, which struck even ancient commentators as cruel in the extreme, led to the discovery of so many new structures and capacities in the human body that the Greek language was simply unable to name them all. Herophilus is credited with the discovery of the nervous system, and the distinction between different types of nerves. Erasistratus mapped the blood-vascular system. Little wonder then that this period witnessed an explosion in the size of the Greek technical vocabulary, some of which found its way into the literary productions of Alexandrian scholars like Callimachus and Apollonius of Rhodes.[12]

None of this, it should be said, *proves* that either of these figures – or any other doctors in early Greek Alexandria – enjoyed an official association with the Museum or Library. We are dealing here for the most part with circumstantial evidence, with balances of probabilities. And if the quality of contemporary evidence for what was going on in the third century BC is poor, later witnesses are not much more helpful; one piece of general testimony about the constitution of the Library itself comes from an odd work by a fourth century AD Christian Bishop of Salamis, Epiphanius. His *On Weights and Measures* contains a short account of how the Library was established and what kinds of books it contained. Epiphanius singles out the writings of doctors and iatrosophists for special mention in his list of texts sought by the first administrators of the Library.[13] We can fill out some of the gaps in Epiphanius' report, since fragments of Callimachus' bibliography and library catalogue, the *Pinakes*, survive, and what we know of other figures like Apollonius of Rhodes (fl. 3rd century BC), Eratosthenes of Cyrene (ca. 285–194 BC), and Aristophanes of Byzantium (ca. 257–180 BC), all of whom worked in Alexandria as librarians, gives some idea of the flavour of the research that was carried out there. And it turns out – hardly surprisingly – that the research was mainly textual and historical. Although the best attested focus of scholarly interest in third century Alexandria was the text of Homer,[14] literary texts were far from the only concern of the early librarians. The physician Galen reports (specifically of medical texts) that customs officials at the port of Alexandria had orders to confiscate any books brought to the city by travellers; the originals were deposited in the Library, marked in the catalogue 'from the ships', and their owners, if they were lucky, were supplied with copies.[15]

Even if we can show that medical *texts* were in the Library from early on, that is not to say that doctors themselves were there too. And even if medical men were present in the royal precinct, what sort of people were they? Were they practitioners? Theoreticians? Researchers? What sort of doctors might have had access to the libraries? Were they, like the other scholars, merely overfed and overrated pet birds in the "cage of the Muses", as the caustic poet Timon of Phlius insisted?[16] Before we can attempt answers to these questions, we must look briefly at the types of medical tradition and intellectual culture the Greek doctors brought with them to Egypt.

Long before Greek medicine reached Alexandria, it had developed many forms. Basic health care could be sought, in the agora of any city or town, from sellers of herbs, roots, charms and amulets. The cult of Apollo, and more particularly of Asclepius, provided another source of medical attention. Incubation in temple precincts seems to have been popular enough for the comic poet Aristophanes to have described the experience of one rather cynical patient in his last surviving play, the *Plutus*.[17] But one strand of ancient medicine had always been deeply bookish, and literate doctors wrote relatively often about their reading and about books. Inevitably, it is this type of medicine which figures most prominently in the medical tradition which has reached us, and which found its earliest expression – so far as we know – in the writings later gathered into the Hippocratic Corpus.

From the middle to late fifth century BC, these literate doctors were asking themselves and telling others what it was, exactly, they did. Whatever the underlying causes, the situation suggests competition, and therefore some degree of oversupply. Hippocratic doctors began to promote themselves, drawing a line between their own practice and the services of competing providers of health care – proselytisers of traditional folk medicine, for instance, who could not, on the whole, read or write. A line was drawn no less firmly between them and certain natural philosophers whose speculations about the nature of physio-logical phenomena and disease tended to attract the ridicule of society at large. Those doctors who could write, however, appropriated the argumentative techniques and physiological doctrines of philosophers, and it comes as no surprise to find that the variety of opinion and the extent of disagreement which characterises ancient philosophy is also central to the flavour of Hippocratic medicine. The strains between the common-sense aims of medicine, and the capacity of the medical art to satisfy these aims were, of course, acutely felt. And rhetoric, more often than not, was the salve prescribed to ease this tension.

The rhetorical character of many of the treatises in the Hippocratic Corpus has often been noticed. It was widely agreed – and not only by doctors, of course – that the techniques of persuasion were no less important than the techniques of investigation and therapy. The sophist Gorgias of Leontini, in a work which sought to absolve Helen from the opprobrium attaching to her after her supposed flight to Troy with Paris, made a telling admission about the importance of rhetoric in the public examination of subjects in which there was no ready route to certainty:

> It may also be seen that when persuasion is added to argument (logos), it can make any impression it likes upon the soul; take first, for example, the arguments of the meteorologists, who take away one opinion and replace it with another, thus making what cannot be seen, and what is unbelievable appear before the mind's eye. And second, consider legal battles, where a crowd may be persuaded by a speech because of the skill of its composition rather than the truth of what is said. And finally, consider philosophical debates, where speed of thought may readily be seen to change opinion.[18]

Hippocratic doctors knew this, too, and many of them poked fun at natural philosophers – much as Aristophanes had done in the *Clouds* – because of their inability to solve the problems they posed. Doctors, of course, were in an even more vulnerable position, dependent as they were on their ability to sell themselves and their services. The authors of the treatises *On Ancient Medicine*, *On the Nature of Man*, and *On Fleshes* all accepted the importance of learning the techniques of persuading their patients of their intellectual, and social, credentials. We know that fifth century doctors sometimes gave public lectures in defence of their doctrines. It is clear they felt that the written word offered the possi-bility of a wider audience, and an enhanced authority.[19]

This rhetorical tradition within Greek medicine was to persist through to the time of Galen and beyond, and it was accompanied by some other, rather more complex prejudices. In the fourth century, Aristotle tried to see off a deep-seated prejudice against pure research into the more intractable areas of nature. In the first book of the *De partibus animalium*, he noted that many students are alienated from the study of the physical world, and of our own bodies, by the fact that these are often disagreeable – even ignoble – objects of study. What seems to have been an early prejudice against the study of anatomy through dissection seems to prove Aristotle's point, although some modern observers feel that such activity was just as much inhibited by taboos concerning the proper treatment of the bodies of the dead. It is not until we reach the Alexandria of the Ptolemies, and Herophilus and Erasistratus, that we find the human body laid open to scientific investigation.

Yet the most striking feature of *this* particular case is that human vivisection was, apparently, never practised again in antiquity. Research of this nature went on for a short time only and doctors in the generations after Herophilus lost the stomach, it seems, for continuing this kind of work. And even less violent forms of anatomical investigation become rare until Galen. (Much of Galen's anatomy is based on his study of the Barbary ape, rather than human subjects). If the Ptolemies had offered initial support, why did their successors seem to show so little interest in appealing for patronage which would allow them to continue these investigations?

This, broadly, is the intellectual context of literary medicine as found in Alexandria. By the middle of the third century BC, many doctors had broad interests in reading, and not merely in reading medical literature. We have already found clear evidence that medical literature featured in the Library's collections. The two following case studies may cast more light on our problem of how the two interacted. The first concerns Herophilus and his followers. Apart from his work in anatomy, Herophilus is credited by several ancient sources with initiating the tradition of lexicographical commentary on Hippocratic texts. The second case centres on the rise of a particularly Alexandrian medical sect known as Empiricism. Both cases offer an indication of the possible role of the Library and its associated culture in the development of several significant tendencies in Hellenistic and Graeco-Roman medicine.

2. THE HEROPHILEANS AND THE RISE OF HIPPOCRATIC LEXICOGRAPHY

The establishment of the Museum and libraries at Alexandria gave medical philosophers and scholars the opportunity to scrutinise far more than the still-breathing bodies of criminals. In the fourth and third centuries, the development of antiquarian scholarship – literary as much as scientific – brought with it a tendency to seek authority in the ideas of the past. In medicine, this change of fashion had important consequences, and in the third century the authority of the Hippocratic writings became a matter of political as much as scientific concern in medical circles, as doctors made competing claims to the 'Hippocratic tradition'. In so doing, they began to re-invent Hippocrates in their own image. The growing fame and importance of Hippocrates – whoever he might have been – meant that the works which bore his name increasingly required explanation and comment.

From the time of Herophilus onwards, doctors – and especially doctors in Alexandria – began to argue over the meaning of difficult terms and the interpretation of difficult passages in Hippocratic texts. Sometimes the difficulties had more to do with the problem of making medical writing acceptable as literature, than with medicine itself. Take, for instance, the debate over the meaning of words used by Homer in one sense, but by the Hippocratics in other, different senses. Herophilus, according to later witnesses, was one of the first to concern himself with what was to grow into the full-scale enterprise of Hippocratic lexicography. His primary concerns seem at least to have been medical rather than literary, and he had a special interest in the resolution of conflicts between his own practical experience, and what he had read.[20] Some, at least, of his work on Hippocrates was polemical, but Herophilus' successors – figures like Callimachus the Doctor, Bacchius of Tanagra, Zeno the Herophilean, and Apollonius 'Byblas' ('the Bookworm') – seem to have been less troubled by the need to criticise and, where necessary, correct their Hippocratic inheritance, reassessing what they had received in the medical tradition in the light of their own practical investigations. On the contrary, they seem to have become increasingly concerned to underline the literary status of early medical texts, and their importance to students of the Greek language. Doctors, it seems, were more and more interested in an audience outside the surgery.

The willingness to attribute literary status to Hippocratics texts reflects a growing authority of texts in general, probably conferred by the Library, and in particular a new-found interest in philological study. Just as earlier generations of doctors had sought to enhance their status with powerful public figures through their association with the intellectual life of the polis, Alexandrian doctors, it seems, began to associate with the scholar/librarians in the Ptolemaic centre of learning. Galen reports that Bacchius, apparently the author of the first Hippocratic lexicon – the first author-specific lexicon in the history of Western scholarship[21] – was provided with lemmata for his dictionary by Aristophanes, the grammarian from Byzantium, who succeeded Eratosthenes of Cyrene as head of the Library in the late third century BC.[22] From what we can tell of the contents of Bacchius' work – it is lost – it sought to illustrate the meanings of words, and not always unusual words, by reference to passages from the early Greek poets. Homer is the favourite source of literary parallels and illustrations of all kinds of medical concepts and terms.[23] Indeed, the best known of all Hippocratic lexicographers, the first century AD grammarian Erotian and our main source for Bacchius' work, characterises the purpose of Hippocratic lexicography in terms which might seem to us odd – as existing to aid in the study of literature in general, and in the appreciation of the Greek language.

Another case may cast light on the nature of medical interest in textual criticism. The odd problem of the so-called *charakteres*, or symbols which somehow appeared in the Alexandrian Library's manuscript of the third book of the Hippocratic *Epidemics*, shows us how far doctors could venture away from their more traditional interests. The *charakteres* were symbols with odd letters and letter-clusters apparently devised as mnemonic guides to words and phrases in the case histories in the original Hippocratic work.[24] The *Epidemics* remained an appealing work to doctors from many theoretical persuasions throughout antiquity, no doubt in part because of their apparent freedom from theoretical baggage. The third book of the *Epidemics* contains a series of notes relating to different cases, which tend to follow a similar pattern. Here is a typical example taken from the beginning of *Epidemics III*:

> At Thasos, a man from Paros who was laid up near the temple of Artemis took a high fever, continuous initially, like *causus* with thirst. At first he was comatose, then wakeful again; the bowels were disordered at first and the urine thin.
>
> Sixth day: passed oily urine; delirious.
>
> Seventh day: all symptoms more pronounced; did not sleep at all, urine unchanged, mind disordered. The stools were bilious and greasy.
>
> Eighth day: slight epistaxis; vomited a small quantity of rust-coloured matter. Small amount of sleep.
>
> Ninth day: no change.
>
> Tenth day: all symptoms showed a decrease in severity.

Eleventh day: sweated all over and became chilled, but quickly got warm again.

Fourteenth day: high fever, stools bilious, thin and copious; urine contained suspended matter. Delirium.

Seventeenth day: distressed, for the patient was sleepless and the fever increased.

Twentieth day: sweating all over, no fever, stools bilious, no appetite, comatose.

Twenty-fourth day: a relapse.

Thirty-fourth day: no fever; bowels not constipated. Temperature rose again.

Fortieth day: no fever, bowels constipated for a short while, no appetite, slight fever returned and was, throughout, irregular; at times he was without fever at others not. Any remission and improvement was followed quickly by a relapse. He took but little food and that poor stuff. He slept badly and showed delirium about the time of the relapses. At these times he passed thicker urine, but it was disturbed and bad. The bowels were sometimes constipated, sometimes relaxed. Slight fever continued throughout, and the stools were thin and copious.

Died after 120 days.

Such case histories preserved a great deal of experience. Yet, it can hardly have been easy to learn from this kind of material. The mysterious characters offered a convenient way of reducing a large amount of material into a short space. On the whole, they involved quite straightforward abbreviations – simply the first·letters of significant words – K for crisis (κρίσις), I for sweat (ἵδρως), θ for death (θάνατος) and so on. By means of a simple concatenation of these letters and appropriate numbers, the gist of a case history could be communicated in short order.

One of Herophilus' followers, a certain Zeno, believed that the characters were the work of Hippocrates himself. Others disagreed and a fierce dispute arose. Galen, who tells the story in his own commentary on *Epidemics III*,[25] says that Zeno's claim about the authenticity of the signs was the subject of fierce controversy for nearly a hundred years. Involvement in this strange argument (which was taken up again and reported in the second century BC by an Empiricist doctor called Zeuxis) confers immortality on a number of otherwise unknown figures, including Apollonius Byblas, another Apollonius of Antioch, and rather later, the empiricist physician Heraclides of Tarentum. Apollonius the Bookworm had insisted that the signs were not the work of Hippocrates at all, but inserted as mnemonic guides by an otherwise unknown physician called Mnemon of Side. In the context, Mnemon's name seems too good to be true. Galen, however, reports Zeuxis' view that Mnemon borrowed a copy of the Hippocratic *Epidemics* from the Great Library at Alexandria, to read it. Before returning it, however, he did what generations of undergraduates have done ever since. He added the mnemonic characters in the margins, but in ink similar to that used on the original manuscript. Those who dissented from this explanation argued that Mnemon arrived in Alexandria with a manuscript already containing the signs, which was seized by officials, and a new copy, completely rewritten was placed in the Library along with the rolls 'from the ships'. Galen goes on to say that Mnemon claimed that he was the only one who held the key to the interpretation of the signs, and that he levied a charge for their decipherment.

The disputes over the meaning of Hippocratic terms, and the debate over the origin of the characters in *Epidemics III*, give us a sense of the extent to which Hellenistic doctors were also readers and critics of texts. One might even be excused for regarding the first Hippocratic lexicographers as philologists as much as doctors. Quite possibly, they would have been flattered by the suggestion. The one work of Hellenistic medicine which survives intact, the *Commentary on the Hippocratic On Joints*, by Apollonius of Citium, contains an acknowledgment of the Ptolemy of his own day – probably Auletes (late second, early first century BC) – thanking him for commissioning such a work, which is as much a piece of literary exegesis as a purely medical commentary.) We are left to ask if this is another case of medicine seeking authority in a wider intellectual culture. The second century BC Greek historian Polybius thought so, and sarcastically dismissed what he called the 'logical' side of medicine which he associated especially with Alexandria, saying that it had led to an absurd situation in which patients who were not even ill entrusted themselves to doctors simply because they were beguiled by seductive rhetoric and intellectual poise.[26] Seductive or not, the extent, circumstances and intensity of these disputes about what Hippocrates really thought, and who Hippocrates really was, point to the developing role of authoritative texts in medical research. Implication of the Library in this seems highly likely.

3. THE RISE OF EMPIRICISM IN ALEXANDRIA

Much of our knowledge of Greek medicine in Alexandria comes from Galen, whose view of what happened in Egypt was complex. On one hand, he was prepared to praise the anatomical research of figures such as Herophilus and Erasistratus, whilst being ultimately disgusted that Erasistratus allowed theory to trump the evidence of his own eyes, and so insist that the arteries carried air rather than blood around the body.[27] Indeed, Galen's relentless attacks on those who allowed theory – in the main, theory which disagreed with his own – to dominate the evidence of autopsy led him to a brittle state of sympathy with a medical sect which almost certainly had its origins in Alexandria during the fifty years following the foundation of the Library and Museum. The sect was called Empiricist, and it forms the basis of my second case study.[28]

The traditional founder of Medical Empiricism – and for some, the founder of sectarian apostasy itself – was a certain Philinus of Cos who broke away from Herophilus early in his career, and was active in Alexandria around 240 BC. Nothing of his own work survives; he is known merely by a few scattered references in later medical authors, gathered by Karl Deichgraeber in the standard work on Greek medical Empiricism, *Die griechische Empirikerschule*.[29] Significantly, several ancient fragments point to an early empiricist interest in lexicography, and it seems that Hippocratic linguistic exegesis was central in the development of this new sect.[30] Other early figures, of whom we similarly know little, include Theodas, Serapion of Alexandria, and Glaucias of Tarentum. Celsus relates that the Empiricists took a strongly sceptical approach to theoretical medicine, insisting that experience was the only teacher of what was right and wrong in the treatment of illness and injury. Abandoning the popular conception of theory (*theoria*) as what could be seen in the mind's eye, the Empiricists argued that true theory (even in the etymological sense of the term) was purely a matter of observation. Armed with a repertoire of observations, or pieces of experience about a given condition (called 'syndromes'), the Empiricist doctor could then readily draw an indication or inference as to the proper method of treatment. Experience teaches everything, they argued; some cited the story in Homer of Odysseus' dog, who was the only one to recognise the master when he finally came back to Ithaca, as a miracle of diagnosis in the proper Empiricist manner.

Faced with a host of rivals in Rome, Galen found the battle of the sects a useful one to exploit, and he wrote no fewer than three substantial works – *On Sects for Beginners*, *On Medical Experience*, and the *Outline of Empiricism* – as guides to the sectarian maze. At the beginning of the *Outline of Empiricism* (*Subfiguratio empirica*), Galen praises the

Empiricists (often disingenuously) for naming themselves after their method, rather than feeding the vanity of some *supposed* inventor of the sect. Consequently, it is not easy to attribute particular details of empiricist philosophy to particular figures. But the sect, as Galen portrays it, was based on the idea that the indication (*endeixis*) for proper treatment always comes from the careful observation of the phenomena. For them, there were three ways in which experience could be gathered, and these three ways were all given special names. Although we know hardly anything about the very earliest Alexandrian Empiricists, the fact that works with titles such as *On the Three*, *On Threes*, and so on, are attributed to them, suggest that this division of the types of medical experience was present in medical Empiricism from the start.[31]

The first leg of the Empiricist tripod was called *teresis* – a Greek word with connotations of careful vigilance. On this view, the doctor's training involved the purely atheoretical collection of a repertoire of observations of what afflicts mankind, and observations of what can be seen to aid in treatment. By 'atheoretical', I mean that the Empiricist doctor was not to waste time wondering why a given remedy might work, but simply to note that it did. On the strictest view of *teresis*, it seems that the Empiricist doctor held that experience of treatment in a given situation was only relevant if precisely the same situation arose again. For example, if I were walking in the mountains, and were bitten on the left leg by a snake, and discovered that the application of a nearby herb to the wound cured me, then this would only mean that the herb in question was useful in the treatment of the bite of that particular snake when it was inflicted on that particular part of my left leg.

However, Empiricism did allow for some degree of extrapolation of experience. The second leg of the tripod was a form of analogical inference, called *metabasis tou homoiou*, which licensed the doctor to say that a treatment which works for, say, one part of the body, may reasonably be expected to work for another part of the body, as long as the other part is similar in nature, and the circumstances of its affection similar too. In other words, a treatment for the left leg could be used with empirical justification on the right leg, too, and perhaps even (in extremis) on the arms.

We have seen that Alexandrian doctors were becoming increasingly pre-occupied with precursor-texts. It might reasonably be objected that medical Empiricism shows signs of precisely the kind of impulse that bookish scholarship discouraged. But the Empiricists took their concept of experience one crucial step further, into the realm of the written word. The last of the three types of experience was derived, in cases where autopsy was of no use or not available, from research, which they termed *historia*. From early on, it is clear that *historia* was pursued through the study of earlier writings.[32] Once doctors thus allowed a formal status to book learning, ancient medicine moved into an altogether new phase. It was from here only a short step to the point where information got from books enjoyed a generally privileged status.

Von Staden has argued that Herophilus, beginning the tradition of the criticism of Hippocratic texts in Alexandria, felt ambivalent and sometimes critical of his Hippocratic heritage.[33] This ambivalence seems not to have been shared by his disciples, and certainly not by the Empiricists. For them, the Hippocratic Corpus and its authority was less problematic – everything that is written in books might reasonably be thought of by an empiricist as *historia*, Galen tells us,[34] reminding us at the same time that this is the way in which most doctors use the term. There is, of course, true history and false history – true history, continues Galen, in the person of an archetypal empiricist, is the reporting of things which have actually been seen, or of things reported as if they have been seen.

The idea that experience could include other people's recorded experience may seem a little odd, even if it does call to mind the method of composition behind the first surviving Greek history, that of Herodotus. But in the context, the Empiricist's threefold classification of the sources of experience is understandable. While most modern scholars rightly regard Empiricism in medicine as a phenomenon which began in third century Alexandria, many later witnesses, some of them Empiricist themselves, saw the origins of their sect in much more ancient terms. (Some even claimed Empedocles as the ultimate father of their group). There is no doubt that the idea that experience is the best teacher is an ancient one. The question is, what kind of experience?

Early Greek philosophers were aware that even if sense perception may contain the truth about natural phenomena, without the mediation of the mind it is impossible to tell true from false. Aristotle took up an ancient slogan when he said that it was the role of the natural scientist to 'save the phenomena' – that is, to reconcile the phenomena with theory aimed at their explanation. It is a slogan which seems strikingly modern in many ways – modern, that is, until we look more closely at what Aristotle means us to understand by 'phenomena'. Literally 'things which appear', they include not only pieces of evidence which we experience directly ourselves, but also reports of what others have similarly experienced. Aristotle does, it must be said, often draw a distinction between what is commonly held to be true – either in literary sources, or in the popular imagination – (the *endoxa*), and what appears to us personally and directly, but the investigation into nature (peri physeos historia) pursued by members of the Lyceum, relied very heavily on literary sources, and hearsay. Aristotle's own investigations into biology and zoology, for instance, were often based on the results of information sent or given him by others – information which he includes under the general banner of 'phenomena'.[35]

Although Galen does not explicitly link this aspect of Aristotelian scientific method with the practice of the medical Empiricists, the connection is clear enough, especially when we recall the historical links between Alexandria and the Lyceum. But there is one very significant point which marks the Empiricists apart. Their insistence that autoptic experience should be pursued entirely without the direction, or even influence, of theory, meant that practical research was ruled out of court. One cannot, they insisted, embark upon a course of practical investigation into a problem without first theorising in some way about it. Experience should be collected accidentally, in the course of one's life, and this is the only way that theory can safely be kept at bay.

Far from encouraging practical investigation and discouraging abstract bookishness, one result of this totalitarian commitment to 'practical' experience was to drive doctors further into their books in their zeal for *historia*. The late third and second centuries BC saw the authority of the Hippocratic writings (not to say the importance of medical literature in general) continue to grow. The high status enjoyed by the philological study of texts in Alexandria no doubt encouraged this; our earliest evidence for critical lexicographical work on Greek texts is focused on medical texts. Gradually, textual critics joined philosophers in the colonisation of medicine. Von Staden notes the way in which textual scholarship became effectively institutionalised in the late third century as a part of medical research. If Athenaeus, writing in Egypt in the second century AD, is to be believed, textual criticism and history had become the sport of kings. Small wonder, then, that those – like doctors – whose livelihoods depended so closely on satisfying the fashions of the moneyed classes, should be so keen to emulate them.[36]

CONCLUSION

We have considered some of the activities of bookish doctors who flourished in the Alexandrian milieu in the fourth and third centuries BC, and seen some of the ways in which Graeco-Roman medical writers sought (and found) their own literary tradition and identity, under the banner of that most elusive yet potent figure, Hippocrates of Cos. In the tenth century AD, Constantine Porphyrogenitus was still able to inveigh against 'doctors who waste their time in libraries'.[37]

The most distinguished example of a literate doctor is perhaps Galen, who tells us that he often resorted to libraries, or to the shops of booksellers specialising in medical books, to resolve problems set by his predecessors. He was distraught when he lost some of his own works in the fire at the library on the Palatine; he regarded himself as something of a connoisseur of texts and their authors; and he affected that self-conscious neo-Attic style characteristic of many intellectuals of the Second Sophistic.[38] Galen's dependence on the literary traditions of medicine is perhaps best seen in his commentaries. He regarded the commentary as a fine pedagogical instrument, and has a great deal to say about most of his predecessors.

Yet Galen must also take credit for rediscovering the importance of practical investigation. Perverse, perhaps, but there are grounds for arguing that as far as practical, autoptic research in medicine was concerned, the Library at Alexandria, the authority with which it endowed early medical texts, and the general intellectual climate of the place proved a dampener of enthusiasm. There is no value judgement meant in this observation. Even though our only direct evidence of patronage of doctors in Alexandria relates to the provision of human victims for vivisection by Herophilus and Erasistratus, the overriding impression one gains is that Royal Patronage ultimately supported textual, rather than practical research. A positivist critic might argue that the presence of the Library could explain the intellectual context within which an active and sustained campaign came to be waged against medical theory – a campaign which flavoured medical writing and practice until the time of Galen. By the time Asclepiades of Bithynia was active in the late second century BC, many doctors were quite explicitly playing down the importance of anatomical research, or the elaboration and development of physiological theory. After Asclepiades, the Empiricists were joined by another medical sect, the Methodist, which was particularly influential in the Rome of Galen's day. The Methodists sought to sidestep even the complicated phenomenological and heuristic arguments into which the Empiricists rapidly fell, by arguing that all disease is of three basic types characterised by three evident states which present in the patient – a state of flux, of stricture, or a mixture of the two. Medicine, they insisted, was not the complex art which former authorities had insisted; on the contrary, anyone could be taught, and taught quickly, to recognise these morbid states, and the treatment then followed from a straightforward indication based on the idea that opposite states are remedied by opposites.[39] That, however, is another story. When medical Methodism was fully established in the first century AD, the power of both philosophical and textual learning to adorn a doctor's reputation had waned. And the great Library at Alexandria had truly become the stuff of legend.

NOTES

1. I use the term 'science', along with 'medicine', 'doctor', and 'scientist' in senses which may appear anachronistic to some readers. On one modern view, science cannot be said to have existed before the late nineteenth century. This seems to me unnecessarily narrow. The terms appear as convenient, if admittedly less than ideal markers for various discrete areas of inquiry, qualitative and quantitative, which formed part of the broad ancient programme of 'investigation into Nature'.

2. This is the view of P.M.Fraser, *Ptolemaic Alexandria* (Oxford: Oxford University Press, 1972), vol. 1, 371, and cf. 1.325–30, 364–5; for the case of the Hippocratic texts, and their supposed early presence in Alexandria, see M. Wellmann, 'Hippokrates des Herakleides Sohn', *Hermes*, 64 (1929), 16–21; L. Edelstein (art. 'Hippokrates (16), Nachträge', *Pauly-Wissowas Realencyclopädie der classischen Altertumswissenschaft*, Suppl. 6. (1935), cols 1310–12; W.D. Smith, *The Hippocratic Tradition* (Ithaca: Cornell University Press, 1979), esp. 199ff; V. Nutton, 'Museums and Medical Schools in Antiquity', *History of Education*, 4 (1), (1975), 3–15.

3. R. Blum, *Kallimachos: The Alexandrian Library and the Origins of Bibliography* (Madison: University of Wisconsin Press, 1991), 95ff.

4. See, for instance M. Clagett, *Greek Science in Antiquity* (New York: Books for Library Press, rev. ed. 1963), 47–48. I am not the first, of course, to advocate caution about this. See L. Edelstein, 'The Interpretation of Ancient Science', in O. and L. Temkin (eds), *Ancient Medicine* (Baltimore: Johns Hopkins University Press, 1987), 431.

5. Later sources often dwell (often, it must be said, for their own polemical reasons) on the jealous (and even vain) zeal with which the Library was stocked in its early years; see Josephus, Ant. Jud. 12.12, 12.36, Simplicius, *Commentary on Aristotle's Categories*, 8.23ff (who speaks not specifically of the Ptolemies, but of 'kings' in general), Athenaeus, *Deipnosophistae* II.1 (74B). See also Seneca, *De tranquillitate animi* (= Dialogi 9.9.4), Aulus Gellius *Noctes Atticae* VI.17. Strabo, *Geographica* 17.1.8 Galen offers a less jaundiced account of their motives, at *Comm. III. in Epid. Hipp. III*, XVIIA.607K.

6. See F. Susemihl, *Geschichte der griechischen Litteratur in der Alexandrinerzeit* (Leipzig 1892, 2 vols), for the standard general account of the protagonists, and the sources for our knowledge of them.

7. Cos and Cnidos, according to Galen, were centres of two influential schools of medical thought in the fifth century. Galen's view of Hippocratic medicine as Coan and Cnidian has come in for criticism in recent years (see A. Thivel, *Cos et Cnide*), just as has the notion that there was a particularly Alexandrian, homogeneous school of medicine.

8. Strabo *Geographica* XIII.1.54: ὁ γοῦν Ἀριστοτέλης τὴν (sc. βιβλιοθηκην) ἑαυτοῦ Θεοφράστῳ παρέδωκεν, ᾧπερ καὶ τὴν σχολὴν ἀπέλιπε, πρῶτος ὧν ἴσμεν συναγαγὼν βιβλία καὶ διδάξας τοὺς ἐν Αἰγύπτῳ βασιλέας βιβλιοθήκης σύνταξιν. (Aristotle, then, handed his own library over to Theophrastus, the man to whom he also left his School, and he in turn was the first we know of who collected books, and trained the Kings of Egypt in the organization of a library).

9. A point made by H. von Staden, *Herophilus: The Art of Medicine in Early Alexandria* (Cambridge: Cambridge University Press, 1989), 27. In other fields – mathematics for instance – the evidence for patronage is rather better. Eratosthenes addressed works on canonical geometrical problems to Ptolemy III (Euergetes), and Euclid is famously supposed to have told

Ptolemy I (Soter), in response to his request for some effective coaching, that 'there is no Royal Road to Geometry' (Proclus, *Commentary on the First book of Euclid's Elements*, 68).

10. Some evidence links Erasistratus with Antioch, but there is modern agreement that he practised in Alexandria. See G.E.R. Lloyd, 'A Note on Erasistratus of Ceos', *Journal of Hellenic Studies*, 95 (1975), 172 – 5; H. von Staden, *Herophilus*, op. cit. 46–8.

11. Celsus, *De medicina* I. pr. 23–25: Praeter haec, cum in interioribus partibus et dolores et morborum uaria genera nascantur, neminem putant his adhibere posse remedia, qui ipsa<s> ignoret. Ergo necessarium esse incidere corpora mortuorum, eorumque uiscera atque intestina scrutari; longeque optime fecisse Herophilum et Erasistratum, qui nocentes homines a regibus ex carcere acceptos uiuos inciderint, considerarintque etiamnum spiritu remanente ea, quae natura ante clausisset, eorumque positum, colorem, figuram, magnitudinem, ordinem, duritiem, mollitiem, l<e>uorem, contactum, processus deinde singulorum et recessus, et siue quid inseritur alteri, siue quid partem alterius in se recipit. (*'Besides these things, since pains, and various types of diseases arise in the interior parts of the body, they thought that no one who was ignorant of these could possibly apply the appropriate remedies. And so they thought it necessary to cut open the bodies of the dead and study the viscera and intestina. It is said that Herophilus and Erasistratus did this in the best way by far. They cut open criminals received out of the Kings' prisons, and they studied, whilst the breath of life remained in them, the things which nature had hitherto concealed – the position of the parts of the body, their colour, shape, size, order, hardness, softness, lightness, communication, processes and recesses of the individual parts, and whether any part is inserted into another, or is itself received into another'*)

12. On the vocabulary, see G.E.R. Lloyd, *Science, Folklore and Ideology* (Cambridge: Cambridge University Press, 1982), 149–167, with references to earlier work.

13. Epiphanius, *De mensuribus et ponderibus* 256–266: Ὁ γὰρ μετὰ; τὸν πρῶτον Πτολεμαῖον δεύτερος βασιλεύσας Ἀλεξανδρείας Πτολεμαῖος, ὁ ἐπικληθεὶς Φιλάδελφος, ὡς προείρηται, φιλόκαλός τις ἀνὴρ καὶ φιλόλογος γεγένηται, ὅστις βιβλιοθήκην κατασκευάσας ἐπὶ τῆς αὐτῆς Ἀλεξάνδρου πόλεως ἐν τῷ Βρουχίῳ καλουμένῳ (κλῖμα δὲ ἔστι τοῦτο τῆς αὐτῆς πόλεως ἔημον τανῦν ὑπάρχον) ἐνεχείρισε Δημητρίῳ τινὶ τῷ Φαληρηνῷ τὴν αὐτὴν βιβλιοθήκην, προστάξας συναγαγεῖν τὰς πανταχοῦ γῆς βίβλους, γράψας ἐπιστολὰς καὶ προσλιπαρήσας ἕκαστον τῶν ἐπὶ γῆς βασιλέων τε καὶ ἀρχόντων τοὺς ὑπό; τὴν αὐτοῦ βασιλείαν τε καὶ ἀρχὴν μὴ κατοκνῆσαι ἀποστεῖλαι ποιητῶν τε λέγω καὶ λογογράφων, ῥητόρων τε καὶ σοφιστῶν καὶ ιφατρῶν καὶ ιατροσοφιστῶν καὶ ιστοριογράφων καὶ λοιπῶν βίβλους (*After the first Ptolemy, the second to rule over Alexandria was called Ptolemy Philadelphus (as I said earlier), and he was an aesthete and a scholar. He established a library in the city of Alexandria in a deserted quarter of the city which still exists, called the Brucheion. He put the library in the hands of a certain Demetrius of Phaleron, enjoining him to collect books from all over the world. He wrote letters, and pressured every king and ruler, and he did not hesitate to send away for the books of poets, logographers, orators, sophists, doctors, iatrosophists, historiographers and the rest.*) The preface to the twelfth century work on Aristophanic comedy, the *De Comoedia* of John Tzetzes adds little of relevance for our purposes here. See also Clement of Alexandria, *Stromateis*, 1.22.148, Eusebius, *Historia Eccl.* 5.8.11; Irenaeus *Adv. Haer.* 3.31, all dependent on similar sources.

14. See H. van Thiel, 'Der Homertext in Alexandria', *ZPE*, 115 (1997) 13–36; A.L. Brown, 'The Dramatic Synopses attributed to Aristophanes of Byzantium', *Classical Quarterly* (1987), 427ff.

15. Galen, *Commentary on Hippocrates, Epidemics* III, XVIIA.606K.

16. ap. Athenaeus, *Deipnosophistae* I. 41 Kaibel.

17. Aristophanes, *Plutus* 653–744.

18. Gorgias of Leontini, *Encomium on Helen* (DK82B11;13).

19. See G.E.R. Lloyd, *Adversaries and Authorities* (Cambridge: Cambridge University Press, 1996), ch. 4.

20. For some detailed examples of the patterns this work took, see von Staden (1989), *op. cit.* Ch. IX, XIV, and H. von Staden, 'Lexicography in the third century B.C.: Bacchius of Tanagra, Erotian,and Hippocrates', in J.A.López Férez (ed.), *Tratados hipocráticos (Estudios acerca de su contenido, forma e influenca) Actas del VIIe colloque international hippocratique (Madrid, 24– 29 de septiembre de 1990)* (Madrid, 1992), 549–569.

21. von Staden, *Herophilus, op. cit.* 549.

22. Galen, *Explanatio vocum Hippocratis*, XIX. 64–5 ταῦτα δὲ καὶ ἄλλοι πολλοὶ τῶν ἐξηγησαμένων ἁμαρτάνουσιν. εἰ τοίνυν ταῦτά τις περιέλοι πάντα, τὰς γλώττας ἂν ἐξηγήστατο μόνας, ὥσπερ ὁ Ἡρόφιλος ἐποίησε καὶ Βακχεῖος, Ἀριστάρχου τοῦ γραμματικοῦ τὸ πλῆθος αὐτῷ τῶν παρα δειγμάων ἀθροίαντος, ὥς φασιῶν.

23. A tradition carried on by Galen; cf. *De optima secta*, I.142–148K; *Adhortatio ad artes addiscendas, 8; De temperamentis*, I.513K etc.

24. Galen offers a convenient key to their decipherment at *Commentary on Hippocrates Epidemics III*, XVIIA.610ffK. The ancient evidence is collected by Deichgraeber, *Die griechische Empirikerschule*, 234–242. On the whole, the system of coding is straightforward enough; the story is well told by W.D. Smith, *The Hippocratic Tradition* (Ithaca: Cornell University Press, 1979), 199ff, and in more detail by von Staden (1989), *op. cit.* ch. XVff.

25. *Commentary on Hippocrates Epidemics III*, XVIIA. 605K.

26. Polybius *History*, XII. 25d.3–4.

27. This attack on Erasistratus is the subject of Galen's *An in arteriis natura sanguis contineatur*, for which see the modern edition of D.J. Furley and J.S.Wilkie, *Galen on Respiration and the Arteries* (Princeton: Princeton University Press, 1984).

28. Hellenistic medicine is characterized by the organization of doctors into these doctrinal groups, called 'sects'. Galen's accounts of the history and significance of the sectarian tradition are translated and discussed by M. Frede, *Galen: Three Treatises on the Nature of Science* (Indianapolis: Hackett Publishing Co., 1985). The best modern introduction to the subject is that of H. von Staden, 'Hairesis and Heresy: the case of the haireseis iatrikai', in B.F. Meyer and E.P. Sanders (eds), *Jewish and Christian Self-Definition, III: Self Definition in the Graeco-Roman World* (London: 1982), 76–100, 199–206. Many of Frede's most important essays on the philosophical affiliations of the sects are collected in his *Essays in Ancient Philosophy* (Oxford: Oxford University Press, 1987).

29. K. Deichgraeber, *Die griechische Empirikerschule* (Berlin: 2nd. ed., 1965).

30. Philinus ap. *GE* 138, 139.

31. Serapion of Alexandria (fl. ?225 BC) is credited with a work διὰ τρίων (Galen, *Subfiguratio Empirica*. 63.13–14 Deichgraeber). On the epistemological background of medical Empiricism, see J. Barnes, 'Medicine, Experience and Logic', in J. Barnes, J. Brunschwig and M. Schofield (eds),

Science and Speculation (Cambridge: Cambridge University Press, 1982), 24–68; Michael Frede, 'The empiricist attitude towards reason and theory ', in R.J.Hankinson (ed.), *Method, Medicine and Metaphysics. Studies in the Philosophy of Ancient Science* (Edmonton: Academic Printing and Publishing, 1988), 79–97.

32. This characterization of *historia* as research pursued through reading quickly becomes current beyond the confines of medical Empiricism; see Galen, *De dignoscendis pulsibus* VIII.788K; *De theriaca* XIV.233K; *Comm. in Hippocratis De natura hominis* XV.25K; Eusebius, *Praeparatio Evangelica* 2.1.55.

33. von Staden (1989), *op. cit.* 453.

34. *Subfiguratio Empirica*, 67–8.

35. For the background to this aspect of Aristotelian scientific method, see G.E.L. Owen, 'Tithenai ta phainomena', in S Mansion (ed.), *Aristote et les problèmes de méthode* (Paris: 1961), 83–103, reprinted in J. Barnes, M. Schofield and R. Sorabji, *Articles on Aristotle 1* (London: Duckworth, 1975), 113–26.

36. Athenaeus, *Deipnosophistae*, II.§19, 58, 84, XVI §15 ctc. Kaibel.

37. *De sententiis*, 152.

38. See, for example, Galen, *De locis affectis* VIII.148K, *De compositione medicamentorum per genera* XIII.362K, (cf. *De antidotis* XIV.31K). At *De libriis propriis* XIX.8K, Galen relates the surprise he felt when he found some forged treatises bearing his own name in a Roman bookshop.

39. For a brief account of the origins of the anti-theoretical character of Methodism in the theory of Asclepiades, see J.T. Vallance, *The Lost Theory of Asclepiades of Bithynia* (Oxford: Clarendon Press, 1990), 131ff.

Chapter 6

The Theatre of Paphos and the Theatre of Alexandria: Some First Thoughts

J.R. Green

INTRODUCTION*

For Greeks in foreign territories or newly-acquired lands, theatre was a signifier of Greekness, a sophisticated activity not shared by other peoples.[1] Modern interpreters read the importance of theatres in the ancient world as resting less in their architecture, than in their social function as sites at which people assembled as a community, bonding, watching and interacting with performances which they enjoyed as a group. In the open air, they were conscious of each others' reactions and shared interests.[2] The architectural importance of theatres is a reflection of their importance to the community, made apparent in their monumentality, in the effort put into their design, and in the care put into their detail.

A team from the University of Sydney has enjoyed three seasons of excavation at the site of the ancient theatre in Nea Paphos, Cyprus.[3] While work there is very far from complete, enough has emerged to justify some speculation about the structure's form and then about its relationships in the wider world of theatre architecture.

Theatres have become a rather unpopular thing to excavate – in part because they are extremely demanding of labour, and difficult to finance at a time when workers in Mediterranean countries such as Italy, Greece and Cyprus receive a reasonable wage (and, for that matter, are often more highly paid than Australian workmen), and in part because theatre excavation is sometimes viewed as old-fashioned. Theatres were, indeed, the focus of a good deal of work in the later nineteenth and early twentieth centuries. However, the excavation techniques of those days did not measure up to what is now expected, and earlier efforts failed to find the answers to questions we ask today, particularly those to do with the chronology of architectural development, their settings within the sanctuaries that housed them, and their relationships to the communities which they were built to serve.

1. PAPHOS AND ALEXANDRIA

The city of Paphos is said to have been founded in the later part of the fourth century BC. This is the time at which it was given some sort of formal recognition, since there is growing evidence of pre-foundation pottery, including imported Athenian, dating from at least the middle of the fifth century, from a number of areas, including our own excavations.[4] Although detail remains unclear, there is reliable historical evidence that soon after the establishment of Alexander's successors, the Ptolemies incorporated Cyprus into their empire and made Paphos its capital. Paphos was situated at a key point for shipping making its way down from the Aegean, and had a good natural harbour which was further improved by a sea-wall. It was also able to draw on an area of fertile plain for its necessary agricultural base. The connections between Paphos and Alexandria are detectable archaeologically – for example, in the trade in Rhodian wine-amphorae which were so popular in both Paphos and Alexandria. In Paphos, they became so important as to become a regular feature in Paphian burials.[5] More important, since more direct, are the clay seal-impressions found in what is thought to have been part of the Governor's offices, made with what are clearly Ptolemaic devices.[6] Ptolemaic coins are, of course, plentiful.[7]

Burials for the élite were also carried out on the Alexandrian model. The so-called Tombs of the Kings on the coast to the north of the city include complex monumental tombs cut into the rock, the more elaborate of them containing peristyles with wells and the burial chambers round the sides. One of them even contained stone Ptolemaic eagles. Other finds include Egyptian faience. There are good parallels for these tombs in the Hadra and Chatby cemeteries of Alexandria itself and now, from more recent excavations, at Marina el-Alamein, a tourist development near a site well known to a generation of Australians, along the coast about 96 km to the west of Alexandria.[8]

2. THE THEATRE OF PAPHOS

The theatre of Paphos lies in the north-east part of the town, diagonally opposite the harbour which lies about 650 m away, and, as we can now determine, arranged so as to give the audience a view across the town towards the harbour. It is partly built into a small hill nowadays known locally as Fábrika, but its importance to the modern architectural historian lies in that its builders chose not to insert the whole of the auditorium into the hill, as was normal practice with Greek theatres, and as would in fact have been quite easy given the nature of the rock, a soft and easily-worked calcareous sandstone. Instead, they excavated into it only for the central part of the seating, and then built up the sides of the auditorium with an earthen embankment on which they placed stone seating.

The auditorium now seems fairly certainly to have been semicircular in plan. (It in fact covers 181.5 degrees.) We have a good stretch of the western parodos or entranceway into the *orchestra* (or central performance area), and on the northern side of this passage the remains of the support wall for the edge of the seating. At what is probably near the western end, there is a strong bastion of squared blocks erected to resist the outward thrust of the embankment; we do not yet have the actual corner, as it runs under a modern road. Tests on the same line on the eastern side have revealed the line of a similar support-wall for the embankment, although much of it has been robbed out.

The auditorium or *koilon* was badly damaged by later quarrying for building stone, but enough is preserved for us to be fairly confident of our reconstruction. It is divided by seven radial stairways into six wedges, each of approximately 30°, with a stairway coinciding with the axial line of the theatre. This arrangement was not unreasonably regarded by Vitruvius as more typical of the Roman rather than the Greek style of theatre (V.vi, 2; V.vii, 2), but one could not claim that the pattern is a regular one. The theatre at Epidauros, for example, has an arrangement like ours. It may, however, be of some ultimate significance in the question we are exploring.

At Paphos, the less defined of the two exposed stairways lies on the eastern edge of the central bedrock section of the cavea. Little of this stairway remains in the area so far excavated. It forms equal angles with the end retaining walls and a right angle with the remains of the stage building, that is it lies on the theatre axis. To the west, the second exposed stairway is well defined from the orchestra level to the twenty-fourth tier of seating. It is possible, though yet to be fully demonstrated, that in the areas supported by an earthen embankment, the stairways were supported from underneath by radial walls which at the same time acted as retaining walls for the earth.

From what has been revealed by excavation so far, the theatre seating rises a minimum of thirty-three tiers. This is equal to a rise in height from the *orchestra* floor to the rear of the theatre of approximately 11.7 m. The rise in seating is uninterrupted: there is no evidence of a central concentric walkway or *praecinctio* to break the auditorium into an upper and lower range. The absence of such a walkway is a little unusual in a theatre of this size as it would have aided in the distribution of such a large number of spectators at times of entry and exit. It may indicate there was at least one major entry and exit point to the auditorium located at the rear, on the brow of Fábrika Hill, although there has been nothing revealed so far to support this suggestion.

The seating rises at an angle of 27° to the horizontal. Individual seat heights range from 35 to 36 cm, and the horizontal run from nosing to nosing is approximately 70 cm. At the base of the nosing, a near straight face meets the seat riser at an angle of approximately 45° and meets the curve of the bullnose with a tangent. In at least the lower parts of the auditorium, the zone for the feet is set slightly lower than that sat on by the people in the row in front. With a radius of 11.2 metres to the front row of seating, and on the basis of a rise of 33 seats – a maximum radius of 33.6 metres – the area of the *cavea* including radial stairways and a rear walkway is roughly 2000 m². This size of auditorium would have accommodated approximately 7,500 seated spectators.

In some places, there remain patches of a fine pebble cement. They are found on the rear halves of the seats, or, failing that, at the very backs of the seats at the junction with the vertical face of the seat behind. The front parts of the seats were the first and most easily removed as building blocks by cutting a vertical channel about halfway back on the seat and then splitting it off horizontally. One of the more remarkable discoveries of the first campaign in 1995 was that the function of this pebble cement served as a bedding for plaster, such as was preserved in a number of places. Indeed, from these traces and many more casual finds, it seems safe to hypothesise that the whole of the seating and the steps of the theatre were covered in a hard fine plaster which gave a better, firmer and more attractive surface to the comparatively poor stone. It was a hard-wearing and waterproof material (unlike the underlying stone which wears readily and is slightly porous). Indeed this plaster was not confined to the seatings and stairs: it is also found on the faces of the major support-wall at the *parodoi*. So far as we know, no other surviving theatre has this treatment, even if there are other kinds of architectural parallels close at hand – for example, in the Tombs of the Kings or in Alexandrian architecture. It must have had a startling and bright effect. In the areas uncovered so far no graffiti or *dipinti* have been detected on the limited areas of plaster preserved.

We have not yet begun the excavation of the stage building itself, but have left it at the level of the Late Roman foundations, the level left by the Byzantine and Medieval occupants of the area. Nonetheless, we have found scattered architectural elements from the pre-Roman structure and they provide interesting links with the architecture of

Alexandria. As examples, we may briefly consider three fragments. The first is a rather battered sandstone fragment with plaster coating.[9] It was found in the packing under the earliest Roman cement floor of the orchestra of the theatre, and must therefore belong to the Hellenistic theatre, although what phase of it we cannot for the moment say. It is from the lower part of a Corinthian capital, preserving the stalks of the acanthus leaves. Its preserved height is 14 cm. No traces of paint remain, nor is there any finished edge above or below. Its importance lies in its Alexandrian technique. Given its state of preservation, however, it is difficult to say more about it.[10]

The second is a cornice fragment made of the local calcareous sandstone.[11] This has a preserved height of 24.5 cm and a length of 44.5 cm. It, too, is worn, without any stucco preserved, and was found in a later context to the south of the theatre. Its style, however, is distinctive. It preserves on its lower face one of a series of simple, flat modillions or brackets with a straight channel along its centre.

The third is another cornice fragment, again made of the local sandstone.[12] Although it is rather worn and battered, it preserves some traces of the plaster which originally coated its surface. The block has a preserved height of 25 cm and a preserved length along the front of 36 cm. It has quite narrow modillions with straight channel. It is worth noting that the front edge of the underside is undercut along a line in front of the modillions. It was found among debris in the western *parodos*.

Although these fragments have some parallels in early Augustan buildings in Rome – for example the Temple of Divus Julius, the Regia and the Temple of Saturn in the Forum Romanum – their best counterparts are in Alexandria, and it is important to note, as did Donald Strong many years ago, that this is where Roman architects found the basis from which they developed this element of the Augustan architectural style.[13] Since 1963, there have been other studies, notably by von Hesberg and Pensabene, which have followed the theme in more detail, characterising the Alexandrian style and publishing much additional evidence.[14]

Our cornice fragments have slightly wide modillions, though not so wide as some of the later examples, nor do they have the Y-shaped channel popular, especially in Cyprus, in the Late Hellenistic and Early Imperial periods.[15] The best parallel is probably a fragment from the Chantier Finney in Alexandria.[16] Daszewski associated it with a structure which also seems to have contained a mosaic with a centaur, which he dated to the second half of the third century BC.[17] Judith McKenzie would rather put it in the second century.[18] From our point of view, for the moment at least, the difference is not of great significance: it is fully Hellenistic.

Given all these demonstrable links with Alexandria and Alexandrian architecture, it is reasonable to hypothesise that the overall design of the theatre at Paphos echoed that of the one at Alexandria. The latter, of course, is not preserved but, given the nature of the site, it is likely that it too was at least partially built up with an artificial embankment, just as the theatre at Paphos. A further guess, but a quite possible one given the closeness of the connections between the two cities and the evidence for Paphian borrowing of Alexandrian architectural elements (indeed one could suppose that it was the design of an Alexandrian architect), may be that the theatre at Alexandria was also semicircular.[19]

3. ALEXANDRIA AND ROME

From this work in Paphos, we may begin to hypothesise that Alexandria had a hitherto largely unsuspected influence upon the development of the Roman style of theatre. Characteristic of classic Roman theatres is the way in which they are built up artificially on flat ground, in their developed form typically with concrete vaulting. The basic plan is semicircular; the stage-building is connected to the seating and comes to the same height as the top of the seating. The theatre at Orange, may be taken as a typical example. From the point of view of the audience, theatres like this created a self-contained world focussed on the stage, and were very different from those of the Greeks which often had extensive views, which were conceived as elements in an outdoor sanctuary.[20]

The leap from the horseshoe-shaped, open Greek theatre to that of the Romans is a considerable one, and it is generally supposed that the theatres of Sicily and Campania acted as intermediaries.[21] Part of the problem is that the theatres of Rome appeared suddenly, after a long history of performance during which permanent theatres were forbidden. The earliest, the Theatre of Pompey, is dated to 55 BC, and the next, the so-called Theatre of Marcellus, to 12–10 BC. It is not unreasonable to suppose some influence from Campania given the close relations between Latium and Campania during the later part of the Republican period. It is clear that Campania acted as a channel for many sorts of contact with the Aegean world during the second and the early first century BC. We see objects both imported and locally-made but dependent on Greek that demonstrate a familiarity with Greek culture. Not least among these is a range of terracotta figurines and moulded vases in the form of actors of Greek comedy. These presuppose not merely a borrowing of motifs, but also an understanding of what they stood for – that is, an understanding of Greek culture.[22] Another good and well-known example is the pair of mosaic *emblemata* from the so-called "Villa of Cicero" at Pompeii signed by one Dioskourides, a Samian. They seem to date to the later part of the second century BC, and were preserved as treasured items until the destruction of the site in AD 79. They illustrate the main scenes from two plays of Menander, his *Women at Breakfast* and his *Girl Possessed* and they copy prototypes created in Athens at the beginning of the third century BC.[23] That the wealthier inhabitants of Pompeii and Herculaneum copied housing styles from the Aegean is also evidence of the strong links between the two areas, as is the appearance of Campanian pottery at sites such as Corinth, Delos and Alexandria.

Perhaps because of pre-existing ties to Greece, through colonial contacts and the continuing use of the Greek language, the Campanians do not seem to have had so much of the ambivalence about the values of Greek culture (and innate resistance to it) that was felt in Rome itself, even if there is evidence that the educated classes in Rome were strongly attracted by elements of Greek literary and performance culture, and by what is perhaps the strongest indicator of cultural influences, food.[24] The peoples of Campania also had on-going links with the other western Greeks in southern Italy and Sicily.

In a recent article, L. Polacco has given a brief but well-annotated overview of Italian theatres of the Campano-Samnite region as background to the form of the Roman theatre. While he emphasises the complexity of the problem, he pursues what he regards as the important rôle as a model of the theatre at Syracuse.[25] Like most other scholars, he rightly attaches little importance to the theatres of Asia Minor as models in the development of Italian theatres (except, perhaps, that at Pergamon), but suggests that there are observable similarities to theatres of Macedonia and Epirus, an area that was to some degree the Alexandrian homeland.

R.J.A. Wilson has also commented recently on the theatres of Sicily, and has provided a useful survey of Hellenistic examples.[26] He presses the argument that Sicily saw the origin – or at least had a major rôle in developing – the semi-circular orchestra that was later taken up by the Romans. One of the difficulties is chronology. Wilson accepts the dates given by Anti and Polacco of the third quarter of the third century BC for the theatre at Syracuse.[27] The earliest known examples of the type known in the West seem to be those of the provincial but important theatre at Monte Iato in Sicily and, of course, that at Metaponto in coastal Basilicata, both of them dated shortly before 300 BC.[28] Wilson argues for a later date for the theatre at Monte Iato, in effect putting it after the theatre of Paphos. That at Metaponto is also important because it is built up in earthen embankment on flat ground.[29] We shall come back to the question of this region.

In my view, the best recent overview of these problems is that by Moretti.[30] He gives a careful summary of the evidence and the principal problems, and emphasises the distinct character of many Sicilian theatres with their auditoria of a semicircle or a little more, the incorporation into the design of the *parodoi* to give access to the orchestra, and then the closeness of the stage to the seating, with the reduction of the emphasis on the orchestra more typical of the theatres of Greece proper. He is unwilling to assign particular priorities within the Sicilian sequence.

Into this picture, Paphos has to be inserted, as among the earliest examples of the style of theatre with semicircular cavea and artificially-built seating. Its obvious links are with Alexandria. Yet, there are hints that theatres in South Italy and Sicily were headed in the same direction. I have argued elsewhere that migrants from that region were a substantial element in the new Alexandria at the time of its foundation.[31] We have literary evidence of the movement of such individuals as the poet Theocritus.[32] We also have inscriptional evidence for their presence.[33] Links have been noted between Alexandrian and Syracusan coinage.[34] And then we have quantities of imported Tarentine and probably Metapontine pottery. Why else import it when other equally good sources were closer to hand except to satisfy a particular need or taste?

CONCLUSION

Alexandrian style emerged from an amalgam of elements, including Macedonian and West Greek in addition to the indigenous Egyptian. Given the wealth accumulated by the early Ptolemies, and their substantial expenditure on public works and related activities, that style developed very quickly. Theatres in Alexandria and Paphos were a part of that expression.

There is no detectable reason why the theatre architecture of Rome should have been influenced by that of Sicily rather than that of any other region. Rather, what is demonstrable is its long connections with Egypt. Alexandria was a major urban centre with which Rome came to compare itself. Moreover, apart from political connections, it was the clear source of Second-Style wall-painting and many other artistic genres such as Nilotic mosaics, not to mention the decorative arts. Alexandria had a lively interest in theatre which, during the course of the Hellenistic period, maintained a stronger tradition than most other centres of the ancient world, including Athens. The particular character of Alexandrian theatre still remains to be explored. It is clear from the material remains, and especially the terracotta figurines of actors of comedy and their masks, that it did have its own identity, even if it must also have drawn on the more general repertoire of Hellenistic theatre. It developed its own figurine types independently of those of other centres. It also created a category of objects which combined the costume of contemporary actors with elements from earlier periods, notably the phallos attached to the front of the body-stocking, thus exploiting that taste for the grotesque and sexual that characterises other aspects of Alexandrian art. Mime also seems to have played an important role. All this awaits fuller discussion, but we can at least be certain that Alexandrian theatre was lively and active and that its theatre must have been a place of some importance. In other words, there are good *a priori* reasons why Alexandria is a likely source of influence in the evolution of Roman theatre design.

As a final point, we may consider the theatre at Aphrodisias in southern Asia Minor.[35] The stage building was constructed probably in the 30s BC by Zoilus, a freedman of Augustus. It was done in some style and at some expense, and one might reasonably have expected that it would have reflected the contemporary theatre designs sponsored by the central government, in the new metropolis. What is remarkable in the reconstructions of the stage-building that are now emerging is the number of Egyptianising elements and motifs. Alexandria was as this date, too, a force to be reckoned with in theatre architecture.

NOTES

* I am grateful to Roy MacLeod for his invitation to contribute to this volume, and to Christie Waddington for much help in the preparation of this article. I owe my thanks, too, to Judith McKenzie for her assistance on a number of aspects of the architecture of Alexandria.

1. See my *Theatre in Ancient Greek Society* (London: Routledge, 1994) for further references. There is no good single study of ancient Greek theatres. For work on theatres in the period 1972–1986, see my bibliographical survey in *Lustrum* 31, 1989, and, for 1987–1995, *Lustrum* 37, 1995 [1998], 7–202. There are also invaluable regular reports and comments in the bibliographical review of ancient architecture in *Revue Archéologique* by Jean-Charles Moretti and others.

2. For example, in the Theatre of Dionysos at Athens, they seem to have sat in their tribal groups. For the ancient evidence collected, see E. Csapo and W.J. Slater, *The Context of Ancient Drama* (Ann Arbor: University of Michigan Press, 1995), 289–290. The best late example for sitting in groups based on shared interests is the evidence of the graffiti on the seats at Aphrodisias. See Ch. Roueché, *Aphrodisias in Late Antiquity. The Late Roman and Byzantine Inscriptions*, (*Journal of Roman Studies* Monograph 5, 1989), 223–226, and *Performers and Partisans at Aphrodisias in the Roman and Late Roman Periods*, (*Journal of Roman Studies* Monograph 6, 1993).

3. The 1995 season was of four weeks, the 1996 and 1997 seasons, of six weeks. The team included both undergraduate and postgraduate students, specialists, and a dedicated group of contributing volunteers. The architect is G. Stennett, and the Assistant Director, A. Rowe. The excavations have been funded by a grant from the Australian Research Council and by private contributions. For preliminary reports, see J.R. Green, 'Excavations

at the Theatre, Nea Paphos, Cyprus, 1995–1996', in C. Petrie and S. Bolton (eds), *In the Field. Archaeology at the University of Sydney*, Sydney University Archaeological Methods Series, 4, (1997), 35–46; idem., 'Excavations at the Theatre, Nea Paphos, 1995–6', *Mediterranean Archaeology*, 9–10, (1996–97), 239–242.

4. Cf J.W. Hayes, *Paphos III: The Hellenistic and Roman Pottery* (Nicosia 1991), 5.

5. See D. Michaelides, 'Οι ροδιακόι αμφορείς και ενα ταφικο έθιμο της Πάφου', in Πρατικα της Β Συναντησης για την Ελληνιστική Κεραμεική (Athens 1990), 187–193. See also Z. Sztetyllo, *Nea Paphos IV: Pottery Stamps (1975–1989)* (Warsaw 1991).

6. I. Michaelidou-Nicolaou, 'Inscribed Clay Sealings from the Archeion of Paphos', *Actes du VIIe Congrès int. d'épigraphie grecque et latine, Constanza, 9–15 septembre 1977* (Bucharest, 1979) 413–416; H.Kyrieleis, 'Η Καυσία στα Πτολεμαικά Σφραγίσματα της Νέας Πάφου', *Kypriake Archaiologia* 2, (1990), 95–103. The publication of the complete series is forthcoming.

7. See, for example, I. Nicolaou and O. Mørkholm, *Paphos I. A Ptolemaic Coin Hoard* (Nicosia 1976).

8. The Tombs of the Kings have not yet received definitive publication, but see, for example ,S. Hadjisavvas, 'Excavations at the "Tombs of the Kings" – Kato Paphos', in V. Karageorghis (ed.), *Archaeology in Cyprus: 1960–1985* (Nicosia 1985), 262–268, or the guide by M. Hadjisavva, *The Tombs of the Kings, A World Heritage Site* (n.d.). For Marina el-Alamein, see the reports by W. Daszewski, *Mitteilungen des Deutschen Archäologischen Instituts in Kairo* 46, (1990), 15–51, and 'The Origins of Hellenistic Hypogea in Alexandria', in M. Minas and J. Zeidler (eds), *Aspekte spätägyptischer Kultur: Festschrift für E. Winter* in *Aegyptiaca Treverensia*, 7 (1994), 57–68, which contains a good series of plans and references to counterparts in Alexandria. For the cemetery at Marina El-Alamein, see the reports by W.A. Daszewski in *Polish Archaeology in the Mediterranean* III (1992) 29–38, IV (1993) 23–31, V (1994) 21–33, VI (1995) 28–36, VII (1996) 41, VIII (1997) 73–81.

9. From trench 1K, deposit 145.

10. For a useful discussion of Corinthian capitals in the Ptolemaic context, see H. von Hesberg, 'Zur Entwicklung der griechischen Architektur im ptolemaïschen Reich', in H. Maehler and V.M. Strocka (eds), *Das Ptolemäische Ägypten: Akten d. internat. Symposions, 27.-29 September 1976 in Berlin* (Mainz, 1978), 137–145.

11. From trench 3B, deposit 052.

12. From trench 1R, deposit 210.

13. D.E. Strong, 'Some Observations on Early Roman Corinthian', *Journal of Roman Studies* 53, (1963), 73–84.

14. For von Hesberg, see above n. 10; P. Pensabene, 'Elementi di architettura alessandrina', (in) S. Stucchi and M. Bonanna Aravantinos (eds.), *Giornate di studio in onore di Achille Adriani, Roma 26–27 novembre 1984* (Studi Miscellanei 28, Rome 1991) 47–54. Pensabene's larger study, *Elementi architettonici di Alessandria e di altri siti egiziani (Repertorio d'arte dell'Egitto Greco-Romano*, 3, Rome 1993) has not been accessible to me.

15. See, for example, R.L. Scranton, 'The Sanctuary of Apollo Hylates' in *Transactions of the American Philosophical Society*, 57 (1967), 5, 72 fig. 66a. There is a block not dissimilar to inv. 100 from a monumental tomb in the cemetery at Salamis in Cyprus: Henner von Hesberg, *Konsolengeisa des Hellenismus und der frühen Kaiserzeit (RM Ergh.* 24, Mainz, 1980), pl. 7, 4. See

esp. 68–73, and for Cyprus 76–78. At 76 n. 342 he notes similar unpublished pieces from the Polish excavations on the western side of the town of Paphos. For a later example, see R. Stilwell, 'Kurion: The Theater', *Proceedings of the American Philosophical Society*, 105, 1, (1961), 74 no. 15, fig. 36; von Hesberg has linked it with the activities of the 60s BC.

16. Alexandria, Graeco-Roman Museum inv. 25659. J. McKenzie, *The Architecture of Petra* (Oxford: Oxford University Press, 1990), 74 no. 9, pl. 211d, f, with refs. See her 69–70 for a discussion of chronology. For a brief overview of Alexandrian architectural style, see also her 'Alexandria and the Origins of Baroque Architecture', in *Alexandria and Alexandrianism* (Malibu: The J. Paul Getty Museum 1996), 109–125.

17. W.A. Daszewski, *Corpus of Mosaics from Egypt*, I (*Aegyptiaca Treverensia*, 3, Mainz: von Zabern 1985) 111–2 no. 5, pll. 13 and 15a.

18. See n. 16.

19. H. Abou al Atta, 'Elements of Theatrical Architecture in the Alexandrian Hypogea', *Classical Papers*, 2 (Cairo University 1992), 101–115 pursues the question of the influence of theatre architecture in the hypogea of Alexandria, and especially the symmetrically-composed false doors and windows, columned façades and so on – in effect, elements of the Second Pompeian Style. One could not claim a demonstrable link with the actual architectural detail of the theatre of Alexandria.

20. See S. Melchinger, *Das Theater der Tragödie* (Munich, 1974), 124, for the notion that a view of the sea was particularly important for early theatres.

21. On the rôle of Campania in transmitting and modifying western Greek models, not least in the development of theatre-temple complexes, K. Mitens gives a fairly traditional view in 'Theatre Architecture in Central Italy: Reception and Resistance', in *Aspects of Hellenism in Italy: Towards a Cultural Unity?*. *Acta Hyperborea*, 5, (Copenhagen, 1993), 91–106. On the sanctuaries at Gabii and Tivoli with their theatrical areas set before the temple, see the excellent study by F. Coarelli, *I santuari del Lazio in età republicana* (Rome 1987) with its further references.

22. See under 2NV and 3NV in J.R. Green and Axel Seeberg, *Monuments Illustrating New Comedy. Bulletin of the Institute of Classical Studies*, Suppl. 50, London, 1995, with further references, and J.R. Green, 'Rolling Drunk. A Comic Slave in Canberra and Some Iconographic Conventions', *Numismatica ed Antichità Classiche. Quaderni Ticinesi* 24, 1995, 189–205.

23. For references and notes, see 3DM 1 and 3DM 2 in Green-Seeberg. n. 22.

24. On food, see E. Gowers, *The Loaded Table: Representations of Food in Roman Literature* (Oxford: Clarendon Press, 1993), esp. chapter 2; on more general issues, there are two important recent analyses by E.S. Gruen, *Studies in Greek Culture and Roman Policy* (Cincinnati Classical Studies n.s. 7, (Leiden - New York: Brill, 1990), and *Culture and National Identity in Republican Rome* (Ithaca , 1992).

25. L. Polacco, 'Rapporti tra i teatri greco-italici e i teatri sicelioti', in L. Franchi Dell'Orto (ed.), *Ercolano, 1738–1988. 250 anni di ricerca archeologica. Atti del Convegno internazionale Ravello – Ercolano – Napoli – Pompei, 30 ottobre – 5 novembre 1988* (Rome, 1993), 147–153. On much the same theme, see also his 'Il teatro greco di Siracusa modello al teatro romano', NumAntCl 6, 1977, 107–117, and 'La posizione del teatro di Siracusa nel quadro dell' architettura teatrale greca in Sicilia', in M.L. Gualandi, L. Massei and S.Settis (eds), *Aparchai: Nuove ricerche e studi sulla Magna Grecia e la Sicilia antica in onore di Paolo Enrico Arias* (Pisa 1982), 431–443.

26. 'Roman Architecture in a Greek World: the Example of Sicily', in M. Henig (ed.), *Architecture and Architectural Sculpture in the Roman Empire*, Oxford University Committee for Archaeology, Monograph 29, 1990, 67–90.

27. C. Anti and L. Polacco, *Il teatro antico di Siracusa* (Pubbl. Ist. Arch. Univ. Padova, Padua, 1976); L. Polacco and C. Anti, *Il teatro antico di Siracusa* (Rimini, 1981); L. Polacco, *Il teatro antico di Siracusa, pars altera* (Padua, 1990).

28. The excavations at Monte Iato have been conducted over 25 campaigns, most of them including work on the theatre, and preliminary reports have appeared regularly in *Antike Kunst* and *Sicilia Archeologica*. The definitive publication of the theatre at Metaponto is that by D. Mertens, 'Metaponto: Il teatro-ekklesiasterion, I', *Bollettino d'Arte*, 67 (16), (1982), 1–57. The second part, on the finds and the details of chronology by A. De Siena, is still to appear.

29. The seating of the theatre at Mantinea in the Peloponnese is also built up artificially: G. Fougères, *Bulletin de Correspondance Hellénique* 14, 1890, 248–256; idem., *Mantinée et l'Arcadie orientale* (Paris 1898), 165–174.

30. J.-Ch. Moretti, 'Les débuts de l'architecture théâtrale en Sicile et en Italie méridionale (Ve-IIe s.)', *Topoi* 3, 1993, 72–100 (see especially his conclusions, p. 97).

31. 'From Taranto to Alexandria', in S.J. Bourke and J.-P. Descœudres (eds), *Trade, Contact and the Movement of Peoples in the Eastern Mediterranean. Studies in Honour of J.Basil Hennessy. Mediterranean Archaeology* Suppl. 3 (Sydney, 1995), 271–274, pl. 18.

32. See recently O.F. Riad, 'Théocrite entre la Sicile et l'Égypte', in *Roma e l'Egitto nell' antichità classica. Atti del I Congresso Internazionale Italo-Egiziano* (Rome, 1992), 305–315.

33. See, for example, the considered comments by L. Koenen in A. Bulloch, E.S. Gruen, A.A. Long, and A. Stewart (eds), *Images and Ideologies: Self-Definition in the Hellenistic World* (Berkeley: University of California Press, 1993), 25–115; also P. Bilde, T. Engberg-Pederson & J. Zahle, *Ethnicity in Hellenistic Egypt* in *Studies in Hellenistic Civilization*, 3, (Aarhus, 1992), and the brief view by D. Delia, '"All Army Boots and Uniforms?": Ethnicity in Ptolemaic Egypt', in *Alexandria and Alexandrianism* (Malibu: The J. Paul Getty Museum, 1996), 41–53.

34. M. Caccamo Caltabianco (ed.), *La Sicilia tra l'Egitto e Roma: la monetazione siracusana dell'eta di Ierone II: Atti del Seminario di Studi Messina 2–4 dicembre 1993* (Messina 1994).

35. See especially K.T. Erim, 'Recent Work at Aphrodisias 1986–1988', in Ch. Roueché and K.T. Erim (eds), *Aphrodisias Papers: Recent Work on Architecture and Sculpture* (Journal of Roman Archaeology Suppl. 1, Ann Arbor, 1990), 9–36 (esp. 30–32), together with the articles by Erim, Reynolds, de Chaisemartin and Theodorescu in R.R.R. Smith and K.T. Erim (eds), *Aphrodisias Papers 2. The Theater (Journal of Roman Archaeology* Suppl. 2, 1991); N. de Chaisemartin and D. Theodorescu, 'La frons scaenae du théâtre d'Aphrodisias: aperçu sur les recherches en cours', *Revue Archéologique* (1992), 181–187; and most recently D. Theodorescu, 'La *frons scaenae* du théâtre: innovations et particularités à l'époque de Zoïlos', in C. Roueché and R.R.R. Smith (eds), *Aphrodisias Papers*, 3 (*Journal of Roman Archaeology* Supplement 20, 1996) 127–148.

Chapter 7

Scholars and Students in the Roman East

Samuel N. C. Lieu

INTRODUCTION

The wanton destruction of the Great Library of Alexandria had probably the same effect on the study, transmission and preservation of
Greek Literature and scientific writing as would the explosion of
nuclear devices simultaneously over Sydney and Canberra, which at
once wiped out the university libraries of Sydney, Macquarie and
Australian National University as well as the Australian National
Library and the New South Wales State Library. The civil war in Alexandria which occasioned the destruction of her famous library also
marked the end of a process of political expansion in which Rome
extended her control over the vestigial kingdoms of the Ptolemies and
the Seleucids. This unification of the Greek world, sharing a common
culture based on that of 5th and 4th C. Athens, meant that Alexandria
would now be only one of several major centres of culture in a world
empire. To return to our Australian analogy: the hypothetical destruction of the major academic libraries at Sydney and Canberra would
certainly have a disastrous effect on the study of history, classics and
oriental studies for which these libraries are famous. It need not spell
the end of these academic disciplines in Australia, of course, so long as
other cities in the Commonwealth had major centres of learning which
escaped destruction. However, the combined strength of these 'provincial' libraries could not possibly match the range and depth of what
would have been lost at Sydney and Canberra.

Similarly, there were other centres of learning and of bibliophilia in the
Hellenistic world besides Alexandria. The city of Pergamum, from which
the Pergamene codex drew its name, had been a major centre of book
production throughout the Hellenistic period, and possessed a library of
some 200,000 volumes – modest by the standard of Alexandria, but not
destroyed by her Roman conquerors. The city of Athens remained the

premier seat of higher learning, especially in philosophy and rhetoric, with libraries to match. To her academies and schools flocked the future famous Roman men of letters like Cicero and his friend and correspondent Atticus. The island of Rhodes boasted a famous finishing school for would-be politicians who needed a dash of Greek culture in their *cursus honorum*, for their political advancement in a world empire in which Latin speakers were a minority. An alumnus of Rhodes was Mark Antony, whose Greek education would have undoubtedly helped his subsequent amorous activities in the Greek-speaking East.[1]

Alexandria continued to be a centre for the study of philosophy and of scientific learning after the civil war among the Ptolemies. It was at Alexandria that the Christian philosopher Clement came under the influence of Pantaenus, head of the Catechetical School of Alexandria. Philo, the famous Jewish author from Alexandria, was a product of the Greek rhetorical schools, judging from his great familiarity with Greek literature, especially the epic and dramatic poets. Once Antioch-on-the-Orontes regained her status as a metropolis in the Roman province of Syria, she, too, would resume her role as a major centre of Hellenic learning – a role which she had played with some distinction under the Seleucids after the loss of the Seleucid eastern capital Seleucia-on-the-Tigris to the Parthians in 165 BC. Nevertheless, the libraries in these centres were not built up by scholars and scientists like those who were active in building up the collection of 700,000 volumes of the Great Library and the 42,800 volumes of the smaller library at Alexandria.

For the educated classes of the predominantly Greek-speaking provinces of the Roman Empire who idolised the culture of Athens, higher education entailed the serious study by young men (aged between 17 to 20) of the Greek literature of the period, from Pericles to Demosthenes and Isocrates. For this they needed books. Under the Empire, urban rivalry had given rise to the city rhetor as the oratorical champion of the city and a training in rhetoric was also seen as essential preparation for the 'fast-track' in the Roman civil service. Many ambitious young men would sacrifice everything to pay for a university education at Athens or Antioch. We are extremely fortunate to possess a considerable body of several famous alumni of the rhetorical schools of Athens on the subject of higher education, especially of rhetorical training, in the imperial period. The first of these is the *Lives of Sophists* (*vitae sophistarum*) of Philostratus (c. 170–205), who studied in Athens but later settled in Rome. This became the literary model of a similarly titled work by Eunapius of Sardis in the fourth century. Above all, we have a large number of orations and private letters of Libanius of Antioch, which shed a great deal of light on higher education both at Athens and Constantinople, as well as on his native city of Antioch, where he held the Chair of Rhetoric from 374 to his death c. 393.

1. RECRUITMENT

Eunapius was born c. 345 AD in Sardis in Asia Minor. In 362 he arrived at Piraeus with some relatives and friends who were all intending to study at Athens.[2] He was in the grips of a raging fever which reduced him to a pitiable state. He was warned that mad enthusiasts, each for his own particular school, used to lie in wait at the docks. The reason was that the number of institutions of higher learning in Athens, especially the schools of rhetoric, had grown enormously as a result of patronage and the availability of fee-paying students. However, demand did not always match the number of places available and to avoid a perpetual state of war between the professors, an agreement was drawn up to divide the potential market on a geographical basis. It was all too common, however, for teachers not to receive enough students from their allocated provinces, and strong arm tactics were employed by their students, sometimes quite openly, to divert recruits to their masters.

Eunapius and his friends docked at midnight. The late hour saved them from being set upon by the agents of the various professors. The ship's captain, however, was in league with Prohaeresius, which was fortunate for the students. Despite the late hour, he took them straight to the house of Prohaeresius in Athens. Poor Eunapius, too feeble to walk, was supported by his friends and relatives in relays. Prohaeresius was staggered by the size of the crowd which he ushered into the house. 'So many in fact', says Eunapius, 'that at a time when battles were being fought to win only one or two pupils, the new comers seemed enough in themselves to man all the schools of the sophists. Some of these youths were distinguished for physical strength, some had more bulky purses, while the rest were only moderately endowed. I, who was in a pitiable state, had as my sole possession most of the works of the ancient writers by heart'.[3] Straight away, there was great rejoicing in the house, and Prohaeresius sent for his own relatives at that time of the night and directed them to take in the newcomers. They were probably only too glad to see so many rent-paying lodgers.

Libanius, who studied in Athens just over two decades earlier (336–340), had a much less fortunate start to his university career. Competition between sophists for students was at an all time high, and professors were said to lure students to their particular schools with offers of lavish dinners. One of the most serious professional accusations that could be levelled against a sophist was that of complicity in the illegal sale of students between institutions. As a native of Antioch, Libanius expected himself to become the pupil of Epiphanius, a teacher who enjoyed an excellent reputation. He arrived at Athens in day-time after staying over night at Geraestus – another harbour of

Athens – and was promptly set upon by the enthusiasts of the school of Diophantus, who locked him up in a cell about the size of a barrel from which he was not allowed out until he had taken an oath to become Diophantus' student.[4]

Libanius' unfortunate experience on arriving at Athens was not the only test which a new student had to suffer at the hands of enthusiasts before he could take up his studies. Students then, as now, bring to university life not only youthful enthusiasm and eagerness to learn but also excess energy. Gregory of Nazianzenus – fellow alumnus of Julian the Apostate and later a leading theologian and bishop – tells us that before a new student was fully accepted into the school, he had to undergo a number of initiation rites administered by his seniors. The student was first conducted to the house of one of his captors, usually someone specially skilled in debate. There he was made the object of jest and banter by all those who wish to take part in the sport through rapid philosophical exchanges. The purpose of this was to humble the conceit of the new student and to bring him at once under the authority of the school.[5] We are told by Olympiodorus of Thebes – a historian who visited at Athens in 415 – that before they were allowed to wear the sophist's cloak, which marked them as students,

> all the novices, junior and senior, were conducted to the public bath. Those of them who, being of the right age, were ready for the philosopher's cloak were pushed to the front by the scholars who were conducting them. Then, while some ran before them and blocked their way, others pushed them and directed them towards the bath; and while all of those blocking their way shouted, 'Stop! stop! don't take the bath', those who were pushing in the opposite direction were determined, of course, to win the struggle in order to bring honour to the scholars who were conducting the novices. After a long time and a long struggle carried out in ritual terms, those who were led into the bath house and washed were then dressed and received the right to wear the philosopher's cloak. Thereafter, having agreed to pay certain sums to the heads of the schools (who are called *Acromitai*), they left the bath in their cloaks escorted by a procession of high-ranking and reputable men.[6]

2. THE STATUS OF PROFESSORS

Once a student had been initiated into a school, he would come under the authority of the head, who would waste no time in reminding him that it was time he should forsake the playing fields and drinking places for serious study.[7] In a university town like Athens, where most students came from the provinces and were safely distant from parental supervision, fighting between rival gangs of students, occasioned undoubtedly by bouts of drinking, were frequent. 'It was', says Eunapius,

> as if the city after those ancient wars of hers was fostering within her walls the peril of discord, that not one of the sophists ventured to go down in to the city and discourse in public, but they confined their utterances to their private lecture theatres and there discoursed to their students.[8]

The professor was generally held in awe by his pupils. Libanius describes him thus in one of his *chriae* (i.e., collection of witty or clever sayings) with the delightful incipit: 'According to Isocrates, the root of education is bitter but its fruit are sweet ...'.

> In fact, think about it. The teacher is established in an imposing chair, like judges are. He seems terrifying, he frowns with anger and shows no sign of calming down. The pupil must go forward in fear and trembling to give an artistically conducted demonstration which he has composed and learnt by heart. If his exercise is bad, there are rages, insults, blows and threats for the future. If everything appears to be worked out to perfection and incurs no criticism, the only thing to be gained is the absence of ill-treatment, the order to do no worse the next time. Even more, a misfortune is in store for whoever fulfilled the whole task well: indeed, as soon as one has been judged to have spoken faultlessly one must submit to a heavier burden, for it seems that one might very quickly be up to more difficult exercises.[9]

Much of the basic teaching in the schools was done by pedagogues – tutors – an academic breed which we all know too well in our own institutions:

> It is the same for all the rest, it's the teacher's part. As for the pedagogue, by Heracles! he is worse than a slavedriver, always on to you, almost stuck to you, continually goading, rebuking all the time, chastising laziness, ordering one to stick to one's task without any praise for what is good, punishing trivia excessively, following you fully armed as it were, brandishing a stick or martinet in his right hand.[10]

The professors would normally teach only until lunch-time, when the pedagogue(s) would take over.[11] Libanius complained that the need to get enough fee-paying students was such that he had to work through his lunch-hour.[12] The pedagogue, because of his role as disciplinarian, was often the butt of student protests:

A blanket is spread out on the ground and held on each side by a varying number of students, depending on the surface area of the blanket itself. Then, in the middle of it is placed the chosen victim of the vilest outrage, and he is thrown into the air as high as possible, and it is very high, in the midst of shrieks of laughter. The circle of spectators also find it amusing, their laughter provoked as much by the unfortunate man's dizziness as by the cries he lets out as he goes up and down. Sometimes the wretched man falls back on to the blanket which is raised up high, sometimes he misses it and lands on the ground: then he goes away with injured limbs, so that this outrage is not without some danger. And the worst of it is that people laugh at it.[13]

A totally fee-paying higher education system, however, has the advantage of parental involvement. Besides putting pressure on both their sons and their teachers to perform well, sometimes the conscientious or ambitious parent would play the part of tutor as Libanius once reminded one of his more wayward pupils by the name of Anaxentius:

It has already happened that a man did not want to return home after having entrusted his sons to me: he joined the class and sat down, and I saw no pedagogue for the children anywhere. As I was asking him one day 'Where is the pedagogue then, and who is he? For surely', I said, 'you are not going to leave your sons without any supervision', he replied that he himself was his sons' pedagogue. He did this though he was already getting on in years. I suppose that because of this occupation he neglected his domestic business, and his worst slaves had a free rein to act wrongly. However, when he was told this, he replied: 'You are speaking to someone who knows it better than anyone, but I consider the damage done to my business as nothing compared with what I am gaining here'. Also remind yourself that your father is with you, that he is putting himself at your disposal in order to take care of you, I think that a father even wishes, to give his son the services of a domestic slave during his studies, and that the problems that your father would experience if he were far from home would surely be no less than those which you are undergoing now. Probably there will even be gods who will help your father and bring him assistance, not least the gods of eloquence, in return for your enthusiasm regarding the disciplines which they have brought to men. Probably men will also show themselves who will not only not reproach you for your conduct, but will prevent others from doing so: the sophist should not mount guard over his chair in this way, but rather by showing that the pupils will not find better sources elsewhere. Pupils must be retained by victory in the struggle for eloquence, not by fear of the evils which will descend upon their fathers if they leave the class. As well as this, even the evils which threaten today would end if a governor who favoured such procedures was succeeded by a more just man who would cause them to stop. And perhaps I would even become his friend.[14]

In the early empire, especially under a Philhellene emperor like Hadrian, institutions of higher learning in the Greek East enjoyed enormous prestige, and professors rubbed shoulders with the leading political figures of the day. One academic who lived life to the full in the Second Century was Polemo of Smyrna.[15] It was through him that Hadrian was persuaded to transfer his patronage from Ephesus, the official capital of Roman Asia, to Smyrna, and he lavished no less than ten million drachmae on the city. With this windfall, the city council was able to construct the famous corn-market – now excellently excavated by Italian archaeologists – as well as a gymnasium and a temple which could be seen from the sea. When the citizens later complained that Polemo had used some of this fabulous sum of money to supplement his extravagant life style, Hadrian replied that he was satisfied with the account given by Polemo on how the money was spent.

Extravagant with the public purse he might have been, but Polemo's personal standing with the imperial authorities was such that he was able to help many of his fellow citizens in law-suits, especially in preventing certain cases to be heard in Ephesus – the official capital of Roman Asia – or at Rome. Much more controversial was his personal crusade for the expulsion from the city of adulterers, murderers and those who had committed sacrilege. His motto was that criminals need a judge with a sword. Unlike modern jet-setting academics, Polemo never travelled light, and was normally accompanied by a large retinue of baggage animals and slaves and various breeds of hunting dogs. He would drive around in the Roman equivalent of a Jaguar or Daimler, viz. a chariot of Phrygian or Gallic design and manufacture, with silver mounted bridles. All this showiness, he claimed was good for the image of his native Smyrna. He wrangled from Hadrian's successor, Trajan, free travel by land and sea to anywhere in the Empire – a privilege that was extended to his descendants. When he was in Rome, he demanded 250,000 drachmae for living expenses and he received it from the Emperor although neither side had agreed to such a figure beforehand.

One of the best illustrations of Polemo's extraordinary standing in relation to the imperial family is the manner in which he was allowed to get away with manifest disregard of royal protocol. Prior to his adoption by Hadrian as successor in 138, Antoninus Pius who was governor of Asia (133–36), once took up lodgings in Polemo's house because it was the best in the city. But this he did without informing Polemo, as the latter chanced to be away at the time. When he got back, he was furious at the show of proconsular presumption that shut him out of his own house. He insisted that Antoninus must move to another house even though it was in the middle of the night. When Hadrian was informed of this, he took no action, as any step taken to charge Polemo of disrespect for his chosen successor would bring into the open his previous indulgence towards the sophist. To save face he named Polemo as the principal adviser for his last will and testament, and thereby silenced all the sophist's critics. Antoninus Pius, despite having been turfed out of bed at midnight, later welcomed the sophist to Rome when he was emperor. He commanded that Polemo should be given the best lodging. Once, when a tragic actor who had performed at the Olympic Games in Asia, over which Polemo had presided, declared that he would prosecute Polemo because he had expelled him at the beginning of the play, the Emperor asked the actor what time it was when he was expelled from the theatre, and when he replied that it happened to be at noon, the Emperor made the witty comment, 'But it was midnight when he expelled me from his house and I did not prosecute him'.

In 267 Athens was sacked by a German tribe – the Heruli, who briefly captured the city. Archaeological evidence yields a clear and definite picture of the effects of the Herulian sack. Extensive burning and destruction of public and private buildings in the sack itself, was followed in the years up to the 280's by substantial use of material from existing buildings for constructing a new inner line of defence (the so-called 'Valerian' wall), which surrounded a small area north of the Acropolis, and left the Agora itself unguarded and deserted. Coin evidence shows that the wall was under construction in the reign of Probus (276–82).[16] The devastation would have undoubtedly been worse had local citizens not rallied round an unlikely leader – Herrenius Dexippus (c. 200?-276?), a professor of rhetoric and later author of an important historical work which would be continued by Eunapius, but which has survived only in part. He was regarded by his contemporaries and later writers as a man of most extensive learning. Over successive generations, members of his family – a leading one in Athens – although possessing Roman citizenship, still preferred to become senators at Athens and to hold office there rather than at Rome. After the capture of his native city by the Heruli, he gathered around him a number of bold and courageous Athenians, and took up a strong position on the neighbouring hills. Though the city itself was in the hands of the barbarians, and Dexippus with his band was cut off from it, he made an unexpected descent upon Piraeus and took vengeance upon the enemy. An account of this act of local defiance without the support of the imperial forces is given in the (now fragmentary) historical work of its daring leader:

> ... and wars are decided by courage rather than numbers. We have no mean force. Two thousand of us have gathered in all, and we have this deserted spot as a base from which we gain an advantage by attacking him in small groups and ambushing him on his way. Once we gain an advantage thus, our forces will swell and we shall strike no small fear into the enemy. If they come against us we shall resist – we have an excellent defence in this rough wooded position. If they assault us from different directions they will be thrown out by fighting against men who are unseen and not fighting like those they have faced before; they will break their line, will not know where to direct their arrows and darts, will miss their aim, and continue to suffer from our attack. We, protected by the wood, will be able to shoot accurately from positions of advantage, and will apply ourselves safely, in minimal danger. As for regular battle, if that is necessary, realise that the greatest dangers call forth the greatest courage, and at the extremity of hope endurance comes more readily. Often the unexpected has happened, when men forced by circumstances, and fighting for things they love in the hope of revenge. We could not have before us a greater cause for anger, since our families and our city are in the hands of the enemy. Those too, who have been forced against their will to fight alongside the enemy, would, once they realise our approach, join in the attack on them in the hope of freedom. ...

Fortune too should be on our side. For our cause is just, we resist those who have gratuitously wronged us, and the divine will plays with human affairs in this way, that it most eagerly relieves misfortune and restores the sufferers. It is a noble fate to spread the glory of our city, to be ourselves an example of courage and the love of freedom to the Greeks, and win among men now and in the future an undying fame, showing by our actions that even in disaster the resolution of Athenians is not broken. Let our watchword in battle be our children and all that is dearest to us, and to save these let us set out together for the conflict, calling on the gods to watch over and aid us.[17]

The victory of Gallienus on the Nestus near Epirus in the same year led to a treaty with Naulobatus the chieftain of the Heruli, by which the latter agreed to serve the Roman Empire and became the first barbarian to receive the honour of becoming a Roman consul. Once peace was restored, Athens quickly recovered her leadership role in higher education. As the imperial administration grew in size in the Late Empire, the need for more graduates in rhetoric rose correspondingly. The increase in the number of institutions, however, led to a perceptible decline in the status of the professor in the eyes of the imperial and provincial authorities. Preoccupied by the need to ensure he had enough fee-paying students to make a reasonable living for himself and for his pedagogues, he had no time to curry the favour of governors and senior officials. The pressures brought about by the need to compete for students were well explained by Libanius in one of his orations (or. XXV) aptly entitled 'On the Slavery of the Teacher':

> Not only is he (i.e. the teacher) the slave of as many masters as he has subjects, he is also the slave of a multitude of pedagogues, parents, yes, mothers, grandmothers, grandfathers. If, thanks to his job, he does not triumph over an obtuse nature, if he does not make the pupil appear to be a son of the gods, though he be made of stone, what a flood of accusations there is of all kinds; he has to cast his eyes down to the ground, not that he lacks excuses, but he seeks to appease the quarrelsome person by his silence.

> He is also the slave of the gate-keepers (sc. of the town) and of the class of innkeepers: of the former so that they do not speak ill of him to strangers entering the town, of the latter so that they praise him in front of their customers. For both of these, and others even humbler than them can do wrong to a sophist's classroom.

> Yes, and furthermore he flatters and coaxes the man who comes from elsewhere and the one who goes from here, the first in order that he does not go and wage war here on the spot and ruin the class, the second so that he does not spread troublesome rumours about the school wherever he goes.

> But the *curia* (i.e. city council) is also a very weighty mistress: in a few lines she can elect him and beat him, turn his destiny as she wishes, drive him out if she wishes, set up a crowd of rivals against him, and all the other annoyances which seem small but cause great distress. I suppose that if he wishes to escape he must not fail to carry out his job as a slave. He will spend his time at the doors of magistrates flattering doormen: let them drive him away, he can bear it; let them admit him, how marvellous his gratitude! And if he has to act in this way towards the master of the door, what does he have to do for the supreme governor?[18]

3. BOOKS AND HIGHER EDUCATION

Higher education could not function in any society, not even in one as highly electronicized as ours, without books, and for a school man like Libanius and his pupils, books were essential. Hence the voluminous writings of Libanius, especially his orations and letters dealing with educational matters, offer us many glimpses into the dissemination of books and personal libraries, especially of those at Antioch, in Late Antiquity.[19]

We learn from his autobiographical oration that it was while he was reading the comedy, the *Acharnians* of Aristophanes, by his teacher's chair at school at Antioch that he had the misfortune of being struck by lightning.[20] Although it did not cause any permanent loss of sight, he would suffer from frequent attacks of migraine as an adult. Old Comedy, then was clearly on the schools' syllabus, and famous plays like the *Acharnians* enjoyed considerable circulation as text-books. Another work which Libanius mentions specifically is the *History* of Thucydides – a great treasure for him which was almost a source of personal tragedy. The relevant passage is worth quoting in full as it is highly informative on books and the theft of books and second-hand book-trade in Late Antiquity:

> Another occurrence deserves mention also. Although a trivial matter, it is significant. Some of you perhaps will regard me as a mere pedant, but I, smitten to my very heart, know that my emotion arose because of a calamity great indeed. I had a copy of Thucydides' History. Its writing was fine and small, and the whole work was so easy to carry that I used to do so myself, while my slave followed behind: the burden was my pleasure. In it I used to read of the war between Athens and Sparta, and was affected as perhaps others have been before me. Never again could I derive such pleasure from reading it in another copy. I was loud in praise of my possession, and I had more joy in it than Polycrates did in his ring, but by singing its praises so, I invited the attention of thieves, some of whom I caught in the act. The last of them, however, started a fire to prevent capture, and I gave up the search but could not grieve at the loss. In fact, all the advantage I could have gained from Thucydides began to diminish, since I encountered him in different writing and with disappointment. However, for this discomfort, Fortune provided the remedy, a tardy one, admittedly, but, none the less, the remedy. I kept writing to my friends about it, so grieved was I, and I would describe its size and what it was like inside and out, and wonder where it was and who had it. Then a student, a fellow citizen of mine, who had purchased it, came to read it. The teacher

of the class set up the cry, 'That's it', recognising it by its tokens, and came to ask whether he was right. So I took it and welcomed it like a long-lost child unexpectedly restored. I went off rejoicing, and both then and now I owe my thanks to Fortune. Let him who likes laugh at me for making a mountain out of a mole hill. I have no regard for the laughter of boors.[21]

Books were highly valued because of their high production cost and rarity. Libanius' copy of Thucydides would have been in the form of a book-roll rather than a codex. Pagan teachers like him eschewed the use of shorthand, and he made frequent mention of the difficulties of finding suitable copyists. The number of those in private service, mainly slaves, was not large and when Libanius' secretary died in the plague which struck Antioch c. 385, he lost an invaluable copyist 'whose writing', he says, 'assisted me greatly in my declamations, since it was much better than my own notes compiled in the process of composition, and allowed me to run through them at a glance'.[22] He was careful not to burden copyists to no purpose, and on one occasion recommended a copyist from Antioch for professional employment in Athens, and asked that he be protected from the insolence of the students there.[23]

The lending of valuable books between scholars was commonplace, but sometimes the practice had to be reinforced by oaths and threats. In one of his shortest letters, Libanius wrote to a friend called Eusebius, who was a descendant of the Odaenathus the Great of Palmyra, the husband of Zenobia: 'I am asking for the speech 'Odaenathus', the speech by Longinus. You must give it in fulfilment of your promise'[24] Libanius was annoyed by rich parents who would not make adequate contributions towards the cost of their sons' school-books. When he saw that a student was in tears because he could not afford to pay for both food and books – an unchanging problem – he wrote immediately to his father Heortius.[25] 'If you were a poor man', he said, 'I would ask you to get contributions from your friends and assist your son, but since fortunately you are one of the foremost men of fortune, my advice is that you spend some of your possessions on the most precious of your possessions. Hunger perhaps is not particularly advantageous for a student either, but the question now is not about the lad's belly but about his books. If he has none, he will be like a man learning archery without a bow'.[26]

The high cost of copying also meant that some works of great literary value but not often read in rhetorical schools were not regularly re-copied. In 361, Libanius wrote to thank his friend Palladius for sending him some books on rhetoric which were of special value to a practising orator like himself.[27] Sadly, the copy of the declamations of the famous Second

Century rhetor Aelius Aristides was 'damaged by age and at first sight, it is a case of to have it and to have it not. One syllable is visible, but you will not see the next for all your searching'.[28]

Besides the high cost of books, the narrow syllabus of the rhetorical schools also contributed to the gradual disappearance of many literary works. At the heart of the rhetorical training lay the great forensic speeches of Attic orators, especially Demosthenes – an author Libanius knew so well – and for whom he wrote a complete set of *hypotheses* (summaries) – that later Byzantine scholars would nickname him a 'Second Demosthenes'. Homer, of course, he would have also known intimately, as indicated by frequent and apt quotations. However, philosophical authors seemed to have been little read by him or by his students and many ancient authors appeared to have been cited through collections of quotations. Of the works of Pindar, the only one he possessed was the *Olympians*, which was probably an example of self-denial as more titles were available. The same selectivity was also evident in his familiarity with Greek drama, which certainly did not extend beyond the received corpus of the works of Aeschylus, Sophocles and Euripides.[29]

ENDS AND NEW BEGINNINGS

As the tempo of the conflict between paganism and Christianity quickened in the fifth century, the nature of higher education for the sons of the ruling elite became a major issue. A rhetorical education was unavoidably pagan in its religious outlook, and the attempt by the Emperor Julian to limit its teaching to pagans who literally believed in the Greek myths as contained in the classics, only invited a fierce backlash from Christian Emperors. The process of gradual attrition was completed by the Emperor Justinian, who ordered the closure of the Platonic Academy in Athens in 529.

Internal conflict within the Christian Church also had a major impact upon the transmission of classical learning. A school of theology in the frontier city of Edessa was closed by the Emperor Zeno in 489 because of the support its staff gave to the banned teaching of Nestorius. The key members fled across the border to Nisibis where, under the protection of the Persian King of Kings, they established a major centre of learning. Although Syriac was their main medium of instruction, their curriculum included the teaching of Greek philosophy (especially that of Plato and Aristotle) and scientific writings. These 'Nestorians' soon established a reputation as a place where Christian theology was taught with the same rigour as Greek philosophy. Another Christian school was established at Gundeshapur, which was particularly famous for its medical studies and teaching hospital. We possess in Syriac the statutes of the school, drawn up in 590, which makes them the oldest surviving statutes of any institution of higher education in the world.

The atmosphere of these Christian institutions was, of course, highly ascetic. The students were bounded by the rule of celibacy during the whole of their training, and dress and hair-style were regulated. At cockcrow, students took their places in the classrooms, and spent the day copying books, reading, hearing lectures, and learning to recite the liturgy. They were forbidden to leave the town of Nisibis without permission from the prefect of discipline, and forbidden to go over the politically sensitive frontier into the Roman empire for any reason whatsoever, not excluding visits to a doctor, or even pilgrimages. They were not allowed to take on paid work in case it would distract them from their studies, and they were prohibited from acting as cross-frontier guides. They ate in a common refectory, and were forbidden to eat in inns or taverns, or in the gardens in the town, or to visit convents or nuns. They lived seven or eight together in a 'cell', under the charge of a chief, and when they were not engaged in their studies, they were supposed to be at their prayers. The better off were not allowed to lend money to their more impecunious brethren at more than 1% interest.

Their course lasted three years, and the basis of it was the transcription of scripture and knowledge of the liturgy. Teaching was in Syriac, but a good knowledge of both Greek and Syriac fathers was necessary. The curriculum began with learning to read correctly, followed by the art of writing, the copying of manuscripts, then philology and grammar, which was more difficult because of the discrepancy between the written and the spoken language of both Greek and Syriac. Music played an important part, too, entailing training in the liturgical chant.[30]

The industry of the Christian Syriac scholars at centres like Nisibis would act as a vital bridge between the classical and the medieval worlds. When the scholars in Toledo translated Aristotle into Latin in the twelfth century, they did not use the Greek originals of Aristotle's works but Arabic translations which were in turn either translations of the Syriac translations of the Greek or translations made from Greek via a Syriac intermediary version made for the purpose of translation. Because it was not a rhetorical school aimed at educating the scions of the Roman ruling class, the syllabus of the School of Nisibis produced scholars with much broader intellectual horizons. These scholars – bilingual in Greek and Syriac – became key figures in the transmission of Greek writings into Arabic under the Abbasid Caliphate. Their endeavours led to the preservation in Arabic not only of the writings of major scientific and philosophical writers including Euclid, Galen, Hippocrates and Aristotle, but also those of many lesser known Greek authors of the Roman period, such as Diosorides, Alexander of Aphrodisias, Themistius, and Nicholas of Damascus. In this roundabout manner, the new centres of learning in the early Islamic period like Baghdad, Cairo and even Alexandria itself, became the heirs of classical Greek learning once so gloriously epitomised by the Great Library of Alexandria.

NOTES

1. For a list of the historically significant alumni of Athens and Rhodes in the Late Republican period, see J. W. H. Walden, *The Universities of Ancient Greece* (London: Routledge, 1912), 55–56.

2. His *Lives of Sophists* which included lives of some of the sophists who had taught him at Athens.

3. Eunapius, *Vitae Sophistarum* X,1,4–7, ed. G. Giangrande, *Eunapii Vitae Sophistarum* (Rome: Istituto Poligrafico dello Stato, 1956), 64–65, Eng. trans. W. C. Wright, *Philostratus and Eunapius, Lives of the Sophists* (Cambridge, Mass. and London: Harvard University Press, 1921), 477–79.

4. Libanius, *Oration* I, 16, trans. A. F. Norman, Libanius, *Autobiography and Selected Letters*, 2 vols., Loeb Classical Library (Cambridge, Mass. and London: Harvard University Press, 1992), [hereafter Norman i and ii], Vol. 1, 71–73. Cf. G. R. Sievers, *Das Leben des Libanius* (Berlin: Weidmannsche Buchhandlung, 1868), 42–49 and A. F. Norman, *Libanius' Autobiography (Oration I)*, (Oxford: Oxford University Press, 1965), 151–52.

5. Gregory Nazianzenus, *Oration* XLIII, 16 (*In laudem Basilii Magni*), in Migne's *Patrologia Graeca* Vol. 36, cols. 516B-517B.

6. Olympiodorus, *Historiae*, frag. 28 from Photius, *Bibliotheca*, Cod. 80, trans. R. C. Blockley, *The Fragmentary Classicising Historians of the Later Roman Empire*, II (Liverpool: Francis Cairns, 1983), 193.

7. See, e.g, Himerius address to his students: *Oration* XXII, esp. §7, ed. F. Dübner, *Himerii Sophistae Declamationum quae supersunt* (Paris: Firmin Didot, 1849), 90. Cf. Walden, *op. cit.* 265–66.

8. Eunapius, *Vitae Sophistarum*, IX,1,6, *ed. cit.* 60, *trans. cit.*, 469. On student unrest see esp. Walden, *op. cit.* 16–20 and A. F. Norman, 'Libanius: The Teacher in an Age of Violence' in G. Fatouros and T. Krischer (eds.) *Libanios*, Wege der Forschung Vol. 621, (Darmstadt: Wissenschafliche Buchgessellschaft, 1983), 149–69, esp 165.

9. Libanius, *chriae* III,7, in Libanius, *Opera*, ed. R. Foerster, Vol. 8, (Leipzig, Tuebner, 1915) 84–85. On Libanius as a teacher in general see F. Schemmel, 'Der Sophist Libanios als Schüler und Lehrer', *Neue Jahrbücher für das klassische Altertum* 20 (1907) 52–69 [Reprinted in Fatouros and Krischer, *op. cit.* 1–25.], P. Petit, *Les Étudiants de Libanius – Un professeur de faculté et ses élèves au Bas Empire* (Paris: Nouvelles Éditions Latines, 1957), 95–192 and A.-J. Festugière, *Antioche Païenne et chrétienne, Libanius, Chrysostome et les moines de Syrie*, Bibliothèque des Écoles Françaises deAthènes et de Rome, vol. 194 (Paris: Éditions E. de Boccard, 1959), 91–179.

10. Libanius, *chriae* III,8, trans. Lieu and Vince, unpubl.

11. On the pedagogues of Libanius, see esp. P. Wolf, *Vom Schulwesen der Spätantike* (Baden Baden: Verlag für Kunst und Wissenschaft, 1952), 60–74.

12. Libanius, *Ep.* 405, 6, trans. Norman, i, 365.

13. Libanius, *Oration* LVIII,18, trans. Lieu and Vince, unpubl.

14. Libanius, *Oration* LV, 28–30, trans. Lieu and Vince, unpubl.

15. For Polemo, see Philostratus, *Vitae Sophistarum* 25 (530–544), trans. W. C. Wright, *Philostratus and Eunapius, Lives of the Sophists* (Cambridge, Mass: Harvard University Press, 1921), 107–37 and Walden, *op. cit.* 163 and 255–57.
16. F. G. B. Millar, 'P. Herennius Dexippus: The Greek World and the Third-Century Invasions', *Journal of Roman Studies*, 59 (1969), 27.
17. Dexippus, *Scythica* Frag. 28, trans. Millar, *op. cit.* 27–28.
18. Libanius, *Oration* XXV,47–49, trans. Lieu and Vince, unpubl.
19. See esp. the masterly study of A. F. Norman, 'The Book Trade in Fourth-Century Antioch' *Journal of Hellenic Studies*, 80 (1960), 122–26. [Reprinted in Fatouros and Krischer, *op. cit.* 267–74].
20. Libanius, *Oration* I,9, trans. Norman, i, 63.
21. *Ibid.* I,148–50, trans. Norman, i, 217–19.
22. *Ibid.* I,232, trans. Norman, i, 289.
23. Libanius, *Ep.* 1258,1–2, no known translation.
24. Libanius, *Ep.* 1078, trans. Lieu in M. H. Dodgeon and S. N. C. Lieu, *The Roman Eastern Frontier and the Persian Wars* (London: Routledge, 1991), 110.
25. On Heortius, see O. Seeck, *Die Briefe des Libanius zeitlich geordnet*, Texte und Untersuchungen zur Geschichte der altchristlichen Literatur, N. F. XV, 1/2 (Leipzig: J. C. Hinrichs'sche Buchandlung, 1906), 171.
26. Libanius, *Ep.* 428, trans. Norman, i, 377.
27. On Palladius see Seeck, *op. cit.* 228 (Palladius VI).
28. Libanius, *Ep.* 631, 2, trans. Norman, ii, 79.
29. On the range and depth of Libanius' personal reading, see esp. A. F. Norman, 'The Library of Libanius' *Rheinisches Museum für Philologie*,107 (1964), 163–64.
30. On the School of Nisibis, see esp. A. Vööbus, *History of the School of Nisibis*, Corpus Scriptorum Christianorum Orientalium, Subsidia 26 (Leuven: Peeters, 1965), passim. I am grateful to the late Rev. Denis Hickley for making available to me a copy of his unpublished work, *Christianity on the Silk Road*, and to Dr. Sebastian Brock, FBA, for doing the same with the text of his important lecture, 'One Church, Two Empires – Christianity in the Sassanian Empire', which he delivered at Warwick University.

Chapter 8

The Neoplatonists and the Mystery Schools of the Mediterranean

Patricia Cannon Johnson

INTRODUCTION

Among the most far-reaching of the achievements of Alexandria was its ability to take the received wisdom of the Hellenistic world and synthesise it into new ideas. It can be said that all the arts and sciences, from an ideal perspective, are generated by the search for wisdom, yet in no sphere is this more apparent than among the philosophers themselves: those 'lovers of wisdom' whose cosmologies reflect and probe the nature of transcendent being.

The dividing line between *Nous* and mystical experience is a fine one, and the Hellenistic world was heir to two great modes of contemplation – the Mystery religions and the schools of philosophy of Greece – which, by the 6th century BC, had begun to coalesce into a new theory of ideas. The initiating genius of this synthesis was Pythagoras (c580–c500 BC), followed in the 4th century BC by the mystically inclined philosophy of Plato (c427–c347 BC).

The doctrines of Pythagoras and Plato were influential in the Hellenising of the eastern Mediterranean between the 4th and 1st centuries BC; a movement which achieved its most creative expression in the milieu provided by the great cultural metropolis of Alexandria.[1] As the foremost centre of philosophy and mathematics, theology, philology and science, Alexandria was a university in the true sense: an awakening of consciousness through the liberal arts in which humanity could find its place as the living image of the philosophic and Hermetic principle of *Nous* or Universal Mind.[2] A remarkable feature of this higher learning was its transcendence of the boundaries of sex and class, philosophy becoming less the preserve of an intellectual elite than the concern of individuals at large.

The same was true of the Mystery religions, which converged on Alexandria to become an essential ingredient of public life: the lesser rites colourful and histrionic, but the higher levels of initiation more akin to the metaphysics of transcendence, and thus to the Platonic theory of Ideas. Consistent with the liberalism of Hellenistic thought, Alexandria gave rise to a new syncretism in the Mysteries, notably with the advent of the god Serapis – consort of Isis – unifying certain Greek attributes of the divine, including healing, a function of the *Logos*, with the Egyptian sacrificial god Osiris.

Perhaps the most significant legacy of Alexandria to the world at large, however, was a philosophic shift in the Platonic concept of the Supreme Principle as identifiable with *Nous* or Mind – and thus encompassed by the boundaries of definition – to a transcendent One, beyond distinct being, limited by no boundaries at all.[3] This is the position of Neoplatonism, which arose through the schools of Alexandria in the 3rd century AD; the metaphysics of which, in later centuries, was to exercise a profound influence upon the mysticism and theology of the western world.

ORPHIC MYSTERIES

The study of Neoplatonism begins inevitably with the Mystery religions, and in particular with the Orphic Mysteries, which are linked with those of Dionysos. The hidden wisdom of the Mysteries serves a double purpose in this context: it provides a theogony against which to read the philosophic doctrines, and also generates an esoteric language, presenting a key to much within the writings of the Neoplatonists and their successors which may otherwise appear obscure.

Both Plato and Pythagoras had been influenced in the development of their ideas by their own experience as initiates of the Mysteries, and by the doctrines expounded in a series of religious writings – usually known as 'the Orphic things' – associated with the name of Orpheus. Pythagoras is said to have gained his knowledge of the Mysteries from Pherecydes the Orphic, who himself had been a pupil of the Chaldeans and Egyptians.[4] Surviving fragments of the Orphic writings which are likely to be genuine include a *Theology* and the *Mystic Hymns*.[5] 'All theology among the Greeks', the Neoplatonist Proclus reminds us in the 5th century AD, 'is sprung from the mystical doctrine of Orpheus'. Philosophy – the love of wisdom – may be defined as the elucidation of theological ideas.

In dealing with the Mysteries of Orpheus there are two separate aspects to consider: firstly, the figure of Orpheus himself and the Greek myths surrounding him; secondly, the complex theology on which the Orphic Mysteries depends, and which derives ultimately from Asia Minor and the *Emanation* theories of Zoroastrianism. The ancients themselves had little real notion of whether Orpheus existed historically as a real man or merely as an allegorical idea. Marsilio Ficino, in the 15th century, traced the line of succession of the great teachers of theology as follows:

> In things pertaining to theology there were in former times six great teachers expounding similar doctrines. The first was Zoroaster, the chief of the Magi; the second Hermes Trismegistus, the head of the Egyptian priesthood; Orpheus succeeded Hermes; Aglaophamus was initiated into the sacred mysteries of Orpheus; Pythagoras was initiated into theology by Aglaophamus; and Plato by Pythagoras. Plato summed up the whole of their wisdom in his letters.[6]

The line of descent of the *Gens Orphica* places ten generations of poets, or schools of poets, between Orpheus and Homer.[7]

The existence of Orpheus as an individual is, however, of less interest than the influence of Orphism in the ancient world. The doctrines of the Orphic school were concerned with mystical salvation, and included a belief in transmigration, or reincarnation, and the means by which the immortal soul might ultimately transcend the cycle of rebirth. It was concerned also with the relationship of number to the nature of the gods, and it is number, in the form of celestial harmonies, to which the power of Orpheus' lyre refers. The seven-stringed lyre had the power to charm not only all who heard it, including rocks and trees, but to hold back the gates of death itself.

In relation to the Orphic theology, we find that any accurate appreciation of it depends upon our understanding of the principle of *Emanation*;[8] which concept has been much misunderstood. The Emanation principle is a theory of Creation. It refers to a Unity or Monad – the Eternally Existent, or Good – which, whilst indivisible within itself, yet emanates Creation – the Many or the All – by a process of multiplicity through a hierarchy of levels or dimensions from one state of being to the next.

When this principle is misunderstood, each succeeding level of Creation is perceived as more distantly removed from God, the world of Matter being most remote of all. The problem is compounded when Matter is seen not as the creation of the Monad, but of the level directly above itself, sometimes referred to as the Soul and sometimes as the Demiurge, depending upon the school concerned. The way is open then for the error of certain Gnostic schools and others in regarding Matter as an evil creation in opposition to the spiritual creation of the Monad, and thus to the devaluing of physical existence.[9]

Dualism, as it is known, is common to a number of religions, and has been the bane of Christianity, recognising as it does the eternal co-existence of Satan with God. It was widespread in southern France in the 12th and 13th centuries in the form of Catharism, which is thought to have originated from a Manichaean Gnostic sect of Asia Minor.[10] Orphism takes a different view. By a mystical process the Monad indwells the whole of its creation, and all the levels of descent are regarded as equally holy. Man – and indeed all life – is a microcosm of the Cosmos. Manifested life is viewed as a final flowering of the harmonically differentiated levels of vibration which underlie the process of the One or the Good into phenomenal existence. Evil is perceived as essentially non-existent, a derivative condition rather than a cosmic constant.

By this manner of perception, the Soul commands a central position between the Intelligible sphere or sphere of Mind and the sphere of the Senses, whence it sends projections of itself into Matter. Each physical projection is re-absorbed into the Soul at death. By this repeated involution the Soul is enabled to evolve. The cycle of rebirth will cease when the projected personality has so transcended material existence, it can learn nothing more by a return. This doctrine is understood in allegory by the myths of Dionysos and Apollo, who are aspects of the same idea: Dionysos represents the Soul fragmented into many incarnations, pursuing his reflection in the mirror which is one of his playthings into the intoxication of the senses; Apollo represents the unifying light of the return. The name 'Apollo' actually means 'not many' – ie., One – in which sense he represents the *Solar Logos*, or mediating principle between the Monad and the material world. The Orpheus of myth suffered the same symbolic fate – dismemberment – as Dionysos, with whom his Mysteries are fused.

Orphism is a doctrine of liberation. A moral and disciplined existence is called for, not because the flesh is evil and to be abjured, but because goodness, being of the nature of the sublime, will manifest the divine nature in the individual, with all the positive effects arising from the cause, according as he is fitted to sustain it. This is in line with the Hermetic axiom, 'As Above, so Below',[11] and the Delphic exhortation, 'Know Thyself' – which means in effect, 'Awaken memory of the divine power behind your physical persona'.

The Mysteries, then, can be described as the personal or experiential aspect of philosophy, giving access at a deep contemplative level to spontaneous, and occasionally ecstatic, moments of insight resulting in the form of knowledge known as *gnosis*, in which the mind comes into a state of oneness with the thing perceived. The Neoplatonist Plotinus describes the experience thus:

All the need is met by a contact purely intellective. At the moment of touch there is no power whatever to make any affirmation; there is no leisure; reasoning upon the vision is for afterwards. We may know we have had the vision when the Soul has suddenly taken light. This light is from the Supreme and is the Supreme... .[12]

The word 'Mystery' is from a Greek word meaning 'to be silent', and the Mysteries by their nature are levels of perception difficult to verbalise. I cannot, for instance, describe to another the scent of a flower; I can only tell him how to find the garden where it grows, so that, if he wishes, he may seek the flower for himself.

PYTHAGORAS AND PLATO

Experience of this kind is central to the Neoplatonist philosophy, and is itself an aspect of the argument for immortality as perceived by Pythagoras and Plato. Pythagoras was concerned with the science of number and the idea that order, or harmony of relation, is the regulating principle of the Cosmos. The principles of music are closely associated with this, and in fact the word 'canon' in Pythagorean usage refers specifically to the template used to mark off the harmonic divisions on the monochord.[13] Pythagoras believed it possible for the study of number and harmony to lead to *gnosis*, since the mathematical patterns in the natural world reflect the archetypal laws on which all phenomena are based.

Pythagoras expressed these principles in terms of numerical ratios and harmonic differentiation. His concept of the *Kosmos* (which word he coined himself) is of a dynamic harmony of opposites or complementary forces. *Harmonia*, meaning a fitting together of parts into the whole, gives rise to the Law of Unity in Multiplicity. Number is treated as a qualitative essence[14] expressing the ideal principles of universal relationship or function. These values, or *Logoi*, are symbolic of the process of Emanation.

The Pythagoreans regarded the number One as not a number at all, but the essence of number out of which the number system emerges. Polarisation into Two – male/female, active/passive – is brought in the triad into a new unity with the harmonic term obtained between the two extremes. With this new unity the possibility of *Logos* is implied. The first emanation of the Monad is perceived as a triangle, which is best symbolically understood by Euclid's definition: point (position only) projecting straight line (dimension) and thus the simplest plane figure traced out by three straight lines (form).

Mystical systems are commonly composed of a series of triads, one following upon another by mediation or relationship of the *Logoi*. The *Solar Logos* is arrived at as a secondary Unity, about which the spheres revolve. This state of harmony is attributed to the divine musician Apollo (as we have seen), whose Muses express the entire number canon emanating from the One.[15] The Jewish philosopher, Philo of Alexandria, refers to God as the Intelligible or Spiritual Sun, and the *Logos*, his offspring, as the 'Son of God'.[16] It is easy, then, to see why the early Christians placed Christ in the position of the Logos; and why Clement of Alexandria could refer to Christ as 'The New Song'.[17]

Plato, in the *Timaeus*, is at one with Pythagoras in depicting the World Soul as being divided according to the ratios of perfect harmony; the *Logos* being the archetype upon which all creation is based. The philosophy of Plato springs from the postulate that wisdom is the attribute of Godhead, and that the impulse to have knowledge or *gnosis* of this wisdom consecrates and lifts the Soul. The impulse to be like the Eternal, however, must imply a prior communion with the realm of Mind, presupposing the divine nature or immortality of the Soul. Plato's arguments are pursued by means of Dialectics, which are defined as 'the art of critical examination into the truth of an opinion'. The Neoplatonists were concerned with a restatement of Plato's rational ideas in the contemporary circumstance of Christianity's appearing to undermine the exercise of intellect and the principles of philosophical inquiry. In illustration of the pagan viewpoint we can refer to the emperor Julian 'the Apostate', whose protest to the Christians was, 'There is nothing in your philosophy beyond the one word, "Believe"!'[18]

PHILO OF ALEXANDRIA

From the 1st Century AD the Platonic mode of thought ran parallel with the development of Christian thinking, producing many points of contact. Nowhere was this encounter more apparent than in Alexandria, which had drawn from the 3rd century BC the greatest minds of the Hellenistic age. Clement 'of Alexandria' (c150–c215 AD), the inspired Christian thinker who perceived the deep spiritual unity between the Platonist philosophy and Christian scriptures, found in Alexandria the teacher he was seeking, after years of travelling.

Greek-speaking Hebrew culture also had its origins in Alexandria, the Jewish colony comprising perhaps a third of the total population. The *Septuagint* (the Greek translation of the Old Testament) was produced in Alexandria; and it is with the Judeo-Hellenistic movement and the work of Philo Judaeus or Philo of Alexandria (c30 BC–45 AD) that we find a new philosophy of religion, closely linked with Platonism, which anticipates the trend of Neoplatonist ideas.

Philo was a mystic who sought to unify the hidden wisdom of the Hebrew scriptures, principally the Torah, with Greek philosophical concepts.[19] Clement of Alexandria called him simply Philo the Pythagorean. He was a member of a wealthy Jewish family; his brother held the post of Alabarch in Alexandria, and made a gift of the gold and silver plates upon the doors of the temple at Jerusalem. Philo's most noted public exploit was to lead an embassy to the emperor Caligula in Rome, to protest against compulsory worship of the emperor's statue.

The Pythagorean and Platonic schools were well-established in Alexandria, and many Jews had long been aware of the parallels between Hellenistic philosophy, which they tended to regard as an early and unrecorded emanation of the *Torah*, and their own mystic doctrines. Others besides Philo had applied themselves to harmonising points of similarity, and there is reason to suppose the ministry of Jesus of Nazareth was an outcome of this Hellenising movement.[20] Philo's prolific writings are a valuable guide to the philosophical and mystical ideas in circulation in the 1st century AD. Whilst scornful of the public pagan rites associated with the Mysteries, he presents us with a fully developed *Logos* doctrine based on Greek sources, which is used allegorically to interpret the symbolism of the Hebrew scriptures.

NEOPLATONISM

Neoplatonism can be said to have originated in Alexandria through the school of a self-taught philosopher called Ammonius Saccas, whose name – if it is a personal epithet – may derive from his official occupation as a corn-porter at the docks. Ammonius died in 242 AD, having taught in Alexandria for over fifty years.[21] He is said to have apostasized from Christianity. Whatever the truth of this, his school received both pagans and Christians, and produced some formidable thinkers, including Plotinus, Longinus, and the church father Origen, whose own prolific writings on theology were conditioned by Stoic reasoning and Platonist ideas.

In Ammonius's teaching, God is perceived as being threefold in Essence, Intellect and Power, the two latter being the emanations of the Primal Unity. This outpouring of divine life manifests on different levels of reality, descending in an hierarchical fashion through the lesser god-forms and daemons who are all aspects of the One. The mass of humanity is limited to worshipping these god-forms, which are all they know. Plotinus presents a different perspective on 'polytheism', however, when he states: 'It is not by contracting the divine into One, but by showing it in the abundance in which God himself has shown it which is proper to those who know the power of God'.[22]

It had been a tenet of Pythagoras that not everything should be told to everybody. That Ammonius' teaching included a mystical or concealed element is clear from the fact that Plotinus, Herennius and Origen[23] are said to have made a pact of silence on the revelation of this aspect of the school. Plotinus only broke the agreement after Origen and Herennius had already done so.[24] That they found themselves unable to keep silence is almost certainly because the teaching of the philosophy in its full glory is not possible without the revelation of the experiential aspect associated with the Mysteries. This aspect, however, brings in a theurgic element, which is doubtless why the injunction to silence was agreed upon in the first place. The theurgic element remains within the Neoplatonist teachings from this time onwards, tending to grow more pronounced as the division between Christianity and paganism increased. There is no denying *gnosis*, and no way to arrive at *gnosis* by means of the human intellect alone. The intellect in isolation produces only opinion or belief, held to be the outcome of failure of memory of the Divine.

The greatest of the Neoplatonists was Plotinus, who was born at Lycopolis in Egypt in about 205 AD. Nothing is known of his family or early life, because Plotinus himself refused to talk about them on the grounds that the temporary housing of his soul was not worth going to the trouble to record. In his late twenties he went to Alexandria to study philosophy, but was dissatisfied with all his teachers until a friend recommended him to try Ammonius. He stayed with Ammonius for eleven years, until, at the age of 39, the desire to study the mystical systems of India and Persia induced him to join the expedition of the emperor Gordian against the Persians. Gordian was assassinated in February 244 AD, after which Plotinus escaped to Antioch, and thence to Rome.

It was in Rome that he established his school. He was never short of funds, and enjoyed the support of some influential friends, including the emperor Gallienus and his wife Salonina. He confined himself to teaching until, under pressure from his pupils Porphyry and Amelius of Tuscany, he began to write down his doctrines in the form of seminars held within his school. Porphyry records that he never read through or revised his work and that his handwriting was appalling. At his death in about 270 AD he left to Porphyry the task of editing his work, the result of which appeared some twenty-eight years later in the form of *The Enneads*. Of this work Porphyry himself writes, 'I had fifty-four treatises before me: I divided them into six sets of nine, which pleased me by the happy combination of the perfect number six with the nines'.[25]

Plotinus' concept of reality is of a hierarchy of causes, moving from the absolute unity of the First Cause to the multiplicity of the phenomenal world. Each succeeding sphere of being is an effect or expression of the sphere above it, by a reciprocal movement of outgoing and return. Thus, the sphere of Intellect, *Nous* or Mind, proceeds from the One. Soul proceeds from Intellect, and is itself the emanator of manifest existence, or Matter. Because the soul originates from the divine it is inherently immortal, and by contemplation of the principles from which it springs it bears within itself its own salvation.

Plotinus conceived of incarnation as an outcome of the soul's forgetfulness of its divine origins, this loss of memory originating in freedom and self will. He writes:

> Ignorance of their rank brings self-depreciation; they misplace their respect, honouring everything more than themselves; all their awe and admiration is for the alien, and, clinging to this, they have broken apart, as far as a soul may, and they make light of what they have deserted; their regard for the mundane and their disregard of themselves bring about their utter ignoring of the Divine.[26]

He goes on to tell us that pursuit of the external is a confession of inferiority, and that nothing counting itself less honourable and enduring than that which it admires could ever form a notion of either the nature or the power of God.

We see here a fundamental difference with the Christians, whom Porphyry was later to criticise in his work *Against the Christians*. The point of most concern to the Neoplatonists was that, whilst Jesus had directed men to contemplate the nature of the One High God, his followers, misinterpreting the meaning of the *Logos*, instructed men to worship Jesus himself instead of God.[27] The Christian viewpoint, that mere belief is enough to secure salvation, appeared to the Neoplatonists to be an undermining of spiritual evolution, for the sphere of Intellect, as they perceived it, may only be transcended by the *use* of intellect.

By placing the One or Good beyond both Intellect and Being, however, Plotinus achieved a radical advance upon his fellow Platonists. By the end of the 2nd century AD the Supreme Principal had come to be regarded as distinct from the Creator of the Cosmos (a derivative aspect of it), whilst remaining identical with Intellect and Being in an act entirely self-contemplative. By this definition the Divine Mind/ Being is distinct and self-aware, and as such exists at the summit of a hierarchy, being attainable through the exercise of intellect alone.

Plotinus' One, in contrast, is beyond self-awareness, being infinite, transcendent and without limitations. Having no distinct nature, it is not merely immanent in the All, but *is* the All; with the consequence that every creature can attain to union with the One according to the resources of its own kind.[28] The path of Intellect is the way appropriate to Man. Speaking as the Cosmos, however, Plotinus writes:

> ... all that is within me strives towards the Good; and each, to the measure of its faculty, attains. For from that Good all the heavens depend, with all my own Soul and the Gods that dwell in my every part, and all that lives and grows, and even all in me that you may judge inanimate.[29]

Plotinus was succeeded as director of his school by his pupil Porphyry, born in Tyre, the capital of Phoenicia, in about 233 AD. In his early twenties, Porphyry went to Athens to study with the rhetorician and philosopher Longinus, who had been a pupil of Ammonius in Alexandria. To Longinus, Porphyry owed the name by which we know him. His proper name was Malchus, or Melech ('the King'), and Longinus suggested Porphyry – meaning purple – as a reference to both his name and his origins at Tyre.

The ideas of the Neoplatonists were too speculative for Longinus, who preferred to confine himself to straight Platonic doctrines. He is described by Eunapius as a 'living library and a walking museum', although Plotinus considered him more of a philologer than a philosopher. It was only to be expected that during his time with Longinus Porphyry was mainly concerned with literary criticism and rhetorical perfection. It was in Athens that he published his first work, the *Homeric Questions*. Porphyry was temperamentally attuned to the synthesis of philosophy and mysticism, however, and at the age of thirty he went to Rome to join Plotinus. He is known to have produced at least seventy-five works, of which many have been lost or destroyed. His work, *Against the Christians* was mainly concerned with criticism of the *Gospels* and the *Book of Daniel*. He pointed out correctly that the latter was a late forgery, the events referred to in the prophecies within it, which the Christians often used to justify their beliefs, having happened before the book was written.[30] The subject matter of his surviving works includes lives of Pythagoras and Plotinus, works on harmonics, theurgy and vegetarianism, and on methods of approach to the realm of Mind. His commentary on the *Cave of the Nymphs* demonstrates that the strange cave referred to by Homer in the *Odyssey* is in fact an allegory of incarnation and ascent back towards the Soul.[31]

Porphyry died in about 305 AD. He was succeeded in the line of Neoplatonist succession by his pupil, Iamblichus of Chalchis in Syria (c260-330 AD), a prolific writer, praised by Julian as 'posterior in time but not in genius to Plato'. Most of Iamblichus' writings have been lost or are preserved only in fragments, but the *Life of Pythagoras* survives,

along with other works including the *Exhortation to Philosophy*, an introduction to the works of Plato in which he contrives to attract pupils to
the cause of philosophy – and presumably away from Christ.[32]

By Iamblichus, the days of intellectual toleration, which had been
well-exemplified in Alexandria, were over. Whereas, in the early days,
Christian scholars like Clement of Alexandria and Origen could
attempt a synthesis of mysticism, philosophy and Christian doctrines in
an open and inquiring manner, we find in Iamblichus a move towards
the dualism which was increasingly a characteristic of the period. The
material world is 'evil' in comparison to spiritual 'good', and whilst
Iamblichus never departs from the central tenets of the Neoplatonist
philosophy we are aware of a narrowing of vision.

The last of the great Neoplatonists was the most mystical of the
school. Proclus came from Xanthus in Lycia, although we are told by
his biographer, Marinus of Samaria, that he was born at Constantinople in 410 AD and died in 485 AD. Proclus was regarded as the
genuine successor to the genius of Plato. He held the official title of
Diadochus or 'the Successor', and was celebrated as a mathematician,
astronomer and poet. As a child, he was sent to study law and rhetoric
in Alexandria, intending to follow the profession of his father, but
abandoned law in favour of philosophy, and became a pupil of Olympiodorus. He was still under twenty when he moved to Athens to
continue his studies, later succeeding Syrianus as head of the Platonic
Academy, which was then leaning towards the mystical theology. These
teachings, which were viewed as heathen, gave Proclus some trouble
with the Christian authorities, and he withdrew to spend a year in Asia
Minor. On his return he was more cautious about the teaching of the
secret doctrines and imparted them henceforth only to his confidential
pupils.

Whilst in Asia Minor, Proclus applied himself to a study of the *Chaldean Oracles*, which are closely associated with Orphism, and wrote a
learned commentary upon them, fragments of which survive.[33] He was
passionately attached to the *Oracles*, and is said to have been initiated
into the Mysteries by Asclepigeneia, the daughter of his old teacher
Plutarchus, who had received them from Nestorius. Proclus wrote
works on the coincidence of the doctrines of Orpheus, Pythagoras and
Plato, and attempted to combine the logical method of Aristotle with
the mysticism of the Neoplatonists. He enlarged upon Plotinus' thesis,
that ascent to the Divine is not a solely rational process, as every creation of the Monad participates in it, whether gifted with reason or not.

The extant works of Proclus include commentaries on works of Plato,
including the *Timaeus*, which he completed by his twenty-eighth year.
His *Institutio Theologica* sets out an account of Neoplatonism together
with his own modifications. Besides astronomical and mathematical

writings, a paraphrase of Ptolemy's *Tetrabiblus*, a commentary on Euclid's *Elements* and a treatise on the effect of eclipses, he wrote seven hymns to various of the gods. Proclus is precise on the subject of emanation, and lays out his concepts in the form of triads in keeping with the schema of the Mysteries. Evil does not originate with God, any more than it derives from the daemons or with matter. The Good has one definite, eternal Cause, which is the Monad. The causes of evil, by contrast, are manifold and indefinite. It has not an original but only a derivative existence, and represents some privation of the Good. We would say today that evil emanates from Fear.

Proclus was one of the last heads of the Platonic Academy. The teaching of pagan philosophy was outlawed by Justinian in 529 AD, in the wake of discord between the exponents of philosophy and the Church. Whilst Neoplatonism never came close to providing a popular alternative to Christianity, it did provide a constant fount of opposition to the new religion, the more so as those in authority within the church became increasingly ambitious and less concerned with studying the Mysteries within their own doctrines. Thus we have the tragic fate of the Neoplatonist Hypatia, daughter of Theon, a philosopher and mathematician torn to pieces by a Christian mob in Alexandria, under the influence of the power-loving bishop Cyril, resentful of her influence and teaching.[34]

Although the schools were suppressed, an extensive body of the literature survived, to reappear in Europe at various periods of renaissance, not without, in many cases, ecclesiastical reprisal. A Latin translation of the *Enneads* of Plotinus was produced by Marsilio Ficino in Florence in 1492 AD, although Ficino's contemporary Pico della Mirandola (1463–94) was forced to make a formal apology to the Church in 1487 for the attempt, in his 72 *Conclusions*, to confirm Christianity by means of Hebrew wisdom.[35] The source material for the *Conclusions* includes Neoplatonic texts, the *Orphic Hymns* and *Chaldean Oracles*, as well as the Hellenic-Egyptian *Logos* teachings known as the *Corpus Hermeticum*,[36] and the Jewish Cabala.

THE CABALA

Whilst the *Corpus Hermeticum* was to become the foundation of the study of mystical alchemy from the Middle Ages onwards, the Cabala provides the framework for the systematising of the many correspondences – planetary, angelic, elemental, etc. – with which the discipline abounds. It was Pico's opinion that the magical aspect of the Mysteries must always be associated with Cabala to be both powerful and safe.[37] The glyph of the Cabala is known as the *Tree of Life*. It has been described as the 'mighty, all-embracing glyph of the soul of man and of the universe'.[38] In this form it was first written down in the 13th century AD, although the hidden wisdom underlies the earliest scriptures of the Jews. New concepts were absorbed from Babylonian, Persian and Greek sources during the exile of the Jews in Babylon in the 6th century BC, although it is likely that the teaching shares a common origin with other Mystery traditions by way of Zoroastrianism. Being a Hellenising diagram, the *Tree of Life* almost certainly expresses in its oral form that same hidden wisdom to which Philo and the Jews of his time applied themselves. Thus, the form it takes today may owe much to its passage through the schools of Alexandria.

The Cabala has survived intact for two reasons: firstly, that being the mystical tradition underlying the Hebrew scriptures it was not subject to Christian manipulation; secondly, it remained an oral tradition until the 13th century AD. For at least two centuries before this, however, schools of Cabala had been established in Europe. In the 13th century, changes in the teaching came about as a result of conflict between religion and philosophy – revelation versus reason, the exact dispute of ancient times – in the Judeo-Arab world. A group of mystics in Gerona in Spain, believing that the Cabala might serve as a medium of reconciliation, pursued this conviction by publishing a Neoplatonic system based upon the secret doctrines of Isaac the Blind, a Cabalist of the French School. Notwithstanding Isaac's disapproval, the product of their labours, the *Book of the Zohar*, was compiled by Moses of Leon. It became a best seller and spread out to influence many European non-Jews.[39]

The Tree of Life is an elegant system, simple but of infinite complexity. It is comprised of ten emanations, or *states of being*, descending from the Source to the level of manifest existence by way of a triadic structure. Each emanation exists in four worlds, or *modes of consciousness* – archetypal, creative, formative and active – from which arises the tradition that there are four ways of viewing a religion: mystically, philosophically, allegorically or literally. The twenty-two paths between them are *experiential journeys*, again in the four modes.

Revelation of the Cabala depends much upon the mystical levels of the Hebrew alphabet and language, but so universal is the glyph that it serves as a key to unlock virtually any religious system. To the emanations are allotted the mundane correspondence of god-names and archangels, equating each to the appropriate state of being; thus the *Solar Logos* is perceived as the central emanation, likened to the Sun. The Source is held to emanate from the Three Veils of Negative Existence, just as in the Orphic Mysteries it is said to derive from the Thrice Unknown Darkness. The Cabala can be both 'known about' and 'known': that is, it can be made the subject of intellectual inquiry or meditated on in pursuit of *gnosis*. The search for Knowledge is a central motivation of the Cabala, which by way of Understanding leads to Wisdom: Plato's attribute of the Divine.

THE MYSTICAL PHILOSOPHY IN EUROPE

The survival of the mystical philosophy in Europe followed two distinct channels of dissemination. That exemplified by the Cabala and Corpus Hermeticum had its flowering towards the period of the Renaissance; but from as early as the 9th century AD the work of a Christian writer deeply influenced by the Neoplatonists was having a profound effect upon the mysticism of the Middle Ages.

Dionysius the Areopagite, a pseudonym adopted in honour of a convert of St. Paul (Acts 17:34), was one of a number of Syrians studying in Athens at the end of the 5th century AD, and a follower of Proclus. The work of Dionysius is dependent both upon the Platonic tradition and the Alexandrian and Cappadocian Fathers, revealing the influence of Proclus and, beyond him, Plotinus, in a mysticism fundamental to Neoplatonism. The corpus of his surviving works include the brief *Mystical Theology* in five books, the *Divine Names*, examining the epithets and concepts attributed to God, and the *Celestial Hierarchy*, dealing with the categories of angel mentioned in the Old Testament and by St. Paùl.[40] Many Christian writers had been influenced by the Neoplatonist tradition, including St. Augustine, but Dionysius was the first to attempt an accurate description of the mystical consciousness and its ecstatic rise to God.

The Greek texts of Dionysius were translated into Latin in the period leading up to 862S.C. AD by John Scotus Eriugena (c810–877), an Irish scholar living at the court of Charles the Bald of France.[41] Thereafter they were to provide, from the 9th to the 17th centuries, inspiration and nourishment to contemplatives throughout Western Europe, who found in them an explanation of their most sublime experience. The influence of Dionysius is apparent particularly in the 14th century, in England with such works as the *Cloud of Unknowing* and, possibly by the same unknown author, *Dionise Hid Divinite*, an English translation of the *Mystical Theology*; whilst in Europe his influence is found, among others, in the works of Thomas Aquinas, John Ruysbroeck and Meister Eckhart.[42]

The line of descent of the Cabala and *Corpus Hermeticum* is clearly recorded from the medieval period onwards. The Hermetic literature in particular owes much to the efforts of the 11th century Byzantine scholar Michael Psellus, who in the face of criticism from the Orthodox church collected and codified the textual material, together with the

Chaldean Oracles and works of Plato and the Neoplatonists: an achievement which was later to fuel the Renaissance.

There is some reason to suppose the Order of the Knights Templar (1118–1314) was acquainted with the Cabala, a fact suggested by certain unofficial aspects of the Rule, such as a reverence for God the Father above the person of Jesus Christ.[43] The name of the alleged idol 'Baphomet', which the Templars were accused of worshipping, has been shown to derive from an Arabic word, *Abufihimat*, meaning 'Father (Source) of Wisdom' or 'Father of Understanding', both of which terms, whilst derived from Sufi mysticism, are titles of the Supernal Sephiroth upon the Tree of Life.[44] Contemporaneous with the Order of the Temple, the Catalan philosopher Ramon Lull (c1232–1316) used Cabalistic methods in his postulation of a system, known as the *Ars Raymundi*, derived from the elemental categories of Aristotle, whereby principles held in common by Christianity, Judaism and Islam might be used to reconcile all three, scientifically, philosophically and mystically.[45]

The emergence of the Cabala into the gentile world was accelerated by the fall of Byzantium in 1453, with the subsequent dispersal into Europe of a large corpus of textual material, including the Hermetic and Platonic works codified by Psellus in the 11th century. Much of this material, through the translations of Marsilio Ficino, who was employed by Cosimo de Medici to undertake this task, came to form the core of Florentine Neoplatonism, into which Pico introduced the Cabala. Pico's contention, that the Tetragrammaton, IHVH, the Holy Name of God, becomes the name of Jesus (IHSHVH, or Ieheshuah) with the addition of the single extra letter *Shin*, thus proving the rightful name of the Messiah, established Christian Cabala as a respected discipline quite separate from Jewish Cabala. Hermetic-Cabalist Neoplatonism thus became viable as a religious philosophy.[46]

In 1492 the expulsion of the Jews from Spain pushed the process of dissemination even further. In Venice, the Franciscan monk Francesco Giorgi (1466–1540), who had access to a wider range of Hebrew literature than the Florentines, taught a Cabalist theology which was unequivocally Christian, yet rested squarely on micro-macrocosmic principles. Giorgi perceived the All as proceeding from the One by way of the four-fold medium of arithmetic, geometry, harmony and music, and sought to incorporate these principles in architecture as well as through the written word.[47]

Important as was the influence of the Italian philosophers, it was through the Reformation that the Hermetic-Cabalist tradition was to become established. The German philosopher Johannes Reuchlin (1455–1522), sought to allay fears of theurgy in Neoplatonism by reference to the wonder-working powers of the Hebrew language, and to

Cabala's stress on holy forces, angels and the sacred names of God. His work, *De Arte Cabalistica* (1517), which is couched as a conversation between three men of differing persuasions, is the first full treatise on the Cabala by a non-Jew.[48] More completely of the Reformation, the Erasmian evangelist Cornelius Agrippa (1486–1535), established the Hermetic-Cabalist tradition as an occult philosophy complete with a full range of correspondences, combining in his great compendium *De Occulta Philosophia* the natural magic of Ficino with the Cabala of Pico. Like Pico, Agrippa held the Cabala to be a fail-safe means of study and stressed the power of the Tetragrammaton.[49]

The thread of the Neoplatonist tradition runs from the Middle Ages to the 17th century, with a reawakening in the 18th century in the work of the Platonist William Law, and the translations and commentaries of Thomas Taylor. In the later 16th century the former Dominican, Giordano Bruno, who was much influenced by Agrippa and the *Ars Raymundi* of Lull, travelled Europe as a missionary to the Hermetic-Cabalist philosophy. He arrived in England in 1583, where, over a period of a year, he expounded his philosophy to English gentlemen and intellectuals at sessions such as the 'Ash Wednesday Supper', held at the house of the poet Fulke Greville.[50] His two chief works on ethics, the *Spaccio* and *Heroici Furore* were dedicated to Sir Philip Sydney.

Both John Dee (1527–1608) and Edmund Spenser (c1552–1599) were Christian Cabalists and Neoplatonists, both drawn in particular towards the Neopythagorean aspects of harmony and number. Spenser was a Puritan, and the Red Cross Knight of his great work, *The Faerie Queen* can be understood as an embodiment of occult Protestantism. That this idea was generally accepted emerges in the *Rosicrucian Manifestos* of 1614–15, two tracts published in Germany purporting to describe the founding, by one Christian Rosenkreutz, or 'Rosy Cross', of a medieval order or fraternity which others are now invited to join. The Manifestos were followed in 1616 by the allegorical work, *The Chymical Wedding of Christian Rosenkreutz*, written by one Johann Valentin Andrea, a Lutheran pastor with Calvinist sympathies, who was one of the authors of the Manifestos. This work, like the Manifestos, is influenced by Giorgi and Agrippa, and by the *Monas Hieroglyphica* of John Dee, emphasising as it does the combination of Cabala, alchemy and mathematics.

Dee had been active in Germany in 1586, as an agent of Elizabeth I of England, in the founding of an esoteric Protestant 'league of defence' known as the 'Confederatio Militiae Evangelica' to counter the French Catholic league, the purpose of which was to prevent the accession of the Protestant king of Navarre.[51] The *Manifestos* used as a figurehead the Protestant Elector Palatine and his English wife Elizabeth Stuart, later to become the Winter King and Queen of

Bohemia, and attracted a sensational degree of interest when they appeared. From these beginnings may be traced the history of the modern Rosicrucian and Masonic orders and their various offshoots.

We can thus point to a line of succession from Pythagoras and the Mystery schools of the first millennium BC, through the Neoplatonist philosophy and the Hermetic-Cabalist tradition to the present day. The highest principle of Platonist philosophy was the exercise of intellect leading to *gnosis*, and thus to wisdom, and the obfuscations of the 'secret arts' are all revealed if we bear this principle in mind. The many aspects of the mystical philosophy are complex, but can be seen to be related to that same quest for truth debated earnestly and openly in Athens and the schools of Alexandria.

NOTES

1. As found, for instance, in the work of Philo of Alexandria. See: E.R. Good-enough, *An Introduction to Philo Judaeus* (New Haven: Yale University Press, 1940), 11–12.
2. David Fideler (ed.), *Alexandria: Journal of the Western Cosmological Traditions* (Grand Rapids: Phanes Press, 1993), vol 2, 7–15.
3. Michael Hornum, 'The Availability of the One: An Interpretative Essay', in *Alexandria: Journal of the Western Cosmological Traditions* (Grand Rapids: Phanes Press, 1993), vol.2, 275–285.
4. G.R.S. Mead, *Orpheus* (London: 1896; London: J.M. Watkins, 1965), 21.
5. Thomas Taylor, *The Hymns of Orpheus* (1792; Los Angeles: The Philosophical Research Society, 1981); R.C. Hogart, *The Hymns of Orpheus* (Grand Rapids: Phanes Press, 1993).
6. Ficino, 'De Immort. Anim., XVII.i.386', in Mead, *op. cit.*, 15.
7. Mead, *op. cit.*, 20.
8. David Fideler, *Jesus Christ, Sun of God* (Wheaton, IL: The Theosophical Publishing House, 1993), 268, 372.
9. Bentley Layton, *The Gnostic Scriptures* (London: SCM Press, 1987), 15–16.
10. Steven Runciman, *The Medieval Manichee* (Cambridge: Cambridge University Press, 1969).
11. Fideler, *Jesus Christ, Sun of God* (Wheaton, IL: The Theosophical Publishing House, 1993), 232–233.
12. Plotinus, *The Enneads*, tr. Stephen MacKenna (Harmondsworth: Penguin Books, 1991), Ennead V.3.xvii.
13. Fideler, *Jesus Christ, Sun of God* (Wheaton, IL: The Theosophical Publishing House, 1993), 87.
14. Fideler, *Jesus Christ, Sun of God* (Wheaton, IL: The Theosophical Publishing House, 1993), 60.
15. Mead, *op. cit.*, 94.
16. Philo of Alexandria, *On Husbandry* 13.51 and *The Confusion of Tongues* 14.63. in the Loeb Classical Library (Cambridge, Mass: Harvard University Press, 1929–1962) vols. III and IV.
17. Fideler, *Jesus Christ, Sun of God* (Wheaton, IL: The Theosophical Publishing House, 1993), 177.
18. Fideler, in *Porphyry's Letter to his Wife Marcella*, tr. Alice Zimmern (London: George Redway 1896; Grand Rapids: Phanes Press, 1986), 17.

19. E.R. Goodenough, *An Introduction to Philo Judaeus* (New Haven: Yale University Press, 1940).
20. In relation to the Jewish/Hellenic controversy, see: Martin Hengel, *Judaism and Hellenism*, tr. John Bowden (London: SCM Press, 1974), vol. 1, 2ff, 309, 312–313; E.R. Goodenough, *op. cit.*, x-xi.
21. S. Lilla, 'Ammonius Saccas', in *Encyclopedia of the Early Church* (London: James Clarke, 1992), 31–32; *Dictionary of Greek and Roman Biography and Myth* (London: W. Smith, 1850).
22. Plotinus, 'The Enneads', II.9.9. 35–36; tr. Fideler, in *Porphyry's Letter to his Wife Marcella*, tr. Alice Zimmern (London: George Redway, 1896; Grand Rapids: Phanes Press, 1986), 14.
23. Considered to be a Neoplatonist distinct from the Christian Origen, also a pupil of Ammonius. See: S. Lilla, 'Origen the Neoplatonist', in *Encyclopedia of the Early Church* (London: James Clarke, 1992), 624.
24. Porphyry, 'On the Life of Plotinus and his Work', in *The Enneads*, tr. Stephen MacKenna (Harmondsworth: Penguin Books, 1991), civ.
25. Porphyry, *ibid.*, cxxiii.
26. Plotinus, *The Enneads*, tr. Stephen MacKenna (Harmondsworth: Penguin Books, 1991), Ennead V.1.i.
27. Fideler, in *Porphyry's Letter to his Wife Marcella*, tr. Alice Zimmern (London: George Redway, 1896; Grand Rapids: Phanes Press, 1986), 15.
28. Michael Hornum, 'The Availability of the One: An Interpretative Essay', in *Alexandria: Journal of the Western Cosmological Traditions* (Grand Rapids: Phanes Press, 1993), vol.2, 275–285.
29. Plotinus, *The Enneads*. Tr. Stephen MacKenna (Harmondsworth: Penguin Books, 1991), Ennead III.2.3.
30. Fideler, in *Porphyry's Letter to his Wife Marcella*, tr. Alice Zimmern (London: George Redway, 1896; Grand Rapids: Phanes Press, 1986), 13–14.
31. Porphyry, *On the Cave of the Nymphs*, tr. Thomas Taylor (Grand Rapids: Phanes Press, 1991).
32. Iamblichus, *The Exhortation to Philosophy*, tr. Thomas M. Johnson (Grand Rapids: Phanes Press, 1988).
33. Proclus, 'Commentary on the Chaldean Oracles', in *The Chaldean Oracles* (Godalming, Surrey: The Shrine of Wisdom, 1979).
34. R.T. Wallis, *Neoplatonism* (London: Gerald Duckworth and Co., 1972); Nancy Nietupski, 'Hypatia of Alexandria: Mathematitian, Astronomer and Philosopher', in *Alexandria, Journal of the Western Cosmological Traditions* (Grand Rapids: Phanes Press, 1993), vol. 2, 45–56.
35. Frances Yates, *Occult Philosophy in the Elizabethan Age* (London: Routledge and Kegan Paul, 1979), 18.
36. G.R.S. Mead, *Thrice-Greatest Hermes* (London: 1906; York Beach: Samuel Weiser, 1992); David Fideler, *Jesus Christ, Sun of God* (Wheaton, IL: The Theosophical Publishing House, 1993), 47–49 and 226–233; Brian P. Copenhaver, *Hermetica* (Cambridge: Cambridge University Press, 1992).
37. F. Yates, *op. cit.*, 24.
38. Dion Fortune, *The Mystical Qabalah*. (London: 1935; York Beach: Samuel Weiser, 1993), 17.
39. Z'ev Ben Shimon Halevi, *Kabbalah, The Divine Plan* (San Francisco: Harper, 1996), 14–19.
40. S. Lilla, 'Pseudo-Dionysius the Areopagite', in *Encyclopedia of the Early Church* (London: James Clarke & Co., 1992), 238–240.

41. Jean Leclercq, in *Pseudo-Dionysius: The Complete Works*, tr. Colm Luibheid (New York: Paulist Press, 1987), 26.
42. Jean Leclercq, *ibid.*, 30.
43. Patricia Cannon Johnson, 'The Knights Templar', in *The Perspective Objective* (OMCE electronic magazine: http://omce.org., 1997), vol.2, no.5.
44. Idries Shah, *The Sufis* (London: Octagon Press, 1964), 225–227.
45. Frances Yates, *Occult Philosophy in the Elizabethan Age* (London: Routledge and Kegan Paul, 1979), 9–15.
46. F. Yates, *ibid.*, 29.
47. F. Yates, *ibid.*, 29–36.
48. F. Yates, *ibid.*, 23–27.
49. F. Yates, *ibid.*, 37–47.
50. Frances Yates, *Giordano Bruno and the Hermetic Tradition* (London: Routledge and Kegan Paul, 1971), 254; A. D. Wraight and V. F. Stern, *In Search of Christopher Marlowe* (London: Macdonald and Co., 1965), 164–174.
51. Frances Yates, *The Rosicrucian Enlightenment* (London: Routledge and Kegan Paul, 1972), 34–35

Chapter 9

Alexandria and its Medieval Legacy: The Book, the Monk and the Rose

J. O. Ward

INTRODUCTION

In this paper, I look at the significance for medieval Europe of the disappearance of the Alexandrian library and its holdings, in the context of the disappearance of the fabric of ancient learning generally. What had survived of this fabric by Carolingian times, and how might this have differed had the Alexandrian library not been destroyed? There was only one 'medieval library' that approached the Alexandrian library in nature and scope, and that forms the subject of Umberto Eco's *Name of the Rose*. Yet this Library never existed, and its description is fundamentally different from any medieval libraries for which we have evidence. It is intriguing to consider the scope and function of the medieval library, and to ask why Eco should have chosen to invent a medieval library that was more like the Alexandrian library in size and scope, than it was like the actual libraries in the period it pretended to portray.

Let me start with a celebrated edifice which ou might imagine to be the monastery in which the events of the year 1327, so intriguingly chronicled by Umberto Eco in the *Name of the Rose*, took place. You would, in fact, be wrong, for the monastery in question is the 'Sac[g]ra di San Michele', or Sant' Ambrogio, built in 998 AD. by Hugh de Montboissier (from Auvergne) above the Dora Riparia valley and the town of Condove, 23 miles west of Turin, in Piedmont,[1] *not* the monastery used to film the *Name of the Rose* (which you can pick out from the acknowledgements at the end of the film)! Both the 'Sagra di San Michele' and Eco's monastery, however, are at least in the same broad mountainous region of this part of Europe.[2] Such a location is an odd kind of place to build a large and important library (Eco describes the library in *his* monastery as 'the greatest library in Christendom').[3] However, there it is – or rather, was, and that is where I begin this paper.

1. ECO'S MONASTIC LIBRARY OF 1327 AD

Umberto Eco is a renowned medievalist, and his *Name of the Rose* – perhaps the finest work of historical scholarship on its subject – is a classic account of a moment of great crisis in European affairs (the putative time of the novel is 1327 AD). All aspects of the novel have been carefully crafted to conform to the medieval social, mental and religious world as we know it from countless documents.[4] Why then, should not his library have been portrayed pretty much as we find in documents?[5] Being a literal sort of academic, I became interested in Eco's library because my research concerns the contents of medieval libraries, and also, perhaps, because many of the libraries I know seem to go back in one way or another to the Middle Ages, or else to derive important features of their design from medieval conditions (such as the poor lighting)!

We should not be surprised to find an important library in Eco's monastery, and I would like to refresh your memory of it. As Benno, the rhetoric scholar from Uppsala says in the novel, 'we (monks) live for books'.[6] It is, of course, quickly apparent that there is something fishy about Eco's library. For a start, it is located on the top floor of a building called an *aedificium*, which had been 'in centuries past ... a fortress',[7] above the scriptorium and, below that, the kitchen. In classical Latin, the term *aedificium* is a neutral word. It just means 'a building'. In fact, in the Italian original of the *Name of the Rose*, the word used is 'edificio' – the normal Italian word for 'building'. Secondly, the library is reached, when the doors are shut, which is abnormally often, through the kitchen on the ground floor of the *aedificium*, via a secret passage from the *ossarium*, which is itself entered from the third altar on the left from the transept of the church proper.[8] When our heroes (Adso and William of Baskerville) finally discover themselves in the library, we learn that it is not a straightforward sort of building.[9] It is large enough to be wandered through for almost an hour, large and complicated enough to get thoroughly lost in. After much wandering and deductive calculation, our heroes work out that the library, in fact, contains fifty-six rooms, four of them heptagonal, each with three blank walls containing huge book cases, and fifty-two of them quadrilateral, squarish or quasi trapezoidal, each with two blind walls covered with book cases. Twenty-four of the rooms are located in the four great towers of the *aedificium*.[10]

How many books might such a library have contained? Let us assume that the heptagonal rooms held three walls each of, say, 800 books per wall (eight shelves with, say, 100 books each),[11] a modest enough estimate, and supported by what we read in the novel. That makes 2,400 per room and 9,600 for all the heptagonal rooms, say

9,000 to make a round figure. Let us also assume that the squarish rooms contained 1,600 books each (two walls, each with 800 books), say 1,500 for round figures. This means an estimated grand total for the squarish *and* the heptagonal rooms of around 87,000 books.

You can scour the *Name of the Rose* to test this figure, but I will round it down to 85,000 and assume that is about the number of books Eco wished us to assume was in the library of his particular monastery. It seems to fit the library's great reputation, its long history and its endless classified contents to which the book often refers. How does this number stack up with so-called 'real' book numbers in real libraries in antiquity and the middle ages?

Almost all the libraries of antiquity were destroyed by neglect, fire or war, we are told, and that takes into account some 26 or 28 public libraries in Rome alone. The celebrated library of Alexandria, founded by Ptolemy I in c300 BC and the subject of the present book, contained, according to varying estimates, between 70,000 and 700,000 scrolls, perhaps, to accept the figure accepted by Reynolds and Wilson,[12] between 200,000 and 490,000 in the third century BC. Now a scroll is not as big as a book. In fact, a scroll would have contained more our idea of a chapter; perhaps as much as a Ciceronian speech. The codex, or book, which superseded the scroll between the 2nd and the 4th centuries AD would, at maximum, have contained twenty to thirty times the contents of a scroll. The medieval books we scholars inspect today in European libraries are not, of course, what circulated during the Middle Ages. It has been established that the circulating medium was more the booklet, perhaps not much bigger than a scroll or two. For conservation and storage purposes, booklets were bound together into the volumes we use today, usually in medieval times, but often in later times. Eco does not tell us what the books in his library were like, but we suspect that they tended to be individual treatises rather than large bound volumes. This means that we should probably only increase the figure of 85,000 books a little to give the equivalent of a scroll collection.

Let us assume that Eco's library contained about 100,000–200,000 scroll-equivalent volumes. This makes it rather on the small size when compared with what we think we know of the great library at Alexandria. Perhaps more the size of the Library of Pergamum, founded by Eumenes II, c160 BC, which seems to have had around 200,000 scrolls by Antony and Cleopatra's time.[13] Or perhaps a little under the size of the Imperial Library at Constantinople, founded in 354 AD and apparently containing around 120,000 volumes under Emperor Basiliscus (475–76 AD) before it was destroyed by fire.[14]

At this stage, are we wrong to take Eco's library presentation seriously? He was after all, the man who advised would-be holiday-makers to take for light reading over tedious beach days, the whole of Migne's

Latin *Patrology*, some 218 volumes, in Latin, each with about 2,000 columns, two per page, each column with up to 60 lines apiece. He was also the wit who wrote a short essay about people who came into his own house, stacked wall to wall, room after room, with books,[15] like the houses of most serious academics in the humanities. When asked the usual question 'My, what a lot of books, have you read them all?' Eco tells us he had two standard replies: 'oh yes, several times over, and more besides'; or 'well, these are the ones I have to read by the end of the month – the rest I keep in my office at work'.[16] In yet another essay, written around the time of the publication of the *Name of the Rose*, Eco fantasised about a library with 3,335 rooms, at least one of which had 33,335 walls, at least one of which had 33,335 bookshelves, at least one of which was capable of holding 33,335 books.[17] Can such a man be taken seriously on the subject of libraries? Let us see.

The first problem is this. If there were 85,000 books in a monastic library of around the year 1327, who would have written them? Were they all medieval creations, or did many of them come from antiquity? We must surely imagine the former. After all, medieval scholars such as the Venerable Bede wrote some 300 works,[18] and modern scholars tell us that, despite the antiquarianism of the 2nd century AD, very little of the literature of antiquity survived into the Middle ages. If, as we are told, all the major libraries of antiquity had disappeared by c600 AD., how *could* anything have survived into the middle Ages? According to Reynolds and Wilson, however, around 500 AD 'the bulk of Latin literature was still extant'.[19] This cannot be true. Many factors argue against it. The shift from scroll to codex must have meant the loss of many treatises that were not thought worthy of the effort of transcription, particularly as tastes were rapidly shifting in the sea-change from pagan to Christian cultural patterns, and because of the general impoverishment of education and learning in the later Roman Empire, which put a premium on the abridgment, the encyclopedic rather than large libraries of individual monographs. We must imagine something like the shift from print to the Internet today, with print being represented by scrolls and the Internet representing the new wave, the codex. If some of our more advanced and fashionable librarians today had their way, what was generally useful would be put on the Internet, and everything else – including 90% of what we set our students and read for our research in the humanities – would be junked.

Besides, tastes and fashions were always changing and outmoding yesterday's classics, even in antiquity. A reading of Tacitus' fragmentary *Dialogue on Orators* makes clear that many of the oratorical speeches of his own and Cicero's day, extant at the time in scroll collections, were no longer being read. From those two centuries we have only fifty-eight of Cicero's 106 speeches, and one panegyric of Pliny. That is all. Masses of scrolls must never have survived even into the time of an Antonines. And how much else of classical Roman literature is not with us today? Here is an off the top of my head list: Varro's *Menippean Satires*, his *Dialogues*, the forty-two books of *Antiquities*, most of his *De lingua latina*, all his *De novem disciplinis* (a celebrated encyclopedia); numerous books of Livy's *Roman History* (the so-called 'lost decades'); most of Cornelius Nepos' *De viris illustribus*, all his *Chronica* and *Exempla*; much of Tacitus' *Annals* and *Histories*; thirteen of the thirty-one books of Ammianus Marcellinus' *History*, and almost *all* of early Roman literature. I could go on, but take the celebrated Suetonius for a close-up example. We have his biographies of the Caesars, and fragments of his *Illustrious Writers,* but his other fourteen books have disappeared. These included fascinating titles like *The Lives of the Famous Whores, The Physical Defects of Mankind, Roman Festivals,* and *Greek Games.*[20] Were these titles in Eco's library we may ask? Were they, for that matter, even in the Alexandrian library?

2. ANCIENT LIBRARIES AND THE MIDDLE AGES

I suspect that the answer to the last question is 'no'. The Alexandrian Library was principally a Greek language institution, though books in other languages were stored there, and, where possible, translated into Greek. By the time that Latin literature became established, however, I suspect that the library's capacity to locate and copy non-Greek works must have been severely reduced. It is difficult to ascertain how much Latin literature lay on its shelves at the time of its destruction. In all likelihood, its fate had little to do with the survival of Latin literature, though its holdings in Greek literature must have been immense, and the consequent losses profound – all, for example, of the 3,000 to 4,000 works of the scholar Didymus (80 10 BC) of the Alexandrian 'School' attached to the Library itself.[21]

The disasters of late antiquity had the general effect of rendering ancient literature a manageable corpus again. Had it all survived, our own libraries would have long since burst–as they will do in the near future unless some similar catastrophe wipes out most of our extant holdings (or puts them onto the Internet!). Not only did the destruction of late antiquity reduce ancient literature to a small and manageable corpus, but it improved its overall quality as only canonised school classics, in the main, survived.

Nevertheless, we should not assume that the survival of even the best items was an easy matter. During the low ebb of the Dark Ages, say 550–750 AD, books almost ceased to be copied, meaning that even such literature as had survived the late antique disasters was at risk of disappearing. Books that in a manuscript culture were not read and copied by each generation had a dim future indeed. As Reynolds and Wilson emphasise, we owe a vast debt to the primarily monastic copying of the Irish, English and Carolingian scribes, who, by the end of the Carolingian period (say c900 AD) had preserved basically what classical Latin literature is in our own libraries today. Many texts hung by a single thread, however, and would require good luck in the centuries to follow. Some, such as Varro's *Encyclopedia*, did not make it, and a very few texts not available to the Carolingians have come down to us today, largely in the form of papyrus fragments from the dry sands of Egypt.

In sum, a very small corpus of antique works must have survived to join the massive production of patristic, biblical, liturgical and other Christian writings that formed the bulk of the average medieval library. Very few indeed of Eco's 85,000 books would have been antique, or even copies of antique books, despite the impression we may gain from what his characters find and leaf through in the library on the top floor of the *aedificium*. Is it likely that the library of Eco's monastery had secured and kept, therefore, such a vast collection of primarily medieval books? For this to be credible, we would have to suppose that much of the collection had been formed very recently, in thirteenth-century scholastic times. Yet this is not the impression given by Eco. The library is portrayed as an ancient, conservative collection, primarily made up of the classics of the past.[22] It is time now to look at what else we know of medieval libraries.

3. MEDIEVAL LIBRARIES

Let me make a general point at the outset. Large medieval books, such as Bibles, were very costly to produce. Even a missal (or book containing the service of the mass for a year) might require up to 156 skins of best calves, and a large pandect or full Bible might require up to 500 skins.[23] Even at a conservative estimate, Eco's 85,000 books might have required the skins of between two and eight million calves. And this does not take into account other libraries around the world at that time. Is this a likely supposition?

To cut a very long story short, almost every aspect of Eco's library, in fact, is in conflict with what we know of medieval libraries from accredited sources. For a start the name of the building housing the library is wrong. I know of no medieval library located in an ex-fortress.[24] Medieval 'libraries' were usually known as *armaria*[25] or *risci* or *arcae* – chests, book-presses or cupboards. The Greek word *bibliotheca*, is also found but meant, originally, much the same thing: 'book boxes'.[26] It is not until the thirteenth century that libraries came to be actually rooms where people consulted books. Some authorities would date the appearance of actual rooms called 'libraries' even later in the Middle Ages.[27] Before that time they were usually niches or storage chests or cupboards, and the books were handed out to the monks to be read in the cloister or the refectory.[28] The 'book-cupboards' were usually kept in the walls or window-boxes of the cloisters of a church, or in a room above the scriptorium near the altar of the church itself. Often the books were stored indiscriminately with archives and valuables of a mixed sort, even tools (*ferramenta*).[29] The situation is well described by Rodney Thomson:[30]

It is well-known that monastic books were kept in different localities according to their use as laid down in the Benedictine Rule, more or less modified by local custom, changing liturgical practice and the progress of learning. No monastery could function without service-books for the performance of the Divine Office, kept in the Sacristy or, if exceptionally large and heavy, in the church itself. In the refectory were kept a few books of homiletic and hagiography for the mealtime reading. By far the largest collection, however, were the books for *Lectio Divina* and study, which with the refectory-books formed the monastic library.[31]

As late as the eleventh century, in the customs of Cluny, the librarian (*bibliothecarius*, *librarius*, *armarius*, *custos librorum*) was the same man as the precentor, in charge of singing and the choir.[32] There is never any mention in the records of any duties of the sort we would associate with library care, service or maintenance. In another eleventh-century collection of monastic customs all the books in the possession of the monastery were brought out once a year and laid on a carpet.[33] The monks brought with them the book they had been assigned the previous year, and were then given, from the pile laid out on the carpet, another book for the ensuing year. The distribution was in the charge of a monk called the 'Guardian of the Books'.

We actually have a picture of an early medieval library, or *armarium*, in a celebrated eighth-century Bible manuscript.[34] It shows the prophet and scribe Esdra or Ezra ('who rewrote the Holy Scripture after the end of the Babylonian captivity') writing,[35] and behind him there is visible an *armarium* in the form of a cupboard with a double door. It contains five shelves, each holding two large volumes lying flat on their sides, making a total for the library of ten books![36] Isidore of Seville, around the same time, is supposed to have had a library consisting of 14 *armaria*, and it was reputed to be the largest in Europe of the time.[37] Even in the late Middle Ages, books were sufficiently localised to be chained to the shelves in which they were stored. Those who wished to consult them had to pull them along on their chains, one end being attached to a ring which slid along a bar attached to the storage shelf, the other to the book cover.[38]

The most extensive and specific reference, however, to a monastic library prior to the thirteenth century, as such, that I know is a famous one, but one that never, in fact, existed (although scholars think that a recently excavated site 30–40 kilometres from Monte Cassino, called San Vincenzo al Volturno,[39] might have once been a monastic complex not unlike that depicted in the St.Gall plan, and we know that the Carolingian monasteries were the largest, richest and most powerful institutions of their time). I am referring to the celebrated ideal monastic plan from St. Gall, found in a manuscript copied between 820 and 830 AD.[40] At the NE corner of the great monastic church itself, on the floor above the scriptorium, next to the altar, is listed a *bibliotheca*. There are no towers, but in the centre is a light well, as in Eco's *aedificium*. The outer dimensions of the 'bibliotheca' seem to have been 30' and 40', with the light well being roughly 10' by 10'. Not quite large enough to contain fifty-six rooms and 85,000 books!!

Early sixteenth century descriptions of the library of the abbey of Clairvaux, one of the two great Cistercian foundations in France, include 1788 manuscripts and a library, situated above a large spiral staircase, beneath which were fourteen study carrels along one side of the cloister. In the library, which was 189' by 17', a dimension appropriate to its cloister location, were forty-eight benches, each with four shelves above it, with books on all subjects, especially theology. A 1723 description says the books were chained to their desks. This is the largest medieval library I have come across in my researches.[41]

It is obvious from all the above that the Eco's book numbers (85,000) are violently wrong. In reality, we must not think of even the 20,000 to 60,000 strong collections of manuscripts to be found in major repositories today, such as the British Library in London, or the Staatsbibliothek in Munich, or the Bibliothèque Nationale in Paris or the Biblioteca Apostolica Vaticana in Rome. These collections have been built up over the modern centuries by the aggregation of numerous lesser libraries or collections and give a totally false picture of what must have been around in any medieval library. We must not even think of collections as large as those private libraries of scholar-gentlemen such as Sir Walter Scott (Abbotsford contains around 9,000 books) or Gibbon (whose library is said to have contained around 7,000 volumes). Occasional reports in our scholarly books of medieval collections as large as 6,500 (Novalese Abbey at the time of its destruction by the Saracens in 905 AD),[42] or 3,000 (Croyland Abbey in the 11th century),[43] must be treated with extreme caution.

In fact, what we find in our accredited sources and in the latest research monographs, is as follows. Early monastic libraries might have contained around 20 or so books,[44] and major monastic libraries by the twelfth century held an upper limit of around 500 volumes each.[45] R.W. Southern seems to think that no library could possibly have contained much more than this number. Writing in 1995, of the period c1050–1325 AD, he says:

> Probably at the moment of widest expansion, three or four hundred volumes of moderate size would have contained all the basic texts on all subjects capable of exact and systematic study.[46]

By the end of this period exceptional libraries were inching over 1,000 titles. The library of the College of the Sorbonne, Paris, in 1338, the richest library in Christendom, had 338 volumes for consultation, chained to its reading desks, and 1,728 works on its registers available for loan (but of these 300 were listed as 'lost'!)[47] The donation by Amplonius Ratinck (1363–1435) of 637 manuscripts gave Erfurt 'the largest stock of books in northern Germany' at the time.[48] Both these collections, significantly, were up-to-the-minute university and college collections, not dusty and archaic monastic collections.

4. ECO'S MONASTIC LIBRARY AS LABYRINTH AND BLIND ALLEY

Why, therefore, is Eco's library so unlike anything that can possibly be said to have existed in its era? The answer is, of course, that it is not a library at all. It is a metaphor, a metaphor for the world. At a certain point 'old Alinardo of Grottaferrata' hints that the library was, in fact, a labyrinth.[49] When questioned by William as to whether the library was, in fact, a labyrinth, he replies in the affirmative and quotes a piece of Latin which, translated, means: 'the labyrinth denotes allegorically this world, large at its entrance, but narrow at the exit'.[50]

Eco, of course, does not tell us where he gets this quotation from, but in fact it comes from an inscription on the floor of the church of San Savino, Piacenza, set into a diagrammatic labyrinth, one of 23 such labyrinths let into the floors of medieval churches 'without including the many open-air labyrinths and mazes made of stones or cut into the turf of Ireland, Britain and Scandinavia'.[51] The quotation on the floor of the Piacenza church continues: 'so he who is ensnared by the joys of the world and weighed down by its vices, can regain the doctrines of life only with difficulty'.[52] That is the symbolism of the large entrance and the narrow exit: the joys of this world are attractive, but once ensnared by them, the path to salvation is difficult to locate. Thus our heroes in the *Name of the Rose* find it easy enough to get into their library, but difficult to get out of it.[53]

The labyrinths on the floors of medieval churches were known as 'pathways to Jerusalem', or 'Jerusalem', or 'City of God'. They are, typically, concentric in arrangement. Though of pagan origin, the idea reaches its Christian apotheosis in the concentric arrangements of the typical rose window of a medieval Gothic church, which George Duby likens to 'the labyrinth which guided profane love from ordeal to ordeal toward its goal'.[54] The same notion of the Rose as the ultimate goal of the Christian and of Christian knowledge will be found in literature, notably in the final verses of the *Romance of the Rose* and the *Divine Comedy*, two almost contemporary masterworks of the age of the Gothic cathedrals:

> The central circle in the labyrinth is the Rose, which is the Lamb described in *Revelation* as being in the centre of the Heavenly Jerusalem. Dante's Christ resides with the great Rose in the centre of Paradise. The rose garden is one of the favourite allegorical devices used by alchemists and courtly painters alike. Mary was called the 'Rosa Mystica' in the litany of Loreto.[55]

The labyrinths are located in floors of the nave of the church and the word nave, which means ship (*navis*),[56] symbolises the journey that the Christian must make in order to arrive at the centre of the Rose, the Lamb, the Heavenly Jerusalem, Salvation. If you compare any picture of a Gothic Rose window with the floor plan of Eco's library, you will see that the latter resembles a Rose Window, more than it does any library that might be thought of as existing at the time.[57]

Eco plays on these ideas. At one point, he has Adso ask how William managed to figure out the plan of the library only when he was outside it. When he was inside it, it was all a mystery to him.[58] The explanation involves an analogy with God and Creation. God can understand the Universe because he created it: he is outside it. We, who are inside it, cannot understand it. At another point Adso says 'the library was at once the celestial Jerusalem and an underground world on the border between *terra incognita* and Hades'.[59] William remarks later on that 'the library is constructed according to a celestial harmony, to which various and wonderful meanings can be attributed'.[60]

But the library has, in the *Name of the Rose*, a much more sinister meaning. It is a symbol of man's wrongful endeavour to control and understand what he cannot control or understand. By establishing a constructed, artificial and ultimately erroneous notion of truth, and vainly surrounding it with a myriad of treatises carefully guarded from profane use, the library and the librarians are contradicting the nature of things. In their insatiable pride, their urge to monopolise and deify knowledge, they go against the desires of their 'loins or the ardour that makes another man a warrior of the faith or of heresy'.[61] The lust for books and knowledge is as sterile as the seed of Onan which is poured in vain upon the ground. Without people to read and use the signs in books, the books themselves are dumb, useless. One former abbot of the monastery knew by heart all the books in the library, but he could not write ... .[62] Blind Malachi, slightly earlier in the novel, is said to have protected the library without knowing what was in it.[63]

Thus, at the end of the novel, William has to admit that even the rational plan, the calculations and deductions he had made in order to work out the truth about the mysterious events in the abbey, were illusory: he had stumbled onto the truth, but not because of his own plans and deductions. Learning is premised upon order and the existence of God; in fact chaos and the non-existence of God are necessary consequences of God's free will. 'Perhaps (says William) the mission of those who love mankind is to make people laugh at the truth, to make truth laugh, because the only truth lies in learning to free ourselves from insane passion for the truth'.[64]

With a final quotation from the twelfth-century Bernard of Morlaix' *De contemptu mundi*, Adso, now an old man, tells us that in the end we are left with *nomina nuda*, only the words and names with which we describe and talk about things.[65] All our structures, our knowledge, our multitudinous and systematic truths are symbolised by the ashes of the burned out *aedificium*, and in that word lies Eco's last laugh, for, according to Hugh of St.Victor, the twelfth-century regular canon whom we have often cited above, 'Divine scripture is like a building (*aedificium*): in its foundations we may see the literal meanings, in its upper stories lie its spiritual meanings'.[66] Perhaps the final spiritual meaning of the *aedificium* of Eco's novel is the contingency of all meaning, the uselessness of all systematic knowledge.[67] What a paradoxical conclusion for a novel about a library![68]

NOTES

1. Curiously, the 1974 Michelin *Guide* to Italy contains more information than the *Blue Guide to Northern Italy from the Alps to Rome* (ed. Alta Macadam, London: Black; New York: Norton, 1988), 45. There are two good views of the abbey in Giovanni Pugliese Carratelli (ed.), *Dall' Eremo al Cenobio: La civiltà monastica in Italia dalle origini all'età di Dante* [Antica Madre: collana di studi sull'Italia antica] (Milan: Schweiwiller, 1987) (figs 19 and 20; cf. also 34 'Come Fruttuaria, anche San Michele, notevole centro culturale, ebbe dipendenze in Piemonte e in altre regioni, che continuarono AD aumentare, almeno fino al secolo XIII').

2. Umberto Eco, The *Name of the Rose* (trans. William Weaver (London: Pan/ Picador [Secker and Warburg, 1984), 3–4: '... the community was some-

where along the central ridge of the Apennines, between Piedmont, Liguria and France'.

3. *The Name of the Rose*, 491. It is the leading character William of Baskerville who offers this description.

4. See the review in *The Observer* by Anthony Burgess, 4 April 1985, 20, column 3: 'For a reader so to be drawn would necessitate ... genuine medieval sources'.

5. '*The Name of the Rose* then, attempts with a rigour never previously shown in fiction to present the inner life of a medieval monastery' (*ibid.*). For the curious, W. M. Miller in his *A Canticle for Leibowitz* (1960, London: Transworld/Corgi Books, 1970) also links monks and books in a bizarre fictional way.

6. *The Name of the Rose*, 112.

7. *The Name of the Rose*, 162.

8. *The Name of the Rose* , 158.

9. *The Name of the Rose*, 169ff.

10. See plan *The Name of the Rose*, 321.

11. *The Name of the Rose*, 168: 'Against the [3] blind walls stood huge cases, laden with books neatly arranged'.

12. L.D.Reynolds and N.G.Wilson, *Scribes and Scholars: A Guide to the Transmission of Greek and Latin Literature* (Oxford: Clarendon Press, 3rd ed, 1991), 7. Hugh of St.Victor, in the twelfth century, thought Ptolemy's library contained 70,000 volumes (*The Didascalicon of Hugh of St.Victor: a Medieval Guide to the Arts*, trans. J. Taylor [New York: Columbia University Press, 1961], 106.

13. Reynolds and Wilson, *op. cit.* 16; Luciano Canfora, *The Vanished Library: A Wonder of the Ancient World*, trans. Martin Ryle, (London: Vintage, 1991) ch. IX; *Encyclopedia Brittanica*, Ninth Edition, vol.XIV (1882), 511a (the whole article on 'Libraries', 509–51 is a mass of relevant and extraordinary information on the present topic). Hugh of St.Victor tells us that 'Pamphilus had in his library nearly thirty thousand volumes' (*Didascalicon*, IV.13, trans. Taylor, 115, and see Taylor's note 42). [On the library at Pergamon see now below n.68].

14. G.H. Putnam, *Books and their Makers during the Middle Ages: A Study of the Conditions of the Production and Distribution of Literature from the Fall of the Roman Empire to the Close of the Seventeenth Century* (1896–97; New York: Hilary House, 1962), vol. I , 161.

15. (Of Eco himself:) 'Meanwhile, he was working on turning his newly bought ruin in Monte Cerignano into a storehouse for his books, 20,000 of which were overflowing from his Milan home, with 5,000 more choking up the small flat he kept in Bologna' – from an undated *Good Weekend* cutting in my collection, 78.

16. Umberto Eco, *How to Travel with a Salmon and other Essays* (London: Minerva, 1995), 24ff, 102ff.

17. Meaning that, according to the system discussed in the essay, at least one book must have had the spine call number of 3335.33335.33335.33335!! See Eco's 'De biblioteca', in *Sette Anni di Desiderio* (Milan: Bompiani, 1983), 237–250. The essay was written for a conference held on 10 March 1981, and the previous year the Italian edition of the *Name of the Rose* was published (the preface is dated 5 January 1980). The speculation about the 'biblioteca con un numero immenso di stanze' is found on 238–39. The rest of the essay is a fascinating romp through Eco's ribald imagination, in

the course of which he takes us into many of the libraries he has himself used, and touches on themes the reader will recognise from the description of the library in the *Name of the Rose*. Speculating as to whether his library with the huge number of rooms may be possible or only fantastic, he says he has, in the course of the research necessary for the writing of the paper, inspected only some of the libraries to which he was able to gain access during night-time hours, 'that of Assurbanipal at Nineveh, that of Polycrates at Samos, that of Pisistratus at Athens, the library at Alexandria which had in the third century B.C. 400,000 volumes, and later, in the first century (BC), with the library of the Serapeum, around 700,000 volumes; then the library at Pergamum and also that of Augustus (in the time of Constantine there were 28 [public] libraries at Rome)'! This excerpt will give some idea of the wicked wit with which Eco conducts his investigations, as also of the kind of thinking that must have surrounded the writing of the *Name of the Rose* ... !

18. *Bedae, Opera de Temporibus*, ed. C.W. Jones (Cambridge, Mass: The Mediaeval Academy of America, 1943), 4.

19. Reynolds and Wilson, *op. cit.* 81.

20. Some idea of the survival of classical works can be gained from the relevant entries in N.G.L.Hammond and H.H.Scullard (eds), *Oxford Classical Dictionary* (Oxford: Clarendon Press, 1970).

21. Reynolds and Wilson (*op. cit.* 17) argue that 4,000 works 'must be an exaggeration'!

22. In *Name of the Rose*, 75, we are told that the library 'dates back to the earliest times'. The books noticed at this point (and elsewhere) are a mixture of ancient and medieval texts. At 320, however, our adventurers come across 'four rooms [packed with] a great hoard of poets and philosophers of pagan antiquity'. In the present paper, I do not examine library classification systems. That set out on 75 of *Name of the Rose* (and elsewhere) is at least 'in the medieval manner'.

23. Christopher de Hamel, *Scribes and Illuminators* (London: British Museum Press, 1992), 13; Bernhard Bischoff, *Latin Palaeography: Antiquity and the Middle Ages*, trans. D.O. Cróinín and D. Ganz (Cambridge: Cambridge University Press, 1990), 10.

24. A few books, of course, would have been stored from time to time in the castles and fortresses of educated lords, but this would have been rare. Books might also have been kept in the Cathar castles, if we accept Fernand Niel's interpretation of their function (cf. Fernard Niel, *Les Cathares de Montségur* (Malesherbes: Seghers, 1973,1978).

25. Charles H.Haskins, *The Renaissance of the Twelfth Century* (New York: Meridian, 1957), 71.

26. By the twelfth century, Hugh of St.Victory (trans. Taylor, 105) tells us that '*biblio-*' is to be understood as meaning 'of books', and '*-theca*' as 'repository'. In the Italian original of the *Name of the Rose*, Eco naturally uses the Italian word 'biblioteca' for 'library'.

27. Putnam, *op. cit.* vol. I, 150. Cavallo (396, *infra*) ascribes the separation of library and scriptorium to the Cistercians, with the mendicants (412), completing the transition from a scriptorium without a library to a library (as an autonomous place for the reading and storage of books) without a scriptorium.

28. *The Rule of St.Benedict* §48 *de opera manuum cotidiana* refers to the handing out of books 'from the library' (*de bibliotheca*) to the monks at the beginning

175

of Lent, for them to read wholly and in proper order. See Attilio Stendardi (ed.), *Gregorio Magno, Vita di San Benedetto e la Regola* (Roma: Città Nuova, 1981, 226, and Giorgio Picasso and Dorino Tuniz (eds), *San Benedetto: La Regola* (Milan: San Paolo, 1966), 148 (Latin text and Italian translations, with notes); and *The Rule of St. Benedict translated witjh an introduction by Cardinal Gasquet* (New York: Cooper Square, 1966), 86. Guglielmo Cavallo, 'Dallo 'Scriptorium' senza biblioteca alla biblioteca senza 'scriptorium'' [331–422 of *Dall' Eremo al Cenobio*], 333, feels that the phrase *de bibiliotheca*' does not refer to a library proper, but to collections of Bibles or parts of Bibles, usually stored in chests, or window niches in and around the cloisters of monasteries (*conservati in qualche modesto ripostiglio*). Hugh of St.Victor in the passage cited above (trans. Taylor 105) is, in fact, talking about the books of the Bible.

29. Cavallo, *ibid.*
30. Rodney Thomson, 'Bury St. Edmunds Manuscripts: A Descriptive Bibliography' (Unpublished M.A. dissertation, University of Melbourne, 1969), 18–19.
31. See R.M. Thomson, 'The Library of Bury St. Edmunds Abbey in the Eleventh and Twelfth Centuries', *Speculum* ,47 (4), (1972), 617–45, and F. Wormald and C.E. Wright (eds), *The English Library before 1700* (London: Athlone Press, 1958).
32. See Cavallo, *op. cit.* 355–56 and Ulrich of Cluny's late eleventh-century A.D. 'Cluniac Customs', III.10 (J.P.Migne, *Patrologia Latina*, 149 cols 748–51. The elaborate reading schedule of the Cluniac monasteries is outlined by Ulrich in I.I (*PL*), cols 643–46. The reading is said to take place *et in ecclesia et in refectorio*. See Putnam, vol. I, 148.
33. Putnam, *op. cit.* vol. I, 151; D. Knowles (ed. and trans.), *The Monastic Constitutions of Lanfranc* (London: Nelson, 1951), 19 and note on 151, where it is stated that the number of books brought out on to the carpet was not the total number in the monastic collection, but a number designed to suit the number of likely book-claimants in the community.
34. The Codex Amiatinus: Bischoff, *Latin Palaeography, op. cit.* 10.
35. Kurt Weitzmann, *Late Antique and Early Christian Book Illumination* (New York: Braziller, 1977), 126. Hugh of St.Victor (*Didascalicon*, IV.3, trans. J.Taylor, 105) writes: 'After the Law had been burned by the Chaldaeans and when the Jews had returned to Jerusalem, Esdras the scribe, inspired by the Divine Spirit, restored the books of the Old Testament, corrected all the volumes of the Law and the Prophets which had been corrupted by the gentiles, and arranged the whole of the Old Testament into twenty-two books, so that there might be just as many books of the Law as there were letters in the alphabet'.
36. The cupboard, which has leatherbound books, presumably Bibles, on its shelves, also goes back to an early tradition when the shelves were still filled with scrolls' (Weitzmann, *ibid.*). Weitzmann [plate 48] shows this manuscript illumination and there is a (better) picture in *Dall' Eremo al Cenobio*, fig. 135, opposite 338.
37. Putnam, *op. cit.* vol. I, 153.
38. The most famous of the medieval 'chained' libraries is that of Hereford Cathedral. See *A Short Account of the Chained Library* (Hereford: Hereford Cathedral, 1961); F.C. Morgan, *Hereford Cathedral Library (including the 'Chained Library'): its History and Contents with Appendix of Early Printed Books* (Hereford: Hereford Cathedral, 1963), and, more recently, the catalogue

of the library by R.M.Thomson. In 1961 there were 1,444 chained books ('the largest collection in the world'), but not all were medieval. An equally famous chained library is 'the oldest public library in the world', dating from the early Renaissance: the Biblioteca Malatestiana in Cesena, Italy. See Antonio Domeniconi *La Biblioteca Malatestiana* (Quaderni della Biblioteca Malatestiana I, Cesena: Bibliotheca Comunale Malatestiana, 1982). According to Domeniconi (13), 'it was a common custom for medieval libraries to be chained, because of the growing cost of books'. The Cesena library contains 340 manuscripts.

39. R. Hodges and J. Mitchell, *San Vincenzo Volturno: The Archaeology, Art and Territory of an Early Medieval Monastery* (Osney Mead: B.A.R., 1985).

40. Adequate general details are given in Lorna Price, *The Plan of St.Gall in Brief* (Berkeley: University of California Press, 1982). The original appearance of the plan is given on xii. The actual Latin inscription from the surviving manuscript has: *infra sedes scribentium* and *supra bibliotheca* – that is, 'below, the location of the scribes' and 'above, the library'.

41. Putnam, *op. cit.* vol. I, 150–51.

42. Putnam, *op. cit.* vol. I, 134. Cf. the comment of Cavallo (389): 'una biblioteca piuttosto ricca, ma ne restano solo scarse tracce'.

43. Putnam, *op. cit.* vol. I, 134. Similar figures are also given in the *Encyclopedia Britannica*, Ninth Edition, XIV, 514.

44. Haskins, *op. cit.*, 71.

45. R. M. Thomson, 'Books and Learning at Gloucester Abbey in the Twelfth and Thirteenth Centuries', in J. P.Carley and C.G.C.Tite (eds), *Books and Collectors, 1200–1700: Essays presented to Andrew Watson* (London: The British Library, 1997), 6. Other figures: Putnam, I, 139, 150, 158, 160, 166, 172; Haskins, 72, 83–84; Martin, 187, 204.

46. R.W. Southern, *Scholastic Humanism and the Unification of Europe* (Oxford: Blackwell, 1995), vol. I , 9.

47. H. J. Martin, *The History and Power of Writing*, trans. Lydia G.Cochrane (1988, Chicago: University of Chicago Press, 1994), 154, 188.

48. *Ibid.* 205.

49. *Name of the Rose*, 157–58; cf. Theresa Coletti, *Naming the Rose: Eco, Medieval Signs, and Modern Theory* (Ithaca: Cornell University Press, 1988), 160. On the medieval idea of the book, see J. M. Gellrich, *The Idea of the Book in the Middle Ages: Language Theory, Mythology and Fiction* (Ithaca: Cornell University Press, 1985).

50. *Name of the Rose*, 158. Readers may like to compare 'The Library of Babel' in Jorge Luis Borges' *Labyrinths: Selected Stories and Other Writings* (London: Penguin, 1962,1964,1970), 78–86.

51. See John James, 'The Mystery of the Great Labyrinth, Chartres Cathedral', *Studies in Comparative Religion*, 11 (2), (1977), [92–115], 92–93.

52. *Ibid.* 93.

53. The reader is invited to follow John James in his journey round the labyrinth at Chartres (James, *idem.*, 7ff), and to compare that journey with the journey undertaken by the heroes in the *Name of the Rose*.

54. Georges Duby, *The Age of the Cathedrals: Art and Society, 980–1420*, trans. E. Levieux and B. Thompson (London: Croom Helm, 1981), 292.

55. James, *op. cit.* 95–96.

56. James, *op. cit.* 113–114.

57. Georges Duby, *History of Medieval Art, 980–1440* (1966–67 in three volumes; one volume edition, London: Weidenfeld and Nicolson, 1986), vol.

II, 203–06 contains excellent illustrations and discussion. James (*op. cit.* 108 ff) comments on the significance of the number of compartments in the Chartres Rose Window. Note that there are even four turret-like extremities reminiscent of the four towers of Eco's library.

58. *Name of the Rose*, 218.
59. *Name of the Rose*, 184.
60. *Name of the Rose*, 217. Cf. also 215: 'The library was built by a human mind that thought in a mathematical fashion, because without mathematics you cannot build labyrinths'.
61. *Name of the Rose*, 395–96.
62. *Name of the Rose*, 421.
63. *Name of the Rose*, 420.
64. *Name of the Rose*, 491.
65. R.E.Pepin, *Scorn for the World: Bernard of Cluny's 'De contemptu mundi"* The *Latin Text with English Translation and an Introduction*, Medieval Texts and Studies No. 8 (East Lansing: Colleagues Press, 1991), xxi. See also R.E.Pepin *'De octo vitiis*: a satire by Bernard of Cluny' *Allegorica* 18 (1997) 31–99, esp. 31.
66. Coletti, *op. cit.* 160. Gellrich elaborates on the meaning of *aedificium scripturae* on 133, 187, 239, 247–48 of his *The Idea of the Book*.
67. *The Name of the Rose* has been described as 'an apologia for nihilism and atheism' (*Annals Australia [Catholic] Magazine*, August-September 1989, 25.
68. Since writing this paper, a number of items have come to my attention. First, research into the furnishings and function of the ancient library at Pergamon are discussed, with illustrations, by Harald Wolter von dem Knesebeck, 'Zur Ausstattung und Funktion des Hauptsaales der Bibliothek von Pergamon', *Boreas: Münstersche Beiträge zur Archäologie*, 18 (1995), 45–56. F.Wormald and C.E.Wright (eds), *The English Library before 1700* (London: Athlone Press, 1958), mentioned in n.31, deals with the monastic library (ch.2,.15ff), the Universities and the medieval library (ch.4, 66ff), and the contents of the medieval library (ch.5, 85ff). In 'the great days of monasticism', books were 'nearly always kept in the cloister' (17) where reading was done; in the 'Dark Ages' they were possibly kept in some of the cells: 'It was desirable that they [the books] should be kept somewhere near the place where they were to be used, and in practice this meant the sacristy of the Church, the refectory and the library proper' (16).
   Two references not mentioned in my paper are: J.W. Clark *The Care of Books: An Essay on the Development of Libraries and their Fittings, from the Earliest Times to the End of the Eighteenth Century*, (Cambridge: Cambridge University Press, 1901, 2nd ed. 1902, reprinted Variorum, 1975), and the entry on 'Libraries', 208–09 in H. R. Loyn, *The Middle Ages: A Concise Encyclopedia* (London: Thames and Hudson, 1989), where the author (R.M.Thomson) says that up to '500 books constituted a large collection such as might be found in a populous monastic house'.
   Marco Mostert in his *The Political Theology of Abbo of Fleury: A Study of the Ideas about Society and Law of the Tenth-century Monastic Reform Movement* (Hilversum: Verloren, 1987), 32ff, discusses the very large medieval library at Fleury in Abbo's time. Between 600 and 800 manuscripts survive today from this library, containing approximately 6000 different texts. 'Both the number of texts and the number of manuscripts which can be connected in some way with the library of Fleury are highly exceptional' (32).
   Patrick Geary's *Phantoms of Remembrance: Memory and Oblivion at the End of*

the First Millennium (Princeton: Princeton University Press, 1994), 127, 208, reminds us that 'Novalesa [monastery] is remembered, even in Umberto Eco's *The Name of the Rose*, for its famous library of either six thousand (or 6,666) books, most of which were lost after the monks' flight to Turin in 906'.

Joan Evans (ed.), *The Flowering of the Middle Ages* (London: Thames and Hudson, 1966), 200–02, discusses medieval libraries and provides many illustrations of them (190–92 show the cupboards in private studies in which books were kept, even into the later Middle Ages). There is also a useful section on 'Medieval Libraries' in K. Strecker, *Introduction to Medieval Latin*, trans. R.B. Palmer (Berlin: Weidmannsche, 1965), 121–126, and further bibliographical orientation in L.Boyle (ed), *Medieval Latin Palaeography: A Bibliographical Introduction* (Toronto: University of Toronto Press, 1984), 203–232.

Since completing this paper, I have come across Helen T. Bennett, 'Deconstructing the monastery in Umberto Eco's *The Name of the Rose*', in Andrew MacLeish (ed.), *The Medieval Monastery* (Medieval Studies at Minnesota No. 2) St.Cloud, Minnesota: North Star, 1988), 77–82. Bennett observes Eco's inaccuracy in regard to the library and cites James F. O'Gorman, *The Architecture of the Monastic Library in Italy, 1300–1600* (New York: New York University Press, 1972). She also makes the same point about the library as a labyrinth that I do, and cites W.H.Matthews, *Mazes and Labyrinths: Their history and Development* (New York: Dover, 1970), and Piero Boitani, 'Chaucer's Labyrinth: Fourteenth-century Literature and Language', *The Chaucer Review*, 17 (1983), 197–220. She claims (80) that Eco modelled his *aedificium* on a pattern in the floor of Rheims cathedral, and, on rhizomatic aspects of labyrinths, cites Eco's *Postscript to the 'Name of the Rose'*, trans. W.Weaver (New York: Harcourt, 1993).

Postscript

See further:
J.W. Thompson, *The Medieval Library* (Chicago: University Press, 1939).
G.E. Bean, Aegean Turkey (London: John Murray, 1989), chpt. 4 (on the Library at Pergamum).

Bibliography

Awad, Mohamed. 'A Note on the Alleged Destruction of the Alexandria Library by the Arabs', *Journal of World History*, 8 (1964), 213–214.

Balsamo, Luigi. *Bibliography: History of a Tradition*, trans. William A. Pettas (Berkeley: B.M.Rosenthal, 1990).

Baratom, Marc et Christian Jacob. *Le Pouvoir des Bibliothèques* (Paris: Albin Michel, 1996).

Barnes, J. 'Medicine, Experience and Logic', in J. Barnes, J. Brunschwig and M. Schofield (eds), *Science and Speculation* (Cambridge: Cambridge University Press, 1982), 24–68.

Bell, Harold Idris. 'Hellenic Culture in Egypt', *Journal of Egyptian Archaeology*, 8 (1922), 139–155.

Bell, Harold Idris. *Juden und Griechen im römischen Alexandreia* (Leipzig: Hinrichs, 1927).

Bell, Harold Idris. *Egypt from Alexander the Great to the Arab Conquest: A Study in the Diffusion and Decay of Hellenism*. Gregynog Lectures for 1946 (Oxford: Clarendon Press, 1948).

Bell, Harold Idris. 'The Custody of Records in Roman Egypt', *Indian Archives*, 4 (1950), 116–125.

Bell, Harold Idris. *Cults and Creeds in Graeco-Roman Egypt* (Liverpool: Liverpool University Press, 1957).

Bennett, Helen T. 'Deconstructing the Monastery in Umberto Eco's *The Name of the Rose*', in Andrew MacLeish (ed.), *The Medieval Monastery* (Medieval Studies at Minnesota No. 2) (St.Cloud, Minnesota: North Star, 1988), 77–82.

Bevan, Edwyn. *The House of Ptolemy: A History of Egypt under the Ptolemaic Dynasty* (London: 1927; reprint Chicago: Argonaut, 1968).

Bing, Peter. *The Well-read Muse: Present and Past in Callimachus and the Hellenistic Poets* (Göttingen: Vandenhoeck & Ruprecht, 1988).

Bischoff, Bernhard. *Latin Palaeography: Antiquity and the Middle Ages*, trans. D.O. Cróinín and D. Ganz (Cambridge: Cambridge University Press, 1990).

Black, Jeremy A. and W. J. Tait. 'Archives and Libraries in the Ancient Near East', in Jack M. Sasson (ed.), *Civilizations of the Ancient Near East* (New York: Scribners, 1995), *IV*, 2197–2209.

Blanck, Horst. *Das Buch in der Antike* (München: C.H.Beck, 1991).

Blum, Rudolf. *Kallimachos: The Alexandrian Library and the Origins of Bibliography*, trans. Hans H. Wellisch (Madison: University of Wisconsin Press, 1991).

Boitani, Piero. 'Chaucer's Labyrinth: Fourteenth-century Literature and Language', *The Chaucer Review*, 17 (1983), 197–220.

Borges, Jorge Luis. 'The Library of Babel', in *Labyrinths: Selected Stories and Other Writings* (London: Penguin, 1962, 1964, 1970), 78–86.

Boyle, L. (ed.) *Medieval Latin Palaeography: A Bibliographical Introduction* (Toronto: University of Toronto Press, 1984), 203–232.

Breccia, Evaristo. *Alexandria ad Aegyptum: A Guide to the Ancient and Modern Town, and to its Graeco-Roman Museum* (Bergamo: Instituto Italiano d'Arti Grafichi, 1922).

Brink, C.O. 'Callimachus and Aristotle', *Classical Quarterly*, 40 (1946), 11–26.

Brinkman, John A. 'Mesopotamian Chronology of the Historical Period', in A. Leo Oppenheim, *Ancient Mesopotamia: Portrait of a Dead Civilization* (Chicago: University of Chicago Press, 2nd ed. 1977), 335–348.

Broek, R. van den. *Studies in Gnosticism and Alexandrian Christianity* (Leiden: E.J. Brill, 1996).

Brown, A.L. 'The Dramatic Synopses attributed to Aristophanes of Byzantium', *Classical Quarterly*, 37 (2), (1987), 427–421.

Bulloch, A., E.S. Gruen, A.A. Long, and A. Stewart (eds)., *Images and Ideologies: Self-Definition in the Hellenistic World* (Berkeley: University of California Press, 1993).

Bushnell, George H. 'The Alexandrian Library', *Antiquity*, 2 (1928), 196–204.

Butler, Alfred J. *The Arab Conquest of Egypt* (Oxford: Clarendon Press, 1902; 2nd ed. by P.M. Fraser, 1978).

Calmer, C. 'Antike Bibliotheken', *Opuscula Archaeologica*, 3 (1944), 145–193.

Canfora, Luciano. *The Vanished Library: A Wonder of the Ancient World*, trans. Martin Ryle (Berkeley: University of California, 1989; London: Hutchinson Radius, 1989, Vintage, 1991).

Canfora, Luciano. *Il viaggio di Aristea* (Roma: Laterza, 1996).

Carratelli, Giovanni Pugliese (ed.) *Dall' Eremo al Cenobio: La civiltà monastica in Italia dalle origini all'età di Dante* [Antica Madre: collana di studi sull'Italia antica] (Milan: Schweiwiller, 1987).

Cary, Max. *A History of the Greek World from 323 to 146 BC* (New York: Barnes and Noble, 1963).

Case, Thomas. 'Aristotle', *Encyclopedia Britannica*, Eleventh Edition (1910), vol. II, 501.

Clagett, M. *Greek Science in Antiquity* (New York: Books for Library Press, rev. ed. 1963).

Clark, John Willis. *The Care of Books: An Essay on the Development of Libraries and their Fittings, from the Earliest Times to the End of the Eighteenth Century* (Cambridge: Cambridge University Press, 1901, 2nd ed. 1902, reprinted Variorum, 1975).

Coletti, Theresa. *Naming the Rose: Eco, Medieval Signs, and Modern Theory* (Ithaca: Cornell University Press, 1988).

Csapo, E. and W.J. Slater. *The Context of Ancient Drama* (Ann Arbor: University of Michigan Press, 1995).

Dalley, Stephanie. *Myths from Mesopotamia* (Oxford: Oxford University Press, 1989).

Dantzig, Tobias. *The Bequest of the Greeks* (London: Allen and Unwin, 1955).

Daszewski, W. 'The Origins of Hellenistic Hypogea in Alexandria', in M. Minas and J. Zeidler (eds), *Aspekte spätägyptischer Kultur: Festschrift für E. Winter* in *Aegyptiaca Treverensia*, 7 (1994), 57–68.

Davis, Harold T. *Alexandria, the Golden City* (Evanston, Ill.: Principia Press, 1957).

Domeniconi, Antonio. *La Biblioteca Malatestiana* (Quaderni della Biblioteca Malatestiana I, Cesena: Bibliotheca Comunale Malatestiana, 1982).

Duby, Georges. *The Age of the Cathedrals: Art and Society, 980–1420*, tr. E. Levieux and B.Thompson (London: Croom Helm, 1981).

Duby, Georges. *History of Medieval Art, 980–1440* (1966–67 in three vols; one vol ed, London: Weidenfeld and Nicolson, 1986).

Durrell, Lawrence. *Justine* (London: Faber and Faber, 1957).

Düring, Ingemar. *Aristoteles* (Heidelberg: Winter, 1966).

Dzielska, Maria. *Hypatia of Alexandria* (Cambridge, Mass.: Harvard University Press, 1995).

Eco, Umberto. 'De biblioteca', in *Sette Anni di Desiderio* (Milan: Bompiani, 1983).

Eco, Umberto. *The Name of the Rose*, trans. William Weaver (London: Secker and Warburg, 1984).

Eco, Umberto. *Postscript to the 'Name of the Rose'*, trans. W. Weaver (New York: Harcourt, 1993).

Eco, Umberto. *How to Travel with a Salmon and other Essays* (London: Minerva, 1995).

Edelstein, L. 'The Interpretation of Ancient Science', in O. and L. Temkin (eds). *Ancient Medicine* (Baltimore: Johns Hopkins University Press, 1987), 431.

Eisler, Robert. *Orpheus the Fisher: Comparative Studies in Orphic and early Christian Cult Symbolism* (London: J.M. Watkins, 1921).

Ellis, Walter. *Ptolemy of Egypt* (New York: Routledge, 1994).

Empereur, J.Y. *A Short Guide to the Graeco-Roman Museum* (Alexandria: Sarapis Publishing, 1995).

Encyclopedia Britannica. 'Libraries', Ninth Edition (1882), vol. XIV, 509–51.

Englund, Robert K. and Jean-Pierre Grégoire. *The Proto-Cuneiform Texts from Jemdet Nasr I: Copies, Transliterations and Glossary* (Berlin: Materialien zur frühen Schriftzeugnissen des Vorderen Orients, 1991).

Englund, Robert K. and Hans J. Nissen. *Die Lexikalischen Listen der archaischen Texte aus Uruk* (Berlin: Ausgrabungen der Deutschen Forschungsgemeinschaft in Uruk-Warka 13, 1993).

Englund, Robert K. *Archaic Administrative Texts from Uruk: The Early Campaigns* (Berlin: Ausgrabungen der Deutschen Forschungsgemeinschaft in Uruk-Warka 15, 1994).

Evans, Joan (ed.) *The Flowering of the Middle Ages* (London: Thames and Hudson, 1966).

Fales, F.M. and J.N. Postgate. *Imperial Administrative Records, Pt. I. Palace and Temple Administration* (Helsinki: Helsinki University, 1992).

Falkenstein, Adam. *Archaische Texte aus Uruk* (Leipzig: Ausgrabungen der Deutschen Forschungsgemeinschaft in Uruk-Warka 2, 1936).

Festugière, A.-J. *Antioche Païenne et chrétienne, Libanius, Chrysostome et les moines de Syrie*, Bibliothèque des Écoles Françaises de Athènes et de Rome, vol. 194 (Paris: Éditions E. de Boccard, 1959).

Fideler, David. *Porphyry's Letter to his Wife Marcella*, trans. Alice Zimmern (London: George Redway, 1896; Grand Rapids: Phanes Press, 1986).

Fideler, David (ed.) *Alexandria, Journal of the Western Cosmological Traditions* (Grand Rapids: Phanes Press, 1991).

Fideler, David. *Jesus Christ, Sun of God* (Wheaton, Illinois: Quest Books/ Theosophical Publishing House, 1993).

Forster, Edward Morgan. *Alexandria: a History and a Guide* (Garden City: Doubleday, 1961; Gloucester, Mass: P. Smith, 1968; Michael Haag, 1982).

Fortune, Dion. *The Mystical Qabalah* (London: 1935; York Beach: Samuel Weiser, 1993).

Foster, Benjamin R. *Before the Muses: An Anthology of Akkadian Literature* (Bethesda: CDL Press, 1993), 2 vols.

Fraser, P.M. *Ptolemaic Alexandria* (Oxford: Oxford University Press, 1972), 3 vols.

Frede, Michael. *Galen: Three Treatises on the Nature of Science* (Indianapolis: 1985).

Frede, Michael. *Essays in Ancient Philosophy* (Oxford: Oxford University Press, 1987).

Frede, Michael. 'The Empiricist attitude towards reason and theory', in R.J.Hankinson (ed.) *Method, Medicine and Metaphysics: Studies in the*

Philosophy of Ancient Science (Edmonton: Academic Printing and Publishing, 1988), 79–97.

Gardthausen, V.E. 'Die Alexandrinishe Bibliothek, ihr Vorbild, Katalog und Betrieb', *Zeitschrift des Deutschen Vereins fur Buchwesen und Schriftum*, 5 (1922), 73–104.

Geary, Patrick. *Phantoms of Remembrance: Memory and Oblivion at the End of the First Millenium* (Princeton: Princeton University Press, 1994).

Gellrich, J.M. *The Idea of the Book in the Middle Ages: Language Theory, Mythology and Fiction* (Ithaca: Cornell University Press, 1985).

Giangrande, Giuseppe. *Scripta minora Alexandrina* (Amsterdam: Hakkert, 1980–1985).

Goodenough, E.R. *An Introduction to Philo Judaeus* (New Haven: Yale University Press, 1940).

Grant, Sir Alexander. *Ethics of Aristotle* (London: Parker, 1857).

Green, J. R. *Theatre in Ancient Greek Society* (London: Routledge, 1994).

Green, J.R. 'From Taranto to Alexandria', in S.J. Bourke and J.-P. Descœudres (eds). *Trade, Contact and the Movement of Peoples in the Eastern Mediterranean. Studies in Honour of J.Basil Hennessy*, in *Mediterranean Archaeology*, Suppl. 3 (Sydney, 1995), 271–274.

Green, J.R. 'Excavations at the Theatre, Nea Paphos, Cyprus, 1995–1996', in C. Petrie and S. Bolton (eds). *In the Field. Archaeology at the University of Sydney*, Sydney University Archaeological Methods Series No. 4, (1997), 35–46.

Green, J.R. 'Excavations at the Theatre, Nea Paphos, 1995–6', *Mediterranean Archaeology*, 9–10 (1996–97), 239–242.

Green, Margaret W. 'The Construction and the Implementation of the Cuneiform Writing System', *Visible Language*, 15 (4), (1981), 345–372.

Griffin, Jasper. 'The Library of our Dreams', *The American Scholar*, 65 (1), (Winter 1996), 59–70.

Guthrie, W.K.C. *A History of Greek Philosophy* (Cambridge: Cambridge University Press, 1981), vol. VI, 'Aristotle, an Encounter'.

Haag, M. *Alexandria* (Cairo: The American University in Cairo Press, 1993).

Haller, Arndt. *Die Heiligtümer des Gottes Assur und der Sin-Samas-Tempel in Assur* (Berlin: Wissenschaftliche Veröffentlichungen der Deutschen-Orient Gesellschaft 67, 1955).

Hamel, Christopher de. *Scribes and Illuminators* (London: British Museum Press, 1992).

Hamilton, J.R. *Alexander the Great* (London: Hutchinson University Library, 1973).

Haskins, Charles H. *The Renaissance of the Twelfth Century* (New York: Meridian, 1957).

Hessel, Alfred. *A History of Libraries*, trans. Reuben Peiss (New Brunswick, NJ: Scarecrow Press, 1955).

Hodges, R. and J. Mitchell. *San Vincenzo Volturno: The Archaeology, Art and Territory of an early Medieval Monastery* (Osney Mead: B.A.R., 1985).

Hogart, R.C. *The Hymns of Orpheus* (Grand Rapids: Phanes Press, 1993).

Holmes, Anne. 'The Alexandrian Library', *Libri*, 30 (1980), 285–294.

Hugh of St.Victor. *The Didascalicon of Hugh of St. Victor: a Medieval Guide to the Arts*, trans. J.Taylor (New York: Columbia University Press, 1961).

Hussein, M.A. *Origins of the Book: Egypt's Contribution to the Development of the Book from Papyrus to Codex* (Greenwich, Conn.: New York Graphic Society, 1972).

Hutchinson, G.O. *Hellenistic Poetry* (Oxford: Clarendon Press, 1988).

Iamblichus. *The Exhortation to Philosophy*, trans. Thomas M. Johnson (Grand Rapids: Phanes Press, 1988).

Irwin, Raymond. *The English Library* (London: George Allen & Unwin, 1966).

Jaeger, Werner. *Aristotle—Fundamentals of the History of his Development* (Oxford: Oxford University Press, 2nd ed. 1962).

James, John. 'The Mystery of the Great Labyrinth, Chartres Cathedral', *Studies in Comparative Religion*, 11 (2), (1977), 92–115.

Johnson, Elmer D. and Michael H. Harris. *History of Libraries in the Western World* (Metuchen, NJ: Scarcrow Press, 1970, 3rd ed. 1976).

Kamil, Jill. *Upper Egypt: Historical Outline and Descriptive Guide to the Ancient Site* (New York: Longman, 1983).

Kenny, Antony. *The Aristotelian Ethics* (Oxford: Oxford University Press, 1978).

Kenyon, F.G. *Books and Readers in Ancient Greece and Rome.* (Oxford: Clarendon Press, 1932).

Knowles, D. (ed. and trans.) *The Monastic Constitutions of Lanfranc* (London: Nelson, 1951).

Koster, W.J.W. (ed.) *Scholia in Aristophanem* (Groningen: Bouma, 1975).

Landels, John G. *Engineering in the Ancient World* (London: Chatto and Windus, 1978).

Leo, Friedrich. *Die griechische-römische Biographie* (Leipzig: B.G. Teubner, 1901).

Lloyd, G.E.R. 'A Note on Erasistratus of Ceos', *Journal of Hellenic Studies*, 95 (1975), 172–175.

Lloyd, G.E.R. *Science, Folklore and Ideology* (Cambridge: Cambridge University Press, 1982).

Lloyd, G.E.R. *Adversaries and Authorities* (Cambridge: Cambridge University Press, 1996).

Loyn, H.R. 'Libraries', in *The Middle Ages: A Concise Encyclopedia* (London: Thames and Hudson, 1989), 208–09.

McKenzie, Judith. 'Alexandria and the Origins of Baroque Architecture', in *Alexandria and Alexandrianism* (Malibu: J. Paul Getty Museum, 1996), 109–125.

Maehler, H. and V.M. Strocka (eds). *Das Ptolemäische Ägypten: Akten d. internat. Symposions, 27–29 September 1976 in Berlin* (Mainz am Rhine: Von Zabern, 1978).

Marlowe, John. *The Golden Age of Alexandria: From its Foundation by Alexander the Great in 331 BC to its Capture by the Arabs in 642 AD* (London: Gollancz/Trinity Press, 1971).

Marshall, D.N. *History of Libraries, Ancient and Mediaeval* (New Delhi: Oxford and IBH Publishing, 1983).

Martin, H. J. *The History and Power of Writing*, trans. Lydia G. Cochrane (1988, Chicago: University of Chicago Press, 1994).

Matthews, W.H. *Mazes and Labyrinths: Their History and Development* (New York: Dover, 1970).

Milne, J. Grafton. *A History of Egypt under Roman Rule* (London: Metheun, 1924).

Minio-Paluello, L. 'Artistotle', *Dictionary of Scientific Biography* (New York: Charles Scribner's Sons, 1970), vol. 1, 250–281.

Mostafa, El-Abbadi. *Life and Fate of the Ancient Library of Alexandria* (Paris: UNESCO, 2nd ed. 1992).

Mutahhari, Murtazá. *The Burning of Libraries in Iran and Alexandria*, trans. N.P. Nazareno, M. Nekoodast (Tehran: Islamic Propagation Organization, 1983).

Nissen, Hans J. 'The Development of Writing and of Glyptic Art', in Uwe Finkbeiner and Wolfgang Röllig (eds). *Gamdat Nasr: Period or Regional Style?* (Wiesbaden: Tübinger Atlas des Vorderen Orients, Beiheft B 62, 1986), 317–319.

Nissen, Hans J. *The Early History of the Ancient Near East, 9000–2000 BC* (Chicago: University of Chicago Press, 1988).

Norman, A.F. 'The Book Trade in Fourth Century Antioch', *Journal of Hellenic Studies*, 80 (1960), 122–126.

Norman, A. F. 'The Library of Libanius', *Rheinisches Museum für Philologie*, 107 (1964), 158–175.

Norman, A. F. 'Libanius: The Teacher in an Age of Violence', in G. Fatouros and T. Krischer (eds) *Libanios* (Darmstadt: Wissenschafliche Buchgessellschaft, 1983).

Nutton, V. 'Museums and Medical Schools in Antiquity', *History of Education*, 4 (1), (1975), 3–15.

O'Gorman, James F. *The Architecture of the Monastic Library in Italy, 1300–1600* (New York: New York University Press, 1972).

O'Hara, James J. *True Names: Vergil and the Alexandrian Tradition of Etymological Wordplay* (Ann Arbor: University of Michigan Press, 1996)

O'Leary, De Lacy. *How Greek Science Passed to the Arabs* (London: Routledge, 1949).

Ollé, James G. *Library History: An Examination Guidebook* (London: C. Bingley, 1979).

Oppenheim, Leo. 'The Position of the Intellectual in Mesopotamian Society', *Daedalus*, 104 (2), (1975), 37–46.

Oppenheim, Leo. *Ancient Mesopotamia: Portrait of a Dead Civilization* (Chicago: University of Chicago Press, 2nd ed. 1977).

Parpola, Simo. 'Assyrian Library Records', *Journal of Near Eastern Studies*, 42 (1983), 1–29.

Parsons, Edward Alexander. *The Alexandrian Library: Glory of the Hellenic World: Its Rise, Antiquities and Destruction* (London: Cleaver-Hume Press/New York/Amsterdam: Elsevier Press, 1952).

Peremans, W. 'Bibliothek en Bibliothecarissen te Alexandrië', in Etienne van Cauwenbergh. *Schinium Lovaniense: Historische Opstellen*, Recueil de Travaux d'Histoire et de la Philologie, ser. 4, fasc. 24 (Louvain: Université de Louvain, 1961), 79–88.

Pfeiffer, Rudolf (ed.) *Callimachus* (Oxford: Clarendon Press, 1949–1953).

Pfeiffer, Rudolf. *History of Classical Scholarship from the Beginnings to the End of the Hellenistic Age* (Oxford: Clarendon Press, 1968).

Pinner, H.L. *The World of Books in Classical Antiquity* (Leiden: A.W. Sijthoff, 1948).

Potts, Daniel T. *Mesopotamian Civilization: The Material Foundations* (London and Ithaca: Athlone and Cornell University Press, 1997).

Putnam, G.H. *Books and their Makers during the Middle Ages: A Study of the Conditions of the Production and Distribution of Literature from the Fall of the Roman Empire to the Close of the Seventeenth Century* (1896–97; New York: Hilary House, 1962), 2 vols.

Reynolds, L.D. and N.G. Wilson, *Scribes and Scholars: A Guide to the Transmission of Greek and Latin Literature* (Oxford: Clarendon Press, 1974, 3rd ed. 1991).

Riché, Pierre. *Daily Life in the World of Charlemagne*, trans. Jo Ann McNamara (1973; Philadelphia: University of Pennsylvania Press, 1978).

Rist, John M. *The Mind of Aristotle: A Study of Philosophical Growth* (Toronto: Phoenix, 1989), Supplementary Series XXV.

Rogers, A. Robert and Kathryn McChesney, with the assistance of F. Laverne Carroll *et al*. *The Library in Society* (Littleton, Colo: Libraries Unlimited, 1984).

Rose, Valentin. *Aristotle's Fragmenta* (Stuttgart: Teubner, 1966).

Ross, Sir David. *Aristotle* (London: Methuen, 1966).

Rowe, Alan. *Discovery of the Famous Temple and Enclosure of Serapis at Alexandria* (Caïre: Institut français d'archéologie orientale, 1946).

Rowe, Alan. 'A Contribution to the Archaeology of the Western Desert, IV: The Great Serapeum of Alexandria', *Bulletin of the John Rylands Library*, 39 (1956–57), 485–520.

Runciman, Steven. *The Medieval Manichee* (Cambridge: Cambridge University Press, 1969).

Schwinge, Ernst-Richard. *Künstlichkeit von Kunst: zur Geschichtlichkeit der Alexandrinischen Poesie* (München: C. Beck, 1986).

Sievers, G. R. *Das Leben des Libanius* (Berlin: Weidmannsche Buchhandlung, 1868).

Skiadas, Aristoxenos D. (ed.) *Kallimachos* (Darmstadt: Wissenschaftliche Buchgesellschaft, 1975).

Smith, W.D. *The Hippocratic Tradition* (Ithaca: Cornell University Press, 1979).

Sorjabi, R. (ed.) *Aristotle Transformed* (London: Duckworth, 1990).

Southern, R.W. *Scolastic Humanism and the Unification of Europe* (Oxford: Blackwell, 1995).

Staquet, J. 'César à Alexandrie: l'Incendie de la Bibliothèque', *Nova et Vetera*, 12 (1928), 157–177.

Steen, G.L. (ed.) *Alexandria, the Site and the History* (New York: New York University Press, 1993).

Strecker, K. 'Medieval Libraries', in *Introduction to Medieval Latin*, trans. R.B. Palmer (Berlin: Weidmannsche, 1965), 121–126.

Thompson, J.W. *Ancient Libraries* (Berkeley: University of California Press, 1940).

Thomson, R.M. 'The Library of Bury St. Edmunds Abbey in the Eleventh and Twelfth Centuries', *Speculum*, 47 (4), (1972), 617–45.

Thomson, R.M. 'Books and Learning at Gloucester Abbey in the Twelfth and Thirteenth Centuries', in J.P. Carley and C.G.C. Tite (eds). *Books and Collectors, 1200–1700: Essays presented to Andrew Watson* (London: The British Library, 1997).

Turner, E.G. 'l'Érudition Alexandrine et les Papyrus', *Chronique d'Égypte*, 37 (1962), 135–152.

Vallance, J.T. *The Lost Theory of Asclepiades of Bithynia* (Oxford: Clarendon Press, 1990).

Veenhof, Klaas R. (ed.) *Cuneiform Archives and Libraries* (Leiden: Uitgaven van het Nederlands Historisch-Archaeologisch Instituut te Istanbul, 57, 1986).

Vleeschauwer, H.J. de. 'Afterword: The Musieon', in H. Curtis Wright. *The Oral Antecedents of Greek Librarianship* (Provo, Utah: Brigham Young University Press, 1977).

Von Arnim, H. *Die Drei Aristotelischen Ethiken* (Wien: Akademie der Wissenschaften zu Wien, Phil-Hist. Klasse Sitzurgberichte 202, Abh 2, 1924).

von dem Knesebec, Harald Wolter. 'Zur Ausstattung und Funktion des Hauptsaales der Bibliothek von Pergamon', *Boreas: Münstersche*

Beiträge zur Archäologie, 18 (1995), 45–56.

von Staden, H. *Herophilus: The Art of Medicine in Early Alexandria* (Cambridge: Cambridge University Press, 1989).

von Wyss, Wilhelm. *Die Bibliotheken des Altertums und ihre Aufgabe* (Zurich: Beer, 1923).

von Wyss, Wilhelm. 'The Libraries of Antiquity', *Living Age,* 316 (1923), 217–249.

Walden, J.W.H. *The Universities of Ancient Greece* (London: Routledge, 1912).

Wallis, R.T. *Neoplatonism* (London: Gerald Duckworth, 1972).

Weber, Gregor. *Dichtung und höfische Gesellschaft: die Rezeption von Zeitgeschichte am Hof der ersten drei Ptolemäer* (Stuttgart: F. Steiner, 1993).

Weitzmann, Kurt. *Late Antique and Early Christian Book Illumination* (New York: Braziller, 1977).

Wendel, Carl 'Bibliothek', in Theodor Klauser (ed.). *Reallexikon für Antike und Christentum* (Stuttgart: Anton Hiersemann, 1954), Bd II, 231–274.

Westermann, William Linn. *The Library of Ancient Alexandria*, Lecture given at University of Alexandria Reception Hall (Alexandria: University of Alexandria Press, 1954).

White, Heather. *Studies in Theocritus and other Hellenistic Poets* (Amsterdam: Gieben, 1979).

White, John Williams. *The Scholia on the Aves of Aristophanes* (Boston: Ginn, 1914).

Winter, Bruce W. *Philo and Paul among the Sophists* (Cambridge: Cambridge University Press, 1997).

Witty, F.J. 'The Other *Pinakes* and Reference Works of Callimachus', *Library Quarterly,* 43 (1973), 237–244.

Wormald, F. and C.E. Wright (eds). *The English Library before 1700* (London: Athlone Press, 1958).

Yates, Frances. *Giordano Bruno and the Hermetic Tradition* (London: Routledge and Kegan Paul, 1971).

Yates, Frances. *The Rosicrucian Enlightenment* (London: Routledge and Kegan Paul, 1972).

Yates, Frances. *Occult Philosophy in the Elizabethan Age* (London: Routledge and Kegan Paul, 1979).

Zeller, Edward. *Outlines of Greek Philosophy* (London: Longmans, 1885).

Index